SEE BRITAIN AT WORK

A whole world of fascinating visits to craft workshops and factories

Exley Publications

To my husband Trevor, who likes to take things apart, in the hope that he will visit Hoover and find out how to put the toaster back together.

By the same author:
Enquire Within Upon Travel And Holidays 1976 Barrie & Jenkins
The A to Z of Shopping By Post 1978
Exley Publications

First edition published 1977
Second edition 1978
Third (completely revised) edition 1981
Copyright © Exley Publications Ltd, 12 Ye Corner, Chalk Hill, Watford, Herts WD1 4BS.
ISBN 0 905521 54 4 (paperback)
ISBN 0 905521 56 0 (hardback)

Front cover illustration: Mary Potter's silk screen and batik work
Back cover illustration:
Llechwedd Slate Caverns

Printed in Singapore by Tien Wah Press (Pte) Ltd.
Typesetting by Ardek Photosetters (Division of Mainline Typesetters), St Leonards, Sussex.

CONTENTS

Introduction 4
The South West 8
The South 46
The Midlands and East Anglia 87
Wales 123
The North 153
Scotland 189
Index 219

Scotland

The North

The Midlands
and East Anglia

Wales

The South West   The South

We would like to record our thanks to the hundreds of firms, workshops and individuals who sent in photographs to accompany entries in this book; without their help it would have been impossible to choose such an attractive selection of illustrations. We are grateful to those who sent in pictures which could not be included for space reasons and we thank the British Tourist Authority, The Heart of England Tourist Board and the Welsh Tourist Board. We also owe special thanks to the Central Electricity Generating Board, who patiently answered all our questions and lent us photographs. Occasionally firms were not able to supply illustrations and we had to seek additional pictures elsewhere, and we record our thanks to: Thames Television (page 124), Kevin Redpath and Huw Evans (page 130), Elizabeth Haines (page 133), Arthur Williamson (page 134), Tegwyn Roberts & Y Cymro (page 137), Council for Small Industries in Rural Areas (pages 143 and 148), Derbyshire Countryside Ltd (page 99), Birmingham Post & Mail Ltd (page 110) and P. Tate (page 181).

INTRODUCTION

This book lists and describes over 400 factories, workshops and small scale industries which the public can visit throughout Britain. These include small potteries and workshops where individual craftsmen will demonstrate their skills, as well as huge distilleries, nuclear power stations and textile factories which sometimes accept thousands of visitors a year. Included are also several agricultural and industrial museums which show how work was carried out in the past. There are visits which provide insight into aspects of everyday life, such as the processes behind your cup of tea: how the cow was milked, how the clay for the cup was mined, how the cup was manufactured, how the electricity to boil the water was generated. You can learn about unusual skills, too: how bagpipes are made and how butterflies are bred. Whether you are on holiday looking for places to visit, or a teacher or club leader planning an outing, *See Britain at Work* will help you.

Choosing a place to visit

How do you choose a place to visit and how will this book guide you?

One way to proceed is to see which places in your area are open to the public. *See Britain at Work* is divided into 6 geographical regions, each listing around 60 places one can visit. The contents page gives a map of these regions, and there is a more detailed map at the start of each region. Each has a variety of places to visit, although you will notice that each has its own distinctive character. The Midlands, for instance, is the pottery region par excellence and boasts some of the best tours of industrial-scale china making. In Scotland you can see the processes in distilling whisky, watch tweeds being woven and Highland cheeses being made. In Wales you can ride through slate caverns or stop to visit a huge hydro-electric scheme.

There is another way in which you can choose a place to visit, if you are not based in any particular area. You may be planning a holiday and would like to incorporate a visit to see how cheeses are made or to see how taxidermists perform their work. Turn to the index and find out what possibilities there are by looking under these subjects. The descriptions may also provide you with some background information and give you a rough idea of what you can expect to see.

Finally, the following section briefly gives a variety of other places to visit, which are either very numerous or can be visited by certain people only.

About visiting places of work

What you can expect to see on a particular visit will vary from place to place: sometimes you will be taken on a guided tour which will show you all the stages involved in, say, the production of a newspaper, while at other times you may be free to wander about at leisure. In some cases tours are held at regular intervals and you can simply join at the appointed hour. But some visits to factories prove so popular that there is a long waiting list and advance booking is essential. Some firms which normally only accept groups will allow individuals to join previously arranged groups. While not every factory or craftsman will accept visitors — they are there to work rather than to entertain trippers — you will often find that those with products to sell are likely to offer free visits.

Some firms and craftsmen, on the other hand, are no longer accepting visitors. The Post Office, coal mines and several businesses have discontinued mass popular visiting for security reasons or to comply with new safety regulations. Children come in for special mention and are often tolerated rather than encouraged.

Even if it is not possible to visit the place of your choice, remember that if you have a special reason for wanting to visit *any* place of work — perhaps because you are thinking of working in that trade, or already do so — many doors will open to you. It is always worth asking.

You can also visit . . .

There are more than 20 lighthouses open to the public throughout Britain, more than 30 city farms where a working farm is brought right into a city, and there are radio and television studios serving different parts of Britain.

Lighthouses. To obtain a list of the 28 lighthouses open to the public write to the Press Officer, Corporation of Trinity House, Tower Hill, London EC3N 4DH (Tel: 01-480 6601). The list covers lighthouses in England, Wales and the Channel Islands. Lighthouses in Scotland and the adjacent islands, including the Isle of Man are administered by the Northern Lighthouse Board, 84 George Street, Edinburgh EH2 3DA (Tel: 031-226 7051).

City Farms. City Farms are educational and leisure projects involving animals and gardening on plots of land in towns and cities that would otherwise remain unused. They give children from urban areas first hand experience of rural activities — a description of one in London is given on page 70. For further information on where to find City Farms in Britain, contact The Hon. Secretary, The National Federation of City Farms, 15 Wilkin Street, London NW5 3WG (Tel: 01-267 9421).

Theatres, opera houses, radio and television studios. Theatre and opera houses sometimes admit groups to rehearsals. The London and Birmingham studios of Associated Television are open to groups from recognised organisations. Write to The Studio Controller, ATV Studio, Eldon Avenue, Boreham Wood, Hertfordshire, or to The Studio Controller, ATV Centre, Bridge Street, Birmingham B1 2JP. Tickets to watch shows are available from the ticket offices at the same studios. The studios of BBC television and radio are not open to the public but tickets for television shows can be obtained by visitors aged fourteen and over, and for radio shows aged ten and over. For regions outside London write to the Ticket Unit of the **BBC** studio in that area. For London programmes write, enclosing an sae, to The Ticket Unit, Broadcasting House, BBC, London W1A 4WW. State which show you wish to see or specify the type (eg comedy), give the number in your party and offer a choice of dates. The Independent Broadcasting Authority, at 70 Brompton Road, London SW3 1EY (Tel: 01-584 7011), has models showing how programmes are put together and displays on future techniques such as videocassette recording. Advance booking is essential.

Local residents may be able to arrange visits to the offices of public services. Places to try are:

Fire stations	**Electricity stations**	**Police stations**
Law courts	**Gasworks**	**Waterworks**

Certain groups, especially educational groups, can arrange to visit a wide variety of places. They can look through the commercial classified section of the telephone directory or the yellow pages, or they may be able to obtain lists compiled by the Youth Employment Office, Teachers Centre, county library, or local authorities. Some places you could approach are:

Banks	**Insurance companies**	**Solicitors**
Accountants	**Estate agents**	

Coal mines. Careers visits from schools can be arranged for a colliery in the National Coal Board's Western Area which covers Lancashire, Cumbria, North Wales and Staffordshire. Normally numbers are restricted to twelve per group. Write to The Deputy Director (Mining), National Coal Board Western Area, Staffordshire House, Berry Hill Road, Fenton, Stoke-on-Trent, Staffordshire ST4 2NH (Tel: Stoke-on-Trent 48201).

School parties and educational groups can also arrange visits to:
Lifeboat stations. There are over 200 lifeboat stations run by the Royal National Lifeboat Institution. Descriptions of those at Rhyl and at Whitby are given on pages 143 and 174. To obtain a map of lifeboat stations and the address of your nearest one, write, enclosing an sae, to Mrs Heather Deane, RNLI, West Quay Road, Poole, Dorset (Tel: Poole 71133).
Dairies and creameries. The Milk Marketing Board has creameries and dairies in various parts of England and Wales. Write to the Visits Officer, MMB, Thames Ditton, Surrey (Tel: 01-398 4101).

Another group of people who may be able to arrange visits to places not normally open to the public are overseas visitors and business people. Chambers of Commerce in every town maintain lists of members, and invitations may be given to people in the same businesses. The tourist organisations in each region can put tourists in touch with relevant companies. Contact the English Tourist Board, 4 Grosvenor Gardens, London SW1 0DU (Tel: 01-730 4300), The Scottish Tourist Board, 23 Ravelston Terrace, Edinburgh EH4 3EU (Tel: 031-332 2433), The Wales Tourist Board, Brunel House, 2 Fitzalan Road, Cardiff CF2 1VY (Tel: Cardiff 499909); or the British Tourist Authority, 64 St James's Street, London SW1 (Tel: 01-629 9191).

How to arrange a visit

The key to a warm welcome and successful visit is planning ahead. In some cases advance booking, either by telephone or in writing, is necessary. It is always a good idea to telephone before setting out to check that details about visiting arrangements have not changed. When visiting individual craftsmen, in particular, it is a courtesy to check that your arrival will not interfere with their domestic arrangements.

For information on hours of opening and whether advance booking is necessary, refer to the paragraph headed *Practical details* which accompanies each entry. Additional information indicates whether group and/or individual visits are possible, whether age or other restrictions apply, whether tours are provided, whether goods are on sale, and there are details on admission charges, refreshment facilities, parking facilities, provision for the disabled, and advice on how to get there.

✱ Do remember

1. That a phone call to check that visiting arrangements have not changed may save you from possible disappointment.
2. That some places accept visitors in organised groups only, while others cannot accommodate more than four or five people at a time.
3. That some visits need to be booked in advance.
4. That some places provide supervised tours, while others allow visitors to browse on their own.
5. That age restrictions may be imposed for reasons of safety or security.
6. That groups from schools or other organisations may be able to arrange visits to places not normally open to the public.

THE SOUTH WEST

Cornwall, Devon, Dorset, Somerset, Avon, Wiltshire

1   Tin Mine

Geevor Tin Mines Limited
Pendeen
Near Penzance, Cornwall TR19 7EW
Tel: Penzance 788662

Visitors can learn about the history of tin
mining in Cornwall. They can then visit the
working tin treatment plant where they will
see today's method of recovering tin. Tin
mining is one of Cornwall's traditional
industries, and there have been underground
workings in this area since the seventeenth
century. Geevor Tin Mines Limited was
founded in 1911.
Practical details: Visits to the tin treatment
plant can be arranged on weekdays. The
museum is open on weekdays from April to
October from 10 am to 5.30 pm. There are
refreshments, a shop and a picnic area. The
mine is situated between Land's End and St.
Ives.

2   Textured Pottery

Tremaen Pottery Limited
Newlyn Slip, Penzance, Cornwall
Tel: Penzance 4364

The pottery is sited in a large old fish loft
overlooking the busy harbour of Newlyn. It
specialises in asymmetric stoneware decorated

with textures and glazes inspired by the
natural weathered beachstones that surround
the Cornish coast. From the showroom, or on
a guided tour you can see the clay being
prepared, and slip casting and pot finishing.
It is certainly worth a visit. Princess Anne
called here in 1972 during her official visit to
Cornwall.
Practical details: The workshop and
showrooms are open all year Monday to

Textured ware from Tremaen Pottery

Friday, from 9 am to 1 pm and 2 pm to 5.30 pm. They are closed on bank holidays. Individuals and groups of up to 20 people, including school children, can observe work in progress, and guided tours can be arranged. Advance notice is essential. Contact Peter Ellery a week ahead.

3 The Leach Pottery

The Leach Pottery
St. Ives, Cornwall
Tel: St. Ives 6398

This famous pottery, established in 1920 by Bernard Leach after a visit to Japan, was the first studio pottery in the Western hemisphere to use Oriental techniques in the production of hand-thrown stoneware and porcelain. Many well-known potters have studied at the pottery which is now run by Janet Leach. There is a permanent crew of exhibiting potters.
Practical details: Professional potters only can visit the workshop. The public, including the disabled, are welcome to visit the showroom which is open from 9 am to 5 pm Monday to Friday and from 9 am to 12.30 pm on Saturdays in summer. The pottery is closed on bank holidays.

4 Real Ale Brewery

Bird Paradise
Hayle, Cornwall
Tel: Hayle 753365

The Bird Paradise has 130,000 visitors a year. Most people go to see the birds but as part of the complex the public can see a brewery which produces 'real ale'. Visitors can see the installation through glass and receive a description of the various processes. They will then be able to move on a few yards and sample the real ale in the pub, which is called "The Bird in Hand" and belongs to The Bird Paradise. At night there are illuminated tours.

Practical details: The Bird Paradise is open from 10 am to dusk and the brewery is open from 10 am to 11 pm. There is no admission charge.

5 Tin Mine

Poldark Mine
Wendron, near Helston, Cornwall
Tel: Helston 3173 or 3531

At Wendron the whole family can go underground in an 18th century tin mine. They can see the levels and chambers hewn by the miners of long ago. There is also the largest collection of bygones in the west. Many are still working daily. Britain's only underground working waterwheel can be seen.
Practical details: The museum is open every day from 10 am to 6 pm, from April 1st to October 31st. There is an entrance charge. There are showrooms and a cafeteria as well as children's amusements and picnic lawns. Car parking is free and plentiful.

6 Tin Mill

Tolgus Tin Company
Portreath Road, Redruth, Cornwall
Tel: Redruth 5171

This is both a place where tin is produced commercially and a working museum. The Tolgus Tin complex covers an area of 20 acres, and a guided tour of half an hour starts at the museum with a slide presentation which tells you about the history of tin mining in the county.
Practical details: The tin mill is open April to October from 10 o'clock in the morning. It remains open on bank holidays. There is no need for individuals and families to give notice, but groups should book in advance. Coach parties are welcome and there are special admission rates for groups of twenty or more people. Articles made of tin are sold in

the large craft centre and mineral shop which shares its building with a restaurant. There is also a picnic site. As you can tell, the place is very well organized for tourists, and you will find it 2 miles from Portreath on the B3300.

7   Ancient Handcraft Pottery

W H Lake & Son Limited
Truro Pottery
Chapel Hill, Truro, Cornwall
Tel: Truro 2928

Before the days of the Staffordshire potteries small rural potteries provided for local needs, and these little potteries sprang up in areas where there was suitable clay and a supply of fuel. As kilns were wood-fired, areas near forests were often chosen and remains of Roman potteries have been found in such places. The Chapel Hill pottery is above the clay seam which runs through Truro. The city of Truro was built over the clay area and the clay now comes from Devon. But the nearness of the clay seam probably suggests that the pottery dates back several hundred years, especially as the pitcher design which is unique to this pottery dates back to Tudor times.

There are now only two ancient handcraft potteries left in Great Britain (which were in

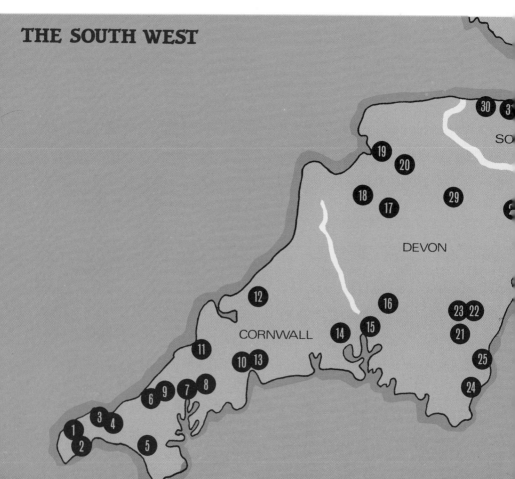

THE SOUTH WEST

production before the days of mass production) — and Lake's is one of them. Visitors are given a brief history of the pottery and are shown around the museum. Amongst the exhibits is the Ancient Cornish Cloam (meaning clay) Oven. These ovens used to be built into cottages for household baking, before the days of the iron stove, and thousands were made here. In recent times one was ordered for the British Museum.

A potter can usually be seen at work, hand throwing on electrically driven wheels. The tour ends in the large, pleasant showroom where the history of some of the pots and the uses of many more are described. Souvenirs (seconds) are sold at greatly reduced prices.

After belonging to the Lake family for four generations the pottery has now become part of the Dartington Trust.

Practical details: The showroom is open Monday to Friday from 9 am to 5 pm, with the exception of bank holidays.

Individuals and groups are catered for and advance booking is not necessary although it is preferable in the case of large parties or coaches.

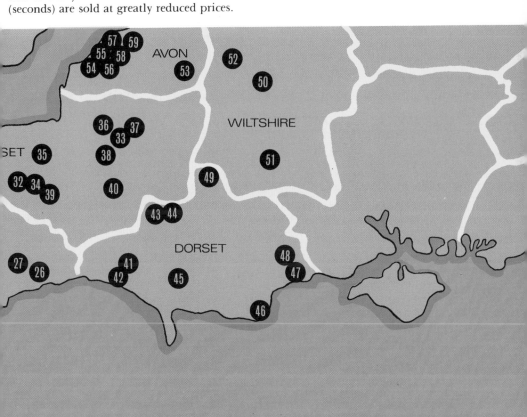

8   Demonstration Garden

Cornwall Education Committee
County Demonstration Garden
Probus, Near Truro, Cornwall

The garden was officially opened in 1972. It is divided into 54 sections and if you follow the numbers you start at the labour-saving garden — then see herbs grown for use in medicines and food, a children's garden, fruit, ferns, vegetables, pruning, plants for shade, windbreaks, a nature trail, pavings and front garden designs. There is even an apiary for would-be bee-keepers.
Demonstrations show how soil can be improved, how shrubs and trees should be cared for and how they can be used to create shelter, and how lawns can be improved. The garden is intended to interest both the public, and architects and planners, whose work involves landscaping.
Practical details: The Demonstration Garden is open to the public all year Monday to Friday from 10 am to 4.30 pm. From May to September it is also open on Sundays from 2 pm to 6 pm. An adviser is on duty on Thursdays from 2 pm to 5 pm.
Guided tours on points of special interest are held on Wednesday afternoons from May to September. Lectures and short practical demonstrations are given on some Sunday afternoons (prior application is not required). Tours last 1½ hours. Application forms and further details can be obtained from P Blake, County Horticultural Adviser, Old County Hall, Truro TR1 3BA, Tel: Truro 74282. There is a small admission charge.

9   Large Popular Pottery

Foster's Pottery Company
Tolgus Hill, Redruth, Cornwall
Tel: Redruth 215754

Some places merely tolerate tourists but here they are really welcomed. The well-organized tour shows you every aspect of making pottery, and one of the enthusiastic guides

(there are 11 of them) may tell you that at the height of the season they get 1,000 visitors a day!
Fifty craftsmen and women are at work using old traditional methods of pottery-making such as handthrowing, or newer methods such as slip casting in moulds, and jigging and jolleying with machinery. Large electric kilns are used to fire the pots, and all sorts of practical pieces — cups, saucers, butter dishes and so on, emerge from them. You can watch the pottery being decorated, some of it in a distinctive mottled green glaze. You may also see row after row of identical teapots being made to go into 'Teasmaid' machines — at the rate of 3,000 a week. The showroom has a range of colourful gifts including slight seconds at reduced prices. 'Try not to leave your visit for a wet day,' they say. Wet days are usually the busiest.
Practical details: In Summer (April to September) the pottery is open Monday to Friday from 9 am to 3.45 pm. The showroom is open Monday to Friday from 9 am to 5 pm, and also on Saturday from 10 am to 12 noon. In Winter (October to March) the pottery and showroom are open for tours Monday to Friday from 10 am to 12 noon and 1.30 pm to 3.45 pm. The pottery is closed on bank holidays and Sundays. Large parties can make arrangements for tours at any time of year. Coach parties (maximum size of group 50) should give at least 24 hours notice. There is a small charge for tours. The pottery is on the A30 Redruth by-pass and there is a free car park.

10   Mining Museum

Wheal Martyn Museum
Carthew
St Austell, Cornwall
Tel: Stenalees 850362

Wheal is a Cornish word meaning a mine. Wheal Martyn Museum is a restored open-air 100-year-old clay works. It has working waterwheels, one of them 35′ in diameter, working machinery, an introductory slide show, other indoor displays and a blacksmith.

Visitors watching 'throwing' at Foster's

A small working craft pottery produces stone-ware and porcelain made from West Country clays.
The pottery products are sold in the museum shop.
Practical details: The museum is open from April to October, 10 am to 6 pm. The last admission is at 5 pm. A small charge is made, with reductions for groups of twelve or more. It is open to groups all year, by prior arrangement only. Most of the site is suitable for the disabled.

11   Dairy Farm

'Dairyland' and Country Life Museum
Tresillian Barton, Summercourt
Newquay, Cornwall TR8 5AA
Tel: Mitchell 246

This is a fascinating outing to a farm where you can see 160 cows being milked to music every afternoon in one of Europe's most modern rotary parlours. It has an 'electric dog' or safety barrier which moves the cows along the entry passage. The platform turns at 7½

Children can meet farm animals

minutes per revolution and two operators milk about 120 cows an hour. Milk is drawn along a vacuum pipe to a collecting jar which shows each cow's yield. This is 'space age' milking and has been featured on television, and is very educational. Children can meet farm animals and pets.

The country life museum is equally interesting with a cider press, Cornish kitchen, different kinds of churns, and a milk and cream separator designed to ring a bell if the person turning it by hand is not going fast enough — 60 revolutions a minute! There are also a blacksmith's, a welding shop and a coffee shop where you can enjoy a pinta.

Practical details: They are open every day April to October from 10 am to 5.30 pm (last admission at 5), and milking takes place from about 3.15 to 4.30 pm. Booked parties of more than 20 are accepted at any time of the year by arrangement. The admission charge covers free parking, picnic area and playground.

12   Quarry and Slate Splitting

Old Delabole Quarry
Delabole, Near Camelford, Cornwall
Tel: Camelford 2242

Slate splitting demonstrations using the traditional bettle and chisel are arranged from 11 am to 4 pm. A small museum and craft shop are open to the public. The charge is 30p with reductions for children and old age pensioners.

The old quarry which has been worked continuously for more than 400 years is 1⅝ miles around and it can be seen from a viewing terrace.

Practical details: The quarry is open during Easter and the season from May to September, seven days a week from 10 am to 6 pm. Both individuals and parties of any size are welcome and no advance notice is required.

13 China-clay Pit

English China Clays Limited
John Keay House, St. Austell
Cornwall PL25 4DJ
Tel: St. Austell 4482

Ask most people what china-clay is used for and they will just say 'for pottery'. But china-clay is used in making dozens of other everyday articles — pills, stomach powders, kaolin mixture, bathroom tiles, plastics, rubber soles for shoes and the coating of glossy pages in magazines and books. China-clay is a fine white powder which is chemically inert, so it is used as a filler or extender in many products.

Surprisingly it is papermaking which uses 80% of all clays. Clay is used in paper as a filler and as a coating for the surface. A good quality magazine paper may contain up to 30% of clay. As china-clay is much cheaper than pulp, it lowers the cost of finished paper as well as improving the quality. The white coating improves the feel of the paper and enables the printer to reproduce the print and pictures in sharp detail.

Rotary milking parlour at Dairyland

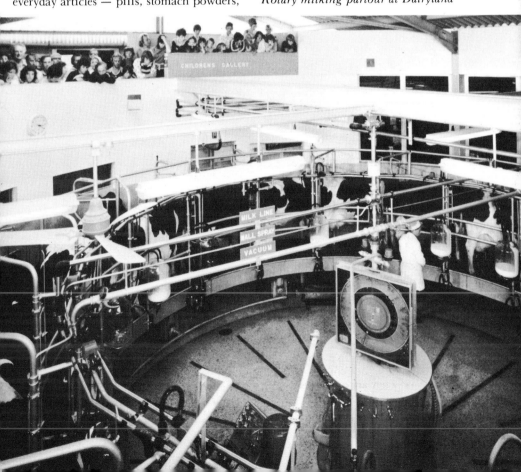

China-clay is also used in the ceramics industry in bone china, earthenware, tiles, sanitary ware and electrical porcelain. Clays differ greatly in quality, even clay taken from only one pit. In order to produce goods of consistent quality, as many as six or more clays are blended to a standard specification.

It would be uneconomical and impractical to make most rubber articles out of purely natural or synthetic rubber. By adding china-clay, the cost is reduced and the article has greater resistance to wear; so china-clay is often used in products like Wellington boots and hot-water bottles.

China-clay is also used in the more expensive prime colour pigments in paints. It disperses easily in a mix and does not quickly settle on the bottom. It flows well and spreads evenly when it is applied.

China-clay is used in pharmaceuticals, too, where it acts as a carrier for the active ingredients. Insecticides in dust form are mixed with china-clay which acts as a bulk carrier. Fertiliser in granular form tends to cake together, so china-clay is used as an anti-caking powder on the granules. Fine quality leathers are dressed with a preparation containing china-clay, which fills the surface pores and helps to produce a smooth surface; and textile manufacturers use china-clay to help strengthen the fibres during weaving. The list of uses is almost endless!

English China Clays Group is the largest single producer of china-clay in the world. Over 75% of the clay is exported and the company won the Queen's Award to Industry in 1966, 1969, 1971 and 1975. It exports about 2½ million tonnes a year.

In the United Kingdom china-clay is found only in Cornwall and on Dartmoor in Devon. The old Cornish method of extracting china-clay was to wash it out of the kaolinised granite, which was broken up with hand tools. The china-clay, suspended in water, was allowed to settle in tanks. The sediment at the bottom was sliced into lumps which were then dried in the air.

Modern methods still rely on water for extracting the china-clay. Very powerful remotely-controlled water hoses are directed at the pit face (the stope). They are strong enough to disintegrate the rock and wash out the china-clay in one operation.

China-clay and quartz sand are now suspended in water and this claystream flows to the bottom of the pit where it is pumped to a sand separation plant. The coarse sand is carried away by a conveyor to large tips. The china-clay and water mixture (called slurry) is pumped out of the pit and passed through a series of tanks which remove the water. The china-clay is then passed through fine mesh screens and enters a drying plant, where it is pressed into a putty-like consistency ready for drying.

Throughout the process samples of clay are tested in laboratories, and computers select the proportions of different clays to be blended for specific grades of clay. Dried clays are transported in bags or in bulk. Special bulk carriers are used to carry china-clay in slurry form by rail to customers in the United Kingdom, and the company has a transport fleet of more than 700 lorries.

The Blackpool pit is 300 ft. at its deepest point and covers more than 120 acres of the surface. At this pit, you see sand being extracted from the clay and dewatering and refining taking place. Because the company cannot get rid of the sand tips at the moment, it has set up a landscaping section to see what can be done to improve their appearance. Experiments are being made to find ways of growing plants on the tips. In a tree nursery 100,000 trees are being brought on for planting in the works areas.

China-clay from the Blackpool and Goverseth refining plants is received at the Blackpool Drying Plant and held in storage tanks. The solid content of the china-clay is increased from fifteen per cent to seventy per cent by screening and then filter pressing. It is then passed to the driers.

Blackpool is one of English China Clays' largest drying plants, producing about five thousand tonnes of china-clay every week. But probably the most striking thing you will see is the complex of eighteen silos. They

A powerful water-jet blasts China Clay

are one hundred and twenty feet high, twenty feet in diameter and can each store six hundred tonnes of china-clay.

Practical details: Conducted tours of the Blackpool open china-clay pit and the drying plant can be arranged from Monday to Friday at any time of year except on bank holidays provided that you book in advance. Write to the information officer at the address above, quoting two or three convenient dates for a tour. Young children under the age of seven cannot be accepted. Up to 25 people are allowed on any one tour.

Tours start at 10 am and 2 pm and consist of a tour of the Blackpool pit and the drying installations. Route maps to the pit are provided and there is a limited amount of free parking.

Thirty-two-foot waterwheel—Morwellham

14   Reproduction Armour

Calcraft Products
Wheal Arthur, Gunnislake
Cornwall PL18 9AB
Tel: Tavistock 832648

Calcraft Products are manufacturers of reproductions of antique pistols, muskets, swords, shields, poleaxes, suits of armour and other items which are used for interior decoration. Visitors can be shown the processes involved.

Practical details: The workshop and showroom are open all the year round from 10 am to 6 pm. Visitors should contact the proprietor a few days in advance. Small groups of up to eight persons can be shown around.

15   Open Air Industrial Museum

Morwellham Quay Centre
Near Tavistock, West Devon
Tel: Tavistock 832766

The Tamar river port lies at the foot of steeply wooded hills. Valuable copper ores were brought from the mines to its quays in the 1800s and the area has so much of interest that it was turned into a visitors' centre by the Dartington Hall Trust in 1970. An audio visual show called 'Introduction to Morwellham' is given in the slide theatre which includes local history and what there is to see.

Visitors can then follow short or long self-guided trails round the quays and docks or travel on a woodland railway going underground into the historic George and Charlotte Copper Mine. They can see waterwheels, a water-powered thresher, farm buildings containing old agricultural implements, lime kilns, inclined railways, the local history museum and trailside displays. A souvenir and craft shop sells trail leaflets including a guide for teachers.

Practical details: Open all year round including bank holidays from 10 am to 6 pm in summer and 10 am to dusk in winter. There is an all-inclusive admission charge.

There are price reductions for coach parties and groups arriving by river from Plymouth. School parties and other groups can contact the warden at the above telephone number to make special catering and educational arrangements.

If you'd like to come by river, the Millbrook

Steamboat Company runs regular sailings on the afternoon tides from Plymouth. Tel: Plymouth 822202. By road: On the A390 travelling from Tavistock to Liskeard, turn left 2 miles west of Tavistock. Travelling from Cornwall turn right 2 miles east of Gunnislake.

16   Hydro-electric Power Station

Mary Tavy Power Station
Tavistock, Devon PL19 9PR
Tel: Mary Tavy 248

Hydro-electric power stations are the ones which most people find easiest to understand. Just as water turns a waterwheel, waterpower moves the turbine, or power generator, which creates an electric current. Free literature is provided.
Practical details: As the power station is in more or less continuous operation visitors can arrange to see it at any time. Groups of up to 50 people can be taken around, but only small groups at evenings and weekends. Telephone or write to the station manager.
Another hydro-electric power station in the Mary Tavy group is at Morwellham. Dartington Trust has a nature trail and waterwheel at the adjoining Morwellham

A turbo-generator at Mary Tavy

Quay and a combined visit to waterwheel and power station can be arranged.

More details about power stations can be obtained from The Public Relations Officer, Central Electricity Generating Board, South Western Region, Bedminster Down, Bridgwater Road, Bristol BS13 8AN.

17   One-man Pottery

Seckington Pottery
Winkleigh, Devon EX19 8EY
Tel: Winkleigh 478

At his North Devon pottery Michael Hatfield makes Devon cider mugs, animal and bird studies and figures, mice on cheese wedges, pendants, vases, miniatures etc, in red or white Devon Clay. Sheila Hatfield makes jewellery.
Practical details: Individuals and small groups welcome daily at this home pottery. Usually open on bank holidays, but phone on weekends or if more than 10 people.

18   Hand-blown Glass Factory

Dartington Glass Limited
Great Torrington, North Devon
Tel: Torrington 3797

Most people have seen Dartington glass — the avocado dishes, the Irish Coffee glasses and modern drinking glasses — even if they do not know the name. Dartington makes unusual modern glassware such as candle-holder vases which are featured at the Design Centre, London. In fact Dartington Glass has won a Design Council award and in 1972 Frank Thrower, the designer, won the Duke of Edinburgh Design Prize for a collection of kitchen and table glass.
The story about how Dartington Glass came to be produced is as pleasing as the glassware itself. For the past 50 years projects undertaken at Dartington, 40 miles away in South Devon, have been concerned with the quality of life. Leonard and the late Dorothy Elmhirst settled at Dartington on a large estate. Together they and their trustees developed

Dartington's woodlands and pioneered selective cattle-breeding. The people who worked on the estate were given the opportunity of learning new skills. Cultural activities were started for the benefit of the community and Dartington Hall School was founded to provide an education for children of people who worked on the estate.

In 1963 the trustees of Dartington Hall decided to repeat the experiment by setting up a small community in North Devon. Ever since the decline of the wool trade, the numbers of people living and working in North Devon had fallen by 6% every 10 years, and North Devon is designated as a development area. It was decided by the Trust that the manufacture of glassware by the traditional Scandinavian method would be an ideal craft for young people in the area to learn, so workers were brought over from Scandinavia. When the glass works was opened in 1967 there were 16 people from abroad and 30 learners. There are now over 200 local employees and 10 from abroad.

The main raw materials used for making glass are sand, soda and lime. Red lead, potash and other chemicals are used to give the glass better quality. Arsenic, barium and antimony are used for purifying the glass. Colouring agents for other types of glass include copper oxide, iron oxide and potassium permanganate.

Factory furnaces contain clay pots known as pot arches. Before melting in these pots, the chemicals are weighed and carefully mixed together to make up a batch. Clean broken glass, called cullet, is added. A new batch takes 10 hours to melt, at a temperature of about 1450°C.

The glass blowers work in teams around each furnace. A full team consists of a master blower, the deputy master blower, the blower, three gatherers and assistants such as mould holders and carriers.

This is how a wine glass is made: a gatherer takes the melted glass from the furnace on a blow pipe which he passes to the blower who blows down the pipe forming the first bubble in the glass. The molten glass is then rolled evenly on a smooth plate. The pipe is then passed to the next blower who points it downwards and blows the bowl for the wine glass in a water cooled mould which gives the glass its shape and pattern. The glass then passes on to the master blower who shapes the stem with extra glass brought from the furnace by another gatherer. Another blower makes the foot of the wine glass by adding another piece of melted glass which is shaped, as the glass is turned, to make a flat base. The piece of glass is now ready for the lehr, which is an extremely slow conveyor belt which takes the glass through a cooling tunnel. This process takes from 4 to 10 hours.

When they emerge open mouthed articles go to the cracking off machines where the tops are removed by propane jets which burn at the correct height as the glass is revolved on turntables. The top edges are ground by belts. Then the glass is placed on another turntable and propane jets melt the top edge to finish it off. After a final inspection, first quality glassware is sent to British retailers (about 1,500 of them) or to any one of 55 countries.

Practical details: The factory is open Monday to Friday from 9.30 am to 10.30 am and from 12 noon to 3 pm. Times subject to alteration without notice. You are advised to telephone Torrington 3797. There is a small charge for adults and children over 12. Parties by prior arrangement. The glass shop is open from 9 am to 5 pm on weekdays and from 10 am to 4 pm on Saturdays. The factory is closed on bank holidays.

19   Hand-thrown Pots

C. H. Brannam Limited
Litchdon Potteries
Barnstaple, Devon EX32 8NE
Tel: Barnstaple 3035

C. H. Brannam is one of the few remaining clay flowerpot manufacturers in the United Kingdom. Using local Fremington which gives the pottery its instantly recognisable terracotta appearance, the pottery produces both garden and domestic ware. An interesting sight is the throwing of large

A glass-blower at Dartington Glass

eighteen-inch pots. Various traditional methods are used at the pottery where pots are decorated by hand, and the pottery uses two old bottle kilns on a weekly firing cycle. **Practical details:** The pottery is in the centre of Barnstaple behind the Imperial Hotel near the Square. Guided tours take place from May to September at hourly intervals starting at 10.45 am, or during winter by appointment for large groups. Coaches should give 24 hours' notice. There is a small charge for the tour. The factory seconds' shop is open Monday to Friday from 9 am to 1 pm and from 2 to 5 pm.

20 Devon and Exmoor Honey

Quince Honey Farm
North Road, South Molton, North Devon
Tel: South Molton 2401

This is the largest honey farm in the country. It is also the largest producer of beeswax, much of which is made into dipped and moulded candles on the premises. In the bee observation room a colony of wild bees can safely be watched behind glass. In the glass observation hives, bees can be seen at work, with their different coloured pollen loads. An exhibition explains the story of honey from

Extracting honey from the comb

flower to table.

The beekeepers are frequently away visiting surrounding farms or working on the moors, caring for bees in their numerous apiaries. Pure Devon honey is on sale in jars or on the comb — also beeswax candles, furniture polish and cosmetics — all at wholesale prices.
Practical details: The honey farm is open 8 am to 8 pm from Easter to September and 8 am to 6 pm from October to Easter. A small charge is made but there is ample free parking space.

21   Wool Mill and Tweed Shop

Dartington Hall Tweeds Limited
Dartington, Totnes, Devon
Tel: Totnes 862271

Dartington Hall Trust emerged from an idea born over fifty years ago, to revitalise the quality of rural life in Devon. Today, Dartington's name is associated with progressive education, music and most recently with glass. The famous Dartington Glass Factory is described elsewhere in this section of the book. Dartington Hall Tweeds is only one of the wide range of ventures in business, farming, education, research and the arts, which has been assisted by the Trust.

The visitor to the mill will see the various stages that the imported lambswool fleeces go through before becoming a length of finished tweed. Visitors see the dyeing, blending and carding of the wool. The yarn is woven into pieces approximately sixty metres in length, ready to be made into 100% wool tweed rugs and garments.
Practical details: The mill is open all year Monday to Friday, except holidays. Parties may book a guided tour for which a fee is charged. Tel: Totnes 862179. Mill tours take place between 9 am and 12 noon and 1.30 pm and 5 pm Monday to Thursday and between 9 am and 3.30 pm on Fridays. The tweed shop, selling travel rugs, clothes, knitwear, scarves and gloves, is open 9 am to 5.15 pm on Monday to Thursday, until 5 pm on Friday, and from 10 am to 5 pm on Saturday. The mill is situated on the Dartington to Plymouth road and has ample car parking.

22 Leather Goods Manufacturer

Devon Leathercrafts Limited
Kingsteignton Road
Newton Abbot, Devon TQ12 2QB
Tel: Newton Abbot 4262

Wallets, purses, shopping list pads in cases, and bookmarks are made here. The leathers used are mainly cow skins and goat skins. Both are tanned with vegetable matter, usually bark, to preserve the skin. Unlike cloth, which can be cut in several thicknesses at once, leather must be cut one thickness at a time to avoid flaws. The more pieces that an article can be made from, the more economical is the use of the skin. But an article made from several parts needs more work done to assemble it.
You will see leather being pared to thin it for hemming and folding. Then it is machined, attached to purse frames, welded with synthetic linings, and stamped in gold lettering.
Practical details: Guided tours are held from early April to late October, Monday to Friday, 9.30 am to 12 pm and 1.30 to 5 pm. The last

tour starts at 4.30 pm. During the lunch hour the shop remains open but the factory itself is closed. There is a charge for a guided tour of the factory but a joint ticket allowing you to visit the nearby New Devon Pottery as well, is good value. There are party rates for groups of 25 or more people. Children under 14 who are accompanied by adults are not charged, and school parties are accepted by special arrangement. Winter bookings, too, can be made by prior arrangement.
Visits to the showroom are free, and seconds and discontinued lines are on sale at reduced prices. There is a picnic area where drinks and ice cream can be bought. Parking is free.

23 Devon Pottery

New Devon Pottery Limited
Forde Road, Newton Abbot, Devon
Tel: Newton Abbot 4262

Seventy-five per cent of the clay used here comes from the West Country. The clay is a mixture of China clay, which is relatively pure, and ball clay which has impurities. The impurities make the clay more malleable, though it does not fire as white. Much of the pottery produced is glazed with a semi-matt or vellum, off-white glaze. One process you will see is jolleying on to a revolving wheel with a semi-automatic cup-making machine. Another process is casting with slip (liquid clay) into a Plaster of Paris mould. The pottery is dipped in glaze, or sprayed, and loaded on to kiln trucks. The kilns are fired at night when electricity is cheaper.
Decorative transfers are applied and these sink into the glaze after firing. Finally the pottery is sorted and seconds are picked out for sale in the factory shop.
Practical details: Guided tours are held from Easter to October 9.30 am to 12 noon and 1.30 pm to 4.30 pm. The factory closes at 5 pm, and during the lunch hour. The shop is open during lunch time. There is a charge for a guided tour of the pottery, but a joint ticket, admitting you to the nearby Devon Leathercrafts, is good value. Children are

admitted free of charge if accompanied. For party rates (groups of 25 or more) and school visits, telephone Mrs. Phyl Johnson. Parking is free.

24   Local Clay Pottery

Brixham Pottery Limited
The Old Pound House
Milton Street, Brixham, Devon
Tel: Brixham 2262

The Old Pound House buildings, believed to be 16th or 17th century, were once used as a cider factory. The pottery's showroom was originally the loading bay for horse-drawn carts carrying cider barrels. Ring bolts, to which the horses were tethered, can still be seen set into the wall.

The clay used in the pottery comes mainly from the nearby Newton Abbot clayfields and you can watch the potters making earthenware and stoneware. There is no guarantee that you will see 'hand throwing' on the wheel, but, at most times during the height of the summer season, someone is working on the wheel. About 20 people are busy throwing, casting, fettling (cleaning up rough edges), decorating, glaze dipping, and firing the pottery in the electric kilns. In the showroom handthrown pottery and stoneware, including many seconds,

Throwing a pot at Brixham Pottery

are on sale.

Practical details: The pottery is open Monday to Friday from 9 am to 12.30 pm and 1.30 pm to 5.30 pm. Only the showroom is open on Saturdays 9 am to 12.30, and on bank holidays. There is a free car park, but because of limited space, visitors in organised groups and coach parties should give advance notice of at least 3 days. Individual visitors are welcome to arrive without prior notice during working hours and walk around the pottery. There is no charge. The staff will gladly answer questions. Young children should be accompanied by an adult.

The pottery is on the Brixham to Kingswear road, about ¾ of a mile from Brixham town centre, opposite a garage.

25   Babbacombe Pottery

Babbacombe Pottery
Babbacombe Road, Babbacombe, Devon
Tel: Torquay 38757

A flag-bedecked entrance welcomes you to Babbacombe pottery with its ornamental gardens, fish ponds and dovecot. You can watch the potters at work, casting, jolleying and decorating the pottery by hand. Seconds, experimental items and discontinued lines are sold at a discount.

Practical details: The pottery is open all year (including bank holidays), Monday to Friday from 9 am to 5.30 pm, and on Saturday morning in the summer season. All visitors are welcome and no advance notice is necessary. Admission free.

26   Carpet Manufacturer

Axminster Carpets Limited
Gamberlake
Axminster, Devon EX13 5PQ
Tel: Axminster 32244

The first Axminster carpet was woven in 1755 by a local man, Mr. Thomas Witty. The buildings which housed his factory can still be

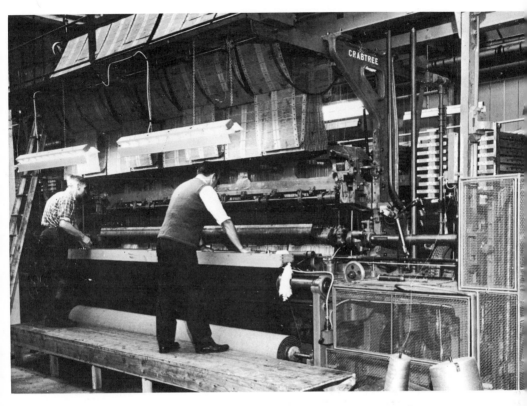

The weaving shed at Axminster Carpets

seen in Silver Street. Those early carpets were hand-knotted. But today's are completely machine produced and the pile tufts are held in place by the threads in the base of the carpet. Axminster carpets are made from three raw materials — wool, jute and cotton. The wool comes from Scottish and Irish blackface sheep and Devon and New Zealand sheep. After the wool has been blended it is scoured, carded, twisted, spun and dyed at Buckfastleigh by a subsidiary of Axminster carpets called Buckfast Spinning Company Limited. Jute is grown in India and Bangladesh and is spun into yarn in Dundee. Cotton is grown in America and spun into yarn in Lancashire. At this factory the first stage you see is coils of wool being wound on to bobbins. The bobbins are placed on 'creels' at the back of the loom and the ends of the wool are fed through to the front of the loom. Then the actual

weaving begins. The pile of the carpet is inserted and held in place at the same time as the back of the carpet is woven. Carpets are inspected for small machine faults. This inspection is called picking. The next process is steaming to 'burst' the yarn to make it cover the base. Then the carpet is sheared to give it an even surface, and a fine coating of vinyl is applied to the backing to improve tuft retention and to enable the carpet to be cut with the minimum amount of fraying. It is then inspected for the last time. Finally each carpet is rolled and measured.

In the showroom there is a variety of carpets on display in patterns ranging from the traditional to modern, from rugs to broadloom carpets. Broadloom carpets, as the name suggests, are made on large machines and so provide a large area of luxury carpet with a minimum of seaming. The showroom manager answers questions and can give information to anyone who wants to know about retail suppliers.

Visitors must observe the factory's rules. No photography is allowed. Do not talk to the people operating the looms, and take care when walking past machinery which has moving parts, because although the machinery is guarded much of it is close together and the company is not responsible for accidents caused by carelessness. Finally, no smoking — a fairly common rule in factories, which applies here even though wool does not flare up like some other fibres.

Practical details: Individuals are welcome without prior booking between 10 am and 12.30, and 2 pm and 4.30 Monday to Friday, and they can walk around the factory on their own. Groups should make an appointment with Mrs. M. Price, Works Management. The guide accompanies groups of between 12 and 35 people, and a guided tour lasts about 1½ hours. School parties are welcome provided that the children are aged 10 or over. There is no charge.

27 Honiton Pottery

Honiton Pottery Limited
30-32 High Street, Honiton, Devon
Tel: Honiton 2106

There are no conducted tours. Just walk round at your leisure. Notices in every department explain the processes. A handout leaflet and children's question paper are available on request.

Pottery making has been carried out in Honiton since the 1700s. The original products were things like bread crocks and milk coolers — made on the potter's wheel but rarely decorated. Local clay was used until about 1947 and it all fired to a red-brown colour. Nowadays the cost of land in the High Street is so high that it is not economic to take the coarse clay from the seam behind the factory, so blends of clays from Devon and Cornwall are used. Traditional vases and jugs

are hand-painted on a cream glaze.

You will see the Making Department where clays are mixed into the creamy liquid slip. This is poured into plaster of Paris moulds for vases or jugs. The shapes of the pieces are designed here, and the moulds are made as well. It must be sound economics to use a mould for a range of pottery in the same shape but each piece looking very different because of the pattern.

In the sponging department pots and vases are 'fettled' to remove the seam line and sponged smooth. The clay pieces are fired in electric kilns and removed in the biscuit state (so called because they have the brittle texture of biscuits). The porous pottery is sealed with a glaze, which is sprayed onto it in powder form. After hand painting with metal oxide colours, the pottery is returned to the kilns where the glaze is fused.

The resident designer can be seen at work in his studio, creating designs on the drawing board or hand-throwing, turning, modelling, hand-painting, decorating or glazing. In the showroom you can see the products and buy export rejects at reduced prices.

Practical details: The *showroom* is open Monday to Saturday from 9 am to 5.30 pm. The *pottery* is open Monday to Thursday from 9 am to 12 noon and 2 pm to 4.30 pm, and on Friday from 9 am to 12 noon and 2 pm to 4 pm. The pottery is closed on bank holidays. Please contact the pottery if you have a party of more than 20 people.

28 Craft Centre and Farm

Bickleigh Mill
Bickleigh, Near Tiverton, Devon EX16 8RG
Tel: Bickleigh 419

Bickleigh is a picture-postcard village complete with thatched hotel and Bickleigh Mill, with its restored waterwheel and ancient mill machinery, provides the perfect setting for a craft centre and working farm showing Devon farming at the turn of the century. Craftsmen and women working in log cabins inside the mill demonstrate a variety of skills:

wood-turning, glass engraving, corn dolly making, spinning and weaving, jewellery making, leather-work, ceramics and pottery. Of particular interest is the glass observation beehive where you can watch the antics of bees as they make honey. There is also a well-stocked shop selling a wide range of craft work from the West Country, a number of items made at the mill and some farm produce. Visitors may also take a tour of the farm. At the dairy you can watch as cows are milked by hand and you can also see shire horses and other farm animals, agricultural equipment and illustrations of a variety of skills.

Practical details: Bickleigh Mill, Craft Centre and Farm is open seven days a week from 10 am to 6 pm April to December, and from 2 pm to 5 pm January to March. There is an admission charge but parking for cars and coaches is free. A restaurant provides home-made food.

Shire mare and Romany caravan

29 Sheep Farm and Countryside Museum

Ashley Countryside Collection
Ashley House, Wembworthy
Near Winkleich, Devon EX18 7RH
Tel: Ashreigney 226

If you have always thought that one sheep looked pretty much like another you will probably change your mind after visiting this farm and seeing the 40 breeds of sheep. You drive up past a large open-fronted shed, full of equipment from the 'horse and open fireplace' era. Having parked your car in the farmyard and paid your admission you are free to wander around looking at the 1,001 items from days gone by. Catalogues are available. You can usually see baby calves and pigs in the pens, 40 different fleeces of wool, and a spinning wheel and small loom used for making woollen goods. There is a wheelwright's and blacksmith's shop too.

When you have finished looking at these you will be able to see the 40 breeds of sheep in the adjoining field. From the field you can see across the valley to Eggesford Fox Hounds Kennels and the Wembworthy Centre where Devon schoolchildren stay for field studies. The visit is suitable whatever the weather because most of the exhibition is under cover and there is a wet weather picnic shelter.

Practical details: The farm and museum are open to the public from 10 am to 6 pm on Mondays, Wednesday, Saturday and Sunday, including bank holiday weekends from Easter to October, and every day in August except Thursdays. Schools, coach parties and other groups are welcome by arrangement with Mr. T. R. Blackford.

Ashley Countryside Collection is halfway between the A337 and the B3220 in North Devon. Those coming off the A377 at Eggesford Station will cross over the river Taw. Then turning right, drive past the first plantings of the Forestry Commission on your left, and the entrance to the mile-long drive of ruined Eggesford House on your right. RAC signs direct you around Wembworthy downhill then up to Ashley.

---

30   Small Remote Pottery

Waistel and Joan Cooper
Culbone Lodge Pottery
Porlock, Minehead, Somerset TA24 8PQ
Tel: Porlock 862539

Culbone Pottery is usually approached on foot along the public footpaths from Silcombe Farm (½ mile), or from Porlock Weir, past the Ashley Combe Toll Gate (where there is a car park). This second route is 2 miles long, but very beautiful. The visitor walks up a slowly winding cliff-path from the toll gate, perhaps stopping occasionally to sit and admire the breath-taking views, until — 450 feet above sea-level — he or she arrives at the opening into Culbone Combe. This is a tiny world of its own, filled with peace and tranquillity. A few yards up the public path, beyond the 12th century Culbone Church, is the Culbone

Lodge Pottery, where Waistel and Joan Cooper make stoneware pottery and sculpture. Culbone Lodge, formerly a keeper's lodge, is a striking building, built of local stone and 4 floors high. Part of it is thought to be 300 years old. The terraces and gardens on the wooded hillside are filled with unusual pottery shapes.

All the pottery is hand-thrown stoneware. Some pieces are repeatable but the Coopers are continuously trying to explore new forms. The pottery is rough-textured and decorated with a variety of oxides, ranging from startling near-white through reddish-brown tones to charcoal-black. Many pieces are glazed with natural wood ashes to produce green-blue to rich gold tones. Bowls, jugs, mugs, vases, table lamps and larger pieces are displayed, and pieces have been acquired by several museums including the Victoria and Albert.

Practical details: The pottery is open every day, including weekends and bank holidays, March to November, from 10 am to 7 pm, and in winter at the weekend or by appointment. Individuals are always welcome, but parties of schoolchildren or groups of 10 or more should write or telephone in advance.

31 Sheepskin Products

John Wood & Son (Exmoor) Limited
'Linton', Old Cleeve
Minehead, Somerset TA24 6HT
Tel: Washford 40291

Visitors are given a potted history of the firm which started its activities about 100 years ago with the great-grandfather of the present owner. Then the guide explains how the skins are bought in the raw state and processed — the skins are scoured, the flesh is removed, the leather is tanned, the pelt is sueded, natural greases are removed, the wool and leather are dyed in some cases, and the wool is finished ready for the skins to be made into various products.

In the cutting department visitors see the skins being cut up for different styles of coats, moccasins and items such as gloves, mitts, seat covers, soft toys, footmuffs and hats.

Practical details: Visitors are welcome to the factory all the year round. From April to October there is a guided tour, Monday to Friday at 11 am, and in addition on Thursday afternoon at 3 pm. There is no charge.

Schools and groups can make appointments to have a guided tour of the factory at any time of year during the day, although these visits are limited as they tend to interfere with production. A limited number of parties can be taken around in the evenings at any time of year — groups can make appointments. The factory seconds shop is open all year round Monday to Friday from 9 am to 4.30 pm, and on Saturday from March to December only, from 10 am to 4 pm.

32 Somerset Cider Farm

R. J. Sheppy & Son
Three Bridges, Bradford-on-Tone, Taunton, Somerset TA4 1ER
Tel: Bradford-on-Tone 233

Somerset has been 'The Cider County' for generations and until the 1930s most farms of any size produced their own cider. Since the Second World War large centralised factories have been set up and nowadays most farms send their apples to these factories. But Sheppy's, who have been making cider since 1925, still produce their own cider from more than 40 acres of orchards. Visitors can see the orchards, cider-making plant and museum. There is a shop on the farm which sells cider, honey, other produce and cider mugs.

Just to tempt you, here are some lines from a poem on their leaflet: 'The juice is extracted like wine. The product—Pure Somerset Cider, de-lightful, de-licious, di-vine!'

Practical details: The farm and cider museum are open to visitors Easter to Christmas, from 8.30 am until dusk Monday to Saturday, and on Sunday from 12 noon until 2 pm. Visitors may wander around as they wish. Coach parties can make prior arrangements for a conducted tour, if the proposed time is

De-fleshing a sheepskin at John Wood's

convenient to the farm's staff. The farm is on the A38, between Taunton and Wellington.

33 Vineyard

The Pilton Manor Vineyard
The Manor House, Pilton
Shepton Mallet, Somerset BA4 4BE
Tel: Pilton 325

The harvest begins in mid-October and carries on to the end of the month and sometimes into November. The stainless steel rotary press used at harvest time can be programmed according to the different types and standard of grape in order to obtain the maximum amount of first-quality juice. All the wines are bottled here. There is a press and bottling room, fermentation and bulk storage room and a small laboratory. Sparkling wine is made by the traditional champagne method, where secondary fermentation takes place in the bottle to produce the sparkle and the bottles have to be turned by hand in the racks.
Practical details: The winery is open to the public from June to September between 12 noon and 2.30 pm on Wednesday, Thursday and Friday. It is also open on Sundays and bank holiday Mondays from 12 noon to 6 pm, from late August through September. Wine with lunch, including stuffed vine leaves, is served on these visits. There is an admission charge.
Groups of over twenty people can enjoy a two-hour conducted tour during the summer by appointment.
The vineyard is open throughout the year for sales of vines and wine by the glass or bottle. Send an sae for a leaflet about the vineyard.

34 Telecommunications Museum

British Telecom Museum Taunton
38 North Street, Taunton, Somerset TA1 1LY
Tel: Taunton 73391

The British Telecom Museum
at Taunton is the largest museum specialising in telecommunications in the country and the only one which is regularly open to the public. The exhibits consist of telephone, telegraph and transmission equipment showing the history and development of one of Britain's most important industries.
Visitors are usually particularly interested in the old manual telephone exchange of 1900 which is reconstructed in the setting of a contemporary private house. The more technically-minded can study the intricacies of automatic exchange equipment and the displays include a complete working automatic exchange of 1929. Through this you can dial a call using telephones of the period, and there are several other working exhibits.
The telegraph section contains some of the oldest apparatus and a large collection of test equipment and tools used by the engineers of years gone by.
Practical details: The museum is open on Saturday from 1.30 pm to 5 pm and at other times by arrangement. Advance notice is needed for mid-week visits. Write to the curator, Mr. P. J. Povey.

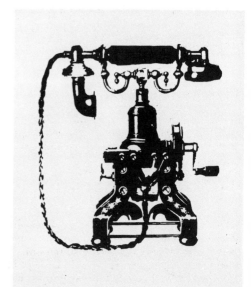

35   Nuclear Power Stations

Hinkley Point 'A' and 'B' Nuclear
    Power Stations
Hinkley Point
Near Bridgwater, Somerset
Tel: Bridgwater 652461

These power stations are of different designs.
The Hinkley Point 'A' power station is of the
earlier 'Magnox' design while the Hinkley
Point 'B' power station has two advanced gas-
cooled reactors and can produce enough
electricity for a city three times the size of
Bristol.
Practical details: It is necessary to contact the
administration officer to arrange a visit.

Wookey Hole — making paper by hand

36   Hand-made Paper

The Caves and Mill
Wookey Hole, Wells, Somerset BA5 1BB
Tel: Wells 72243

Many people have heard of the famous caves at
Wookey Hole, but do not know about the
interesting things you can see in the nearby
mill. The entire site is now owned by Madame
Tussaud's and the tour takes you first to the
caves, then to the mill.
The caves are impressive, rather than pretty,
and legends surround the witch who once
lived here.
The mill, where hand-made paper used to be
made in large quantities, is still producing
high quality hand made paper on one vat for
sale to the paper trade and to visitors. Two
or three men can be seen at work and other
trained mill staff will answer questions on
papermaking and the other exhibits.
Elsewhere in the drying lofts is the collection
of fairground relics, bought by Madame
Tussaud's from Lady Bangor. There are
coloured cats and ostriches, wild gold men and
other fantasy figures. On your way you walk
through the Madame Tussaud storeroom,
where the heads of famous people are kept in
case they suddenly come into fashion again.
You may spot the head of a pop singer, or a

British MP awaiting re-election.
In 1980 a new caves museum and waterwheel
were added to the mill exhibitions.
Practical details: Wookey Hole is open every
day of the year except Christmas Day, from 10
am. The last visitors are admitted at 4.30 pm in
winter and 6 pm in summer. There is an
admission charge, with reductions for
children and pensioners — a cost which covers
the combined tour to caverns and mill. Parties
of 20 or more people can obtain reduced prices
by writing in advance to the party booking
officer. Parking is free. There is a shop, a
picnic area and a cafeteria which is open all
year round. The restaurant serves a roast lunch
between 12 noon and 2.30 pm, every day in the
summer, and on Sundays only in the winter.

37   Steam Railway Centre

East Somerset Railway
Cranmore Railway Station
Shepton Mallet, Somerset
Tel: Cranmore 417

Steam engines fascinate everyone and at
Cranmore they have locomotives of all sizes
from the smallest Lord Fisher up to the
largest — like huge, powerful Black Prince, a
British Rail class 9F (freight). Owned by

the famous artist David Shepherd, who is one of the directors and a founder of the railway, Black Prince has appeared in the film 'Young Winston' and the film 'The Man Who Loves Giants' about David Shepherd's life.

Green Knight, a class 4MT (mixed traffic) engine was one of the first modern engines designed to be powerful enough for main line traffic, yet light enough not to damage old bridges on branch lines.

Practical details: The railway centre is open daily from 9 am to 6 pm, April to October. Steam trains run to Merryfield Lane and back on Sundays, public holidays, Wednesdays in peak season and certain Saturdays. The railway centre is open from 9 am to 4 pm during weekends, from November to March. Steam trains run on Sundays in December. Light refreshments are available and a full meal service is offered on days when trains are running. Cranmore is on the A361 Frome–Shepton Mallet road.

38 Shoe Manufacturer

C & J Clark Ltd
Street, Somerset
Tel: Street 43131 Ext 2321

The museum has documents and photographs showing the early history of C. & J. Clark from the founding of the firm in 1825. Shoes and machinery are displayed in the oldest part of the factory built by Cyrus Clark in 1829. Sole-cutting presses and sewing machines can be seen and there is a collection of slippers, boots and shoes from Roman to modern times, including some high ones which must have sorely tried a lady's sense of balance. Silly shoes are not merely the products of the age we live in. (Clarks, however, have been making children's shoes in a choice of half-sizes and multi-fittings for 100 years. One of their original advertising posters of 1883 advocates correct fitting footwear for children.)

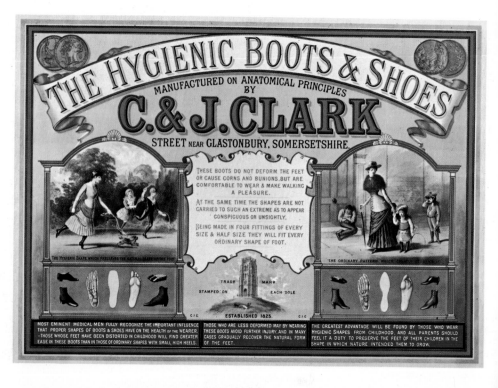

The story of Clark's beginning is of interest. Young James Clark was apprenticed to his older brother in the 1820s. He was bound not to gamble or marry for 5 years. At that time the factory made sheepskin products like rugs and mops and to while away his evenings, and make some extra pocket money, James started using short wool skins to make warm slippers. The sideline was soon so successful that it overtook the main business and the younger Clark became a partner.

In those days the work was largely done by outworkers, who were fined 1d. if they brought in work with soiled linings or tied odd shoes together! Today there are 2,500 employees at these headquarters alone, and Clarks has grown into a world business.

Practical details: Clark's Shoe Museum is open to the casual visitor in the summer months, Monday to Friday from 10 am to 1 pm and 2 pm to 4.45 pm and on Saturday mornings. No pre-booking is necessary. It is closed on bank holidays.

The shoe factories accept pre-booked organised trips. Write well in advance because the demand is so great that these tours are usually fully booked a year ahead. The factory is closed at weekends and at holiday times. Schools, colleges, clubs and so on are welcome. The maximum number allowed in a group is 40 and the lower age limit is 11 years.

39 Animal Hospital

Little Creech Animal Centre
RSPCA, West Hatch, Taunton, Somerset
Tel: Hatch Beauchamp 480384

This is a centre for sick, injured and orphaned wildlife and domestic animals. The national oiled bird cleaning and rehabilitation centre is here. There is a domestic animal section which is interesting for children.

Practical details: The centre is open every day including bank holidays from 9 am to 4.30 pm. It is suitable for the disabled, and casual visitors are welcome.

One of Clark's early posters—1883

40 Naval Air Station

Fleet Air Arm Museum and
Concorde Exhibition
Royal Naval Air Station
Yeovilton, Yeovil, Somerset BA22 8HT
Tel: Ilchester 840551 Ext: 521

The museum now houses the largest collection of historic military aircraft under one roof in Europe which, with an assembly of artefacts associated with the Royal Naval Air Service and the Fleet Air Arm, illustrates the development of naval aviation since 1903. Specialised exhibitions tell stories of events, personalities, ships and aircraft.

Connected to the museum is the Concorde Exhibition Hall in which the Science Museum displays Concorde 002, the first British assembled prototype, and tells the story of the development of passenger supersonic flight.

Practical details: Parking is free and flying may be watched from a free picnic area. Coaches and caravans are welcome. A cafeteria sells snack refreshments and a wide range of articles are available at a souvenir shop. Children and the disabled are catered for. Reduced rates for parties are quoted on request.

The museum and Concorde Hall are open daily (except Christmas Eve and Christmas Day) from 10 am on weekdays and from 12.30 pm on Sundays until 5.30 pm (or dusk when earlier). The museum is two miles east of Ilchester on the B3151, closely linked to the A303, and reached by Western National bus 478 from Yeovil.

41   Custom-made Furniture

The John Makepeace Furniture Workshops
Parnham House, Beaminster, Dorset
Tel: Beaminster 862204

Both individuals and groups are welcome to
the cabinet-making workshops of John
Makepeace and his assistants. Fine furniture is
designed and made here, using solid woods
like oak, cherry, walnut, rosewood, satinwood
and ebony. Suede, ivory and other materials
can be incorporated. Usually only one of each
design is ever produced, and furniture is made
on commission for private customers or
corporations in the UK and abroad.
Parnham itself is a fine Tudor manor house,
built around 1550 with later extensions by
John Nash. It is romantically set in a secluded
valley with the river Brit running through the
grounds. Oaks and cedars, woodpeckers and
peacocks form the setting.
Practical details: The principal rooms of
Parnham House, the gardens, gallery and
workshop are open April to October, on
Wednesdays, Sundays and bank holidays from
10 am to 5 pm.

42   Biscuit Bakery

S. Moores
Goldencap Biscuit Bakery
Morcombelake, Bridport, Dorset DT6 6ES
Tel: Chideock 253

This is a mouthwatering visit, and something
a little bit different. Moores make speciality
Dorset biscuits — the most popular being
Walnut Crunch, Dorset Gingers, Butter
Biscuits, Easter Cakes (January 1st to April
30th) and Dorset Knobs (December to March)
Moores' Dorset Knob Biscuits — rusks shape
like a small bun — originated about 150 year
ago at the old Moores homestead of Stoke

Dorset Knobs being made at S. Moores

John Makepeace Workshops: working with satinwood

Mills in the Marshwood Vale, West Dorset. Homegrown wheat was ground by the watermill and the knobs made from this flour were cooked in a faggot heated oven. Dorset Knobs, with early tea, made a traditional meal for local farm workers at the start of the day. The business is still carried on by the Moores' family and Dorset Knobs are made about three days a week at the rate of about 25,000 a day, in much the same way as they always were. Each biscuit is individually moulded by hand and has three separate bakings lasting a total of four hours. The whole process takes at least 8 hours, starting with the making of the dough at 6 am.

There is no charge for visits but only the most strong-willed will be able to resist the temptation to buy some of the company's products.

Practical details: The bakery is open on Monday to Friday from 9 am to 5 pm except on public holidays. The person to contact is Mr. Keith Moores who writes, 'The bakery is open to the public who are welcome to see whatever production is in progress. We like at least three days' notice for parties. A tour takes only 10 to 15 minutes and because of limited space we have to restrict groups to not more than 20 people at a time. We try to give a guided tour but cannot guarantee one. Depending on the time of day visitors will see the production and perhaps baking and packing of one or two of six lines of biscuits.' Moores' Biscuit Bakery and Dorset Shop are on the south side of the A35 road in Morcombelake, 4 miles west of Bridport.

43 Butterfly Farm

Worldwide Butterflies Limited
Compton House, Sherborne, Dorset
Tel: Yeovil 4608

Living butterflies can be seen flying and breeding in the indoor jungle. There are brilliantly colourful displays of butterflies and collections from every continent and a breeding hall for both butterflies and moths. In Summer there is more to see, as an outdoor section is open. In fine weather butterflies can be seen flying in the Butterfly House and sleeves of caterpillars are on the trees. Apart from butterflies, you can see green, pink and brown stick insects, scorpions and locusts, and the Giant Atlas Moth with a wingspan of nearly 1 foot.

The farm was started in 1960 by Robert Goodden when he was 20 years old. With the encouragement of all the family, he expanded it from an attic collection, bought a printing press to produce catalogues, and toured the Far East. Now the farm supplies live and mounted butterflies to museums, schools, photographers, film-makers and gardeners throughout the world.

As many butterflies live for only 7 to 14 days there are different things to see each time you visit the farm. You can walk through the new Palm house which looks like an equatorial rain forest.

Practical details: The butterfly farm is open from 10 am to 5 pm, including weekends and bank holidays, from Easter to the end of October. Individuals and groups can visit the farm during these hours without an appointment. Groups are advised to book.

Reeling silk from the cocoon

There is an admission charge. Visitors can picnic in the grounds and buy refreshments. Meals are obtainable from the Little Chef Restaurant just outside, but groups telephone Yeovil 23890 to book seats. Worldwide Butterflies is on the A30 and there is free parking space for cars and coaches. Lullingstone Silk Farm is in the same building (see below).

44 Silk Farm

Lullingstone Silk Farm
Compton House, Sherborne
Dorset DT9 4QN
Tel: Yeovil 4608

Lullingstone Silk Farm provides a unique opportunity to view the rearing of silkworms and the reeling of silk, practices which normally occur only in countries with hotter climates. The farm owes its existence to the determined efforts of Lady Hart Dyke who began the farm in the early thirties and

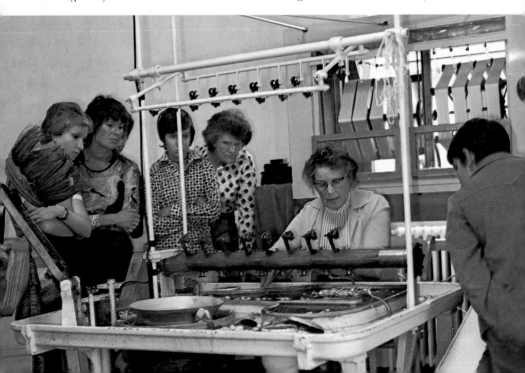

succeeded in establishing it despite the loss of 400,000 silkworms in the early years.

A display room shows visitors how silkworms are reared from the time that the moths lay eggs until the silkworm spins a cocoon, each of which contains as much as two to three miles of silk. Would-be rearers can receive advice on how to proceed. Visitors can also watch the skill of reeling silk on a machine which produces hanks of raw silk. Silk scarves and ties, silkworm eggs and booklets are on sale.

Practical details: Admission to the Silk Farm is included in the ticket for the Butterfly Farm in the same building (see above).

45 Old Ale Brewery

Eldridge Pope & Company Limited
Dorchester Brewery
Dorchester, Dorset DT1 1BR
Tel: Dorchester 4801

Huntsman Ales are brewed here by a family firm which has been independent since 1833. The brewery and wine merchants have unique Victorian premises, built in 1880, and they still brew beers similar to those made at that time — as the old 'Brewing Book', which you can inspect, will prove. The tours include the brewing process, bottling, and Maltings Conference Centre museum.

Practical details: The brewery is open in the afternoon from 2.30 pm to 5 pm. It is advisable to book in advance.

46 Earthenware Pottery

Leslie Gibbons
The Owl Pottery, 108 High Street
Swanage, Dorset BH19 2NY

Leslie Gibbons makes highly decorative domestic pottery and he also makes ceramic jewellery, small animals and hand-decorated tiles. He produces thrown and moulded

Leslie Gibbons makes earthenware pots

earthenware, specialising in individual dishes with pictorial motifs and intricate designs in majolica and slip. Owls and animals often feature in a variety of designs which are colourful and elaborate.

Practical details: The studio can be seen from the shop which is open daily except for Thursday afternoons and Sundays. It is necessary to make a prior arrangement for an educational visit and a charge is made.

47   Modern Pottery Factory

Poole Pottery Limited
Quayside, Poole, Dorset BH15 1RF
Tel: Poole 2866

Poole, the famous pottery based on a quayside, has a history dating back to the nineteenth century. Today it is a large factory where pottery is mass-produced using a variety of methods and tehniques. The pottery is divided into several sections, and visitors may join a tour which takes one through the major production departments of the factory, showing one how modern tableware is produced in large quantities.
Alternatively, one can browse in certain

Left: Inscribing a plaque

Below: Handpainting a stoneware model

Right: Mass production of ashtrays

departments of the factory. These include the craft section where potters work at the wheel, and the traditional handpainting section where Delft or in-glaze techniques are practised. Another section manufactures limited edition plates and the Blue Plaques which are used to commemorate the homes of famous men and women.

Practical details: Certain sections of the pottery, including the hand-throwing and handpainting sections, are open during normal working hours. There is no need to book and a small admission fee is charged. For a one hour tour of the factory which takes place Monday to Friday advance booking is necessary and a fee is charged.

The showroom selling a wide selection of pottery including seconds is open during normal working hours and, sometimes during the summer season, it is open at weekends.

48   Pottery and Craftwork

The Wimborne Pottery
6 West Borough, Wimborne Minster
Dorset BH21 1NF
Tel: Wimborne 887613

This pottery produces hand thrown and decorated pottery and there is also a spinning and weaving workshop in the attic. There are other sorts of craftwork here too, including hand spun and woven garments, corn dollies, woodwork, basketware and tie-dyed clothes.
Practical details: Wimborne Pottery is open from 9.30 am to 5 pm Monday to Saturday. Disabled people are welcome.

49   Wrought Ironwork

Wing & Staples
The Forge, Motcombe
Shaftesbury, Dorset SP7 9PE
Tel: Shaftesbury 3104

Mr. Staples writes, 'Visitors can see blacksmiths at work, and occasionally horse-

shoeing at the forge. Through many centuries the blacksmith has played an important role in his country's heritage. He has forged, bent, twisted, rolled, shaped, cut and welded metals into rugged shapes or beautiful works of art. 'You are welcome to visit our showroom and see for yourself where hand-made pieces are produced for you. The showroom has a few items available for sale but the majority of work is made to customers' specifications.' The forge produces door knockers, lanterns, wall light fittings, gates, boot scrapers, flower pot holders and adjustable flower stands, paper knives, balustrades, weathervanes and a large range of fire and hearth furniture and accessories. Something for everyone.

Practical details: Individual visitors and small parties are welcome to watch work in progress and browse in the showroom on Monday to Friday from 10 am to 4 pm, except lunchtime. Please give at least one week's notice.

50   Stone Carving

Bedwyn Stone Museum
Great Bedwyn, Marlborough, Wiltshire
Tel: Great Bedwyn 234

Mr. Lloyd is a local stonemason who carves monuments and fireplaces and does repairs to churches and other buildings. The museum, which he inherited from his father, is his hobby. He writes that a visit here is 'Humorous — very. Educational — in a way that you had never thought of before. Religious — in a strange and rather vulgar sort of way.'

But it is his theories about the symbolism of carvings which attract coach parties to the museum. At a time which most of us would regard as the Dark Ages, the local villagers believed that learning reading, writing and grammar were dangerous. The mason, often himself illiterate, would carve messages in stone on church buildings and gravestones. Mr. Lloyd, who claims he can crack any code, interprets the moral tales from symbols on the carved and painted headstones which he has restored. Baskets of flowers, surrounded by certain numbers, indicate that the soul had gone to a happy place. A bad man had cherubim on his memorial which showed, says Mr. Lloyd, that sexual experience was his highest ideal.

The local church of St. Mary's is famous for its carvings, and associations with Jane Seymour, wife of Henry VIII. The church authorities, while not agreeing with Mr. Lloyd's interpretation, have no objection to members of the public visiting the church, either guided by Mr. Lloyd or on their own.

Practical details: The museum is out of doors and so it is always open. Visitors are accepted at any time. A guide will be supplied by appointment.

Gravestone of a good woman from Bedwyn

51   Carpet Manufacturer

The Wilton Royal Carpet Factory Limited
Wilton, Wilts. SP2 0AY
Tel: Wilton 2441

This is the oldest carpet factory in the world. A history of the factory is given and the different types of carpet are explained. Four hundred people are employed here and the old buildings are still in use together with new purpose-built ones. Carpet seconds are available at the shop on the premises.

Practical details: A complete tour of the factory is given at 10 am and 11 am each weekday, with the exception of bank holidays.

Up to 10 people can be taken round at a time. Visitors are advised to book in advance, especially during the summer months. The tour lasts 45 minutes and there is a small charge.

52   Agricultural Museum

Lackham Agricultural Museum
Lackham College of Agriculture
Lacock, Chippenham, Wiltshire
Tel: Chippenham 3251

At Lackham Agricultural Museum you can see old farm machines, farm tools, wheelwright and smithy items. There are also reconstructed granaries, a dairy section and livestock implements. Sections on trapping, thatching, ditching and drainage are on view. An increasing number of veteran tractors is being collected.

Practical details: The museum can be seen on open days as advertised locally. It is also open at any other times for groups or individuals if prior arrangements are made. There is a small charge. The college is on the A350 midway between Chippenham and Melksham.

53   Craft Gallery

Wellow Crafts
Bath Hill, Wellow, Near Bath, Avon
Tel: Combe Down 833344

Alison Walker started this gallery after a successful exhibition to celebrate the Silver Jubilee in 1977. On display is the work of some 160 craftsmen and women whose ages range between eleven and ninety. Not only are traditional crafts such as tatting and hand-smocking represented, but also perennial favourites such as soft toys and jewellery. Mrs. Walker is particularly keen to encourage knitters and jam-makers, many of whom are elderly, and whose skills have been taken for granted over the years. Visitors are likely to see skills such as spinning or the making of corn

dollies being performed. During the winter months lectures and demonstrations are held.
Practical details: The gallery is open from Easter to Christmas between 11.30 am and 5.30 pm, from Thursday to Saturday, and on Sundays and bank holidays from 2 pm to 5.30 pm. Demonstrations take place during winter. Wellow Crafts is off the square in Wellow Village, six miles south of Bath on the A367 road to Radstock.

54   Costume Doll Factory

House of Nisbet Limited
Dunster Park, Winscombe, Avon BS25 1AG
Tel: Winscombe 2905

Peggy Nisbet started making dolls in Coronation Year when, with the permission of The Lord Chamberlain, she produced a limited edition of the Queen in her Coronation robes. Historical characters followed in quick succession, the Tudor period being one of the most popular, with King Henry VIII, his six wives and his daughter Queen Elizabeth I stealing the

limelight.
A tremendous amount of research into historical characters and costumes is involved and many of the patterns Peggy Nisbet uses are taken from reproductions of original drawings of clothes of the period, scaled down to fit the Nisbet 'little people'.
One hundred per cent wool tartans are woven for her in miniature in Scotland. The dolls' features are modelled mainly from paintings — often in the National Portrait Gallery.
Visitors are shown the various stages involved in producing the dolls — the art room, the cutting department, the machinists, the finishing section, the checkers, and the boxing and despatch departments. The factory tour takes about 45 minutes. There is no charge and visitors are usually able to obtain a cup of tea or coffee from the small canteen.
The dolls are not sold at the factory, but can be obtained from retail shops.
Practical details: The factory is open Monday to Friday from 8.30 am to 4.30 pm and visitors are welcomed, either individually or in parties of up to 12 people, providing 24 hours' notice is given by telephone or letter. Contact Mrs. D. Mantle.

55   A Variety of Crafts

Clevedon Craft Centre
Newhouse Farm, Moor Lane (off Court Lane),
Clevedon, Avon BS21 6TD
Tel: Clevedon 872867

Clevedon Craft Centre is housed in what was formerly a farm on the Clevedon Court Estate. The outbuildings, some of them up to 300 years old, have been turned into studios where you can see craftsmen and women at work.
There is quite a variety. Crafts include woodturning, leathercraft, carving in the round, handweaving, spinning, glass engraving and glass sculpturing. Unusual items produced by these craftsmen include waxed flowers and tables and trolleys with tile and marble-topped tables.
One of the old barns has been made into a countryside museum where you can look at

SS Great Britain docked at Bristol

old farm implements, craftsmen's tools, early household equipment and a unique collection of remedial horseshoes. An open-ended wagon house, with the original stone walls, has been converted into a licensed restaurant which serves morning coffee, lunch and tea. Admission is free throughout the centre and there is plenty of parking space.

Practical details: The craft centre is open every day of the week. The museum and restaurant are closed on Mondays (but stay open on bank holiday Mondays). Individuals are welcome without notice. Groups should contact Mrs. Pam Huxtable 2 days in advance.

56   Printers and Publishers

The Abson Press and Abson Books
Abson, Wick, Bristol, Avon BS15 5TT
Tel: Abson 2446

Visitors can see a Heidelberg press working and, according to what is going on, a variety of jobs such as typesetting, which lead up to the final printing. An explanation will willingly be given of the mechanics of publishing with visual examples of making a book at all stages from the author's manuscript, designs for covers and proofs, through to the finished book. This small publishing house produces recipe books and dialect books, like American/English glossaries.

Practical details: Heidelberg letterpress printers operate 7 days a week from 9 am to 5 pm and visits — for individuals — are by appointment.

57   Restored Liner

SS Great Britain
Great Western Dock, Gas Ferry Road
Bristol
Tel: Bristol 20680

SS Great Britain was the first ocean going iron

liner that was propeller driven. It was designed by Isambard Brunel and was launched in 1843. After a long and varied career ending in the Falkland Islands in 1886, she was salvaged in 1970 and returned to her original dock in Bristol and is being restored.

Practical details: Visitors may go aboard and there is a museum on the site as well as a souvenir shop and restaurant. There is an admission charge. Visits can be made every day from 10 am to 6 pm in summer and from 10 am to 5 pm in winter.

You can take the opportunity to see the striking suspension bridge at nearby Clifton. This was also designed by Brunel.

58 Nuclear Power Station

Oldbury-on-Severn Power Station
Thornbury, Bristol BS12 1RQ
Tel: Thornbury 416631

Oldbury-on-Severn Power Station is on the east bank of the River Severn, about 15 miles north of Bristol. The site covers 175 acres of land on the bank of the Severn, and a 380-acre reservoir has been excavated in the river bed to ensure that cooling water is available at all states of the tide. It can provide 416 million gallons of cooling water during low-tide. The station buildings consist of three major blocks housing the two nuclear reactors, the turbine house and the main 132,000 volt switchgear.

This is the Central Electricity Generating Board's first station where each of the nuclear reactors is housed in a cylindrical pressure vessel of pre-stressed, high-strength concrete.

The walls are 60 feet high and 16 feet thick. The base and lid of the cylindrical reactor are 22 feet thick.

Two computers are used in the control system. One computer monitors the many thousands of alarms and prints a record of every abnormal occurrence. It also displays on cathode-ray screens an analysis of a fault and the action needed to remedy it. A second computer scans signals from the burst cartridge detection equipment, and if signals are above a certain level an alarm warns the operator.

In the event of a reactor fault the safety system trips all 101 control rods into the core bringing about very rapid reduction in reactor power and temperatures.

Practical details: Write to the station manager or telephone the administrative officer. Individuals or groups of up to 40 people (aged over 14) can be accommodated Monday to Friday or, in

Decanting—Harveys' 13th century cellars

exceptional cases, at weekends. Guides accompany visitors and there is no charge.

59   Wine Museum

Harveys (of Bristol) Wine Museum
12 Denmark Street, Bristol 1, Avon
Tel: Bristol 298011/277661

The Harveys wine museum is the only one of its kind in Britain. Here you can learn how wines are made, and see articles used in production.
The main gallery has a display of sherry butts. Illustrated panels tell the story of the main types of wine from the regions of Bordeaux, Burgundy, Champagne, Rhine, Moselle, Oporto and Jerez the home of Sherry, complete with maps and climate charts.

The bottle gallery shows how Bristol became Britain's most important glass-making centre, exporting all over the world, and explains the development of the bottle, including the mechanisation of bottle-making from 1900. The company's sherry can be bought, and gourmets can lunch or dine in the Harvey's restaurant, selecting complementary wines, which are stored in the cellars seen on the tour.
Practical details: Visits by appointment only. Write to the PR Office, 12 Denmark Street. Organised parties of 35 to 45 persons are welcomed at either 2.30pm or 6.30 pm, Monday to Friday (not at weekends nor on public holidays). There is a charge for the tour, and a guide takes the group around. Under 18's not admitted.
The museum is very popular. It is fully booked for group tours a year ahead. Individuals and small family parties can sometimes arrange to join one of the smaller groups, but even then notice is necessary.

THE SOUTH

Essex, Kent, East Sussex, West Sussex, Surrey, Greater London, Hertfordshire, Bedfordshire, Buckinghamshire, Oxfordshire, Berkshire, Hampshire, Isle of Wight

1   Farmhouse-style Furniture

Ridgewell Crafts
Ridgewell, Halstead, Essex
Tel: Ridgewell 272

Farmhouse-style furniture is handmade in English Elm in a small workshop and sold from a retail shop on the premises. They specialise in Suffolk and Essex oyster stools and tables, and spinning chairs. Visitors can see the furniture being made by age old methods. "We still use handmade type nails" they say.
Practical details: Telephone Mr. and Mrs. Godsell or Mr. Crouch if you wish to visit the workshop. The centre is open all year except on Wednesdays. The workshop is on the A604, six miles south of Haverhill.

2   Dairy and Livestock Farm

Hobbs Cross Farm
Theydon Garnon, Epping, Essex
Tel: Theydon Bois 2808

Hobbs Cross offers children a unique opportunity to see round a farm. Normally members of the National Farmers' Union are obliged to keep to the rule that children accepted on school visits to farms must be aged eleven or older. However, Mr. W. A. Collins has adapted his farm to deal with school groups.

Between 7,000 and 8,000 children a year are taken round the dairy, beef and pig units, and receive an informal lesson in a heated classroom which has wall charts and pictures. At any time the farm has about 500 cattle, all British Friesians. During the summer months, April to September, the cows can be seen grazing or being milked in the milking parlour. The farm aims to produce one calf from every cow each year, and 1,000 gallons of milk.

The beef calves (150 of them) are fed mainly on barley until they are ready for market, when they are about a year old, and weigh about 8 cwt — as much as a small car or a dozen children.

Sows, 450 of them plus 150 replacements, are kept mainly for producing weaners (piglets). When the piglets are three weeks old they go into multi-suckling pens containing five sows and their litters. The pigs are sold when they are eight weeks old and weigh about 50 lbs each, and every sow is expected to produce 20 piglets a year.

Some ewes are kept specially for the entertainment of children, so that lambs can be seen all year round.

The farm has 240 acres of land and the grass is used for making hay and silage for the farm's livestock. Children might see tractors, or machinery for cutting, turning and baling, in operation.
Practical details: Hobbs Cross farm is suitable

for school parties of all ages and other organised groups. It is open in school term time and on some Saturdays, and up to fifty people can be taken on a guided tour. There is a small charge for each child, but adults accompanying children do not have to pay. A picnic area is available. For further information write to Mrs. R. C. Lynn or telephone between 9 and 10 am.

3 Car Manufacturer

Ford Motor Company Limited
Dagenham, Essex
Tel: 01-592 4591 Ext: 439/308

The giant Ford complex at Dagenham has

28,000 employees. Visitors are met by one of the eight full-time guides at the No. 1 Security Gatehouse in Kent Avenue. First stop is the giant engine plant where you see machining and assembling of petrol and diesel engines. From the engine plant a coach takes visitors to the body plant to see body panels being formed from sheet steel in lines of massive presses, some of which exert pressure of up to 2,000 tons per square inch! Cortina and Fiesta bodyshells take shape in the framing, welding and assembly sections and visitors follow the car through to the assembly plant. Here vehicles are painted and fitted with engines, gearboxes, electrical equipment and trim.

Practical details: The complex is open Monday to Friday from 9.45 am to 12 noon and from 1.30 pm to 4 pm. Telephone or write in

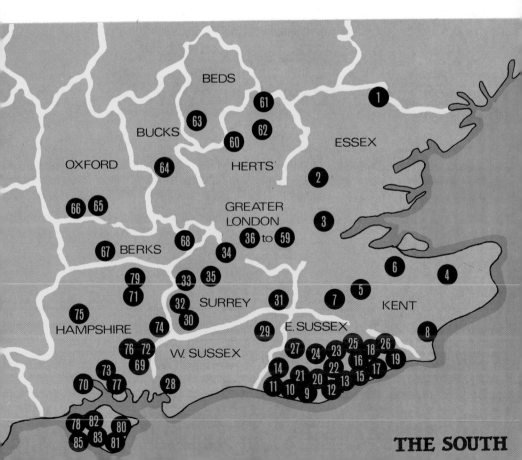

THE SOUTH

advance to the Supervisor of factory visits, Room 4/311a. Individuals or groups of up to 40 are welcome, but not children under 10. Children aged between 10 and 16 must be supervised by an adult. There is no admission charge.

Engine production line at Ford

4   Traditional Weaving

The Old Weavers House Limited
1-3 Kings Bridge, Canterbury, Kent CT1 2AT
Tel: Canterbury 62329

The Old Weavers House in the centre of Canterbury has a riverside shop on the ground floor selling handwoven goods, leatherware, locally made pottery and stones and mounts for jewellery-making. Upstairs this striking Tudor building contains 150 year old looms, spinning wheels and weaving implements.

There are demonstrations of weaving during the summer months.

During the reign of Elizabeth I the Walloons from the Spanish Netherlands came to England because they had faced religious persecution. Many of them were skilled weavers and they settled in Canterbury. The old Weaving House is believed to have been a centre for their work. The weavers' fortunes declined in the 18th century, because of competition from India, but the craft was revived at the beginning of the 20th century **Practical details:** Individuals are welcome to the house Monday to Friday from 9.30 am to 5.30 pm, and in the summer months the shop is open seven days a week. River tours on the Old Weavers Ferry leave from the house. Visitors in groups of twenty or more are given a discount on advance booking for the house or river tours. A tour of the house and weaving room lasts fifteen minutes, and there is a small charge. The river tour takes thirty minutes.

5   Carmelite Friary/Pottery

Carmelite Friary
Aylesford, Maidstone, Kent ME20 7BX
Tel: Maidstone 77272

This is a Friary of the Carmelite Order which was re-founded in 1949 and it is also a Shrine of the Virgin Mary. The site is impressive. Some of the original Cloisters date back to the 14th or 15th century and Samuel Pepys, the diarist, said, 'I was mightily pleased when I saw it'.

Pilgrimages are made to the shrine by Roman Catholics, Anglicans and members of free churches.

The pottery, run by the Carmelites, was started for them by David Leach and it produces typical Leach Japanese stoneware. The friars specialise in ecclesiastical pottery and all kinds of pottery for domestic use. These products have been sent all over the world. The Friary has a cafeteria, a car park, and a shop for postcards, souvenirs, religious

Car bodies taking shape at Ford

articles, books and pottery.

Practical details: The Friary is open from 9 am until dusk throughout the year, including bank holidays. The guesthouse, tea room and shop are closed over Christmas. Admission is free. The pottery is open Monday to Friday. The friars like to have notice of visits by groups, and guided tours are by arrangement — contact the Friary at least a week beforehand. The tour takes an hour. All kinds of groups are welcome as long as they respect the religious character of the shrine. Contact the Pilgrimage Secretary.

Handicapped groups are welcome, including people in wheelchairs.

6   Brewing, Kegging and Bottling

Shepherd Neame
17 Court Street
Faversham, Kent ME13 7AX
Tel: Faversham 2206

The tour lasts about 1 to 1½ hours and covers the brewing, kegging and bottling plants. The visit ends with a sampling session in one of the brewery cellars. You can buy mementoes from the brewery, such as ties and beer mugs.

Practical details: The brewery is open all year round from 10.30 to 12 noon, and 2.30 pm to 4 pm — not including weekends or bank holidays. Applications must be made in writing to the head brewer.

Advance notice of at least one month is needed as the tours are very popular. Individuals can join groups, but groups cannot be larger than forty people.

7   Wrought Ironwork

Hyders Limited
Plaxtol, Sevenoaks, Kent TN15 0QR
Tel: Plaxtol 215

Hyders' 14th century showrooms are of architectural interest and well worth a visit. The wrought ironwork displayed includes a museum of antique ironwork collected over many years. The display covers hand-forged wrought ironwork, gates, grilles, weathervanes, lanterns and brackets, electrical fittings of all kinds, fireplace fittings, firescreens, dog grates, and there is also some garden furniture.

Hyders specialise in restoring wrought ironwork. Groups visiting the works will see blacksmiths making scrollwork parts for gates and railings. Canopies and lanterns are put together in the sheet metal shop. Fitters put together bigger items such as gates and railings. Welders do smaller items such as weathervanes, bootscrapers and chandeliers. Finally, the wrought ironwork is painted.

Practical details: The showroom/museum is open Monday to Friday from 10 am to 4.30 pm, and on Saturday from 9.30 am to 1 pm. Not open on bank holidays or works' annual holiday. Individuals can only see the showrooms and cannot be shown around the works — groups of from ten to twenty people are welcome by appointment.

8   Nuclear Power Station

Dungeness Power Station
Dungeness, Romney Marsh, Kent TN29 9PP
Tel: Lydd 20461

Dungeness has steam plant using heat

supplied from nuclear reactors. Sea water condenses the steam after it has been exhausted from the turbine.

Visits last about one and a half hours and a short film on the principles of nuclear power is shown. Guides then take you on a conducted tour.

Practical details: The station is open to the public on Wednesday afternoons from June to September inclusive. Tours begin at 2 pm and 3 pm. Visitors must be fourteen years of age or over. Admission is by ticket only, available from the Seeboard shops at Bexhill, Rye, Hastings, Tenterden, Ashford, New Romney, Hythe and Folkestone. Details of electricity production are in this book.

9   Shellcraft and Jewellery

The Tropical Shells Company Limited
22 Preston Road, Brighton, Sussex BN1 4QF
Tel: Brighton 63178

The sea shell warehouse is a never-to-be-forgotten setting for all kinds of sea shells. It has a green floor, yellow walls and a brown ceiling. In the shop there are three palm trees and two stuffed crocodiles.

'I never thought there were so many shells,' is the usual exclamation when visitors come into the warehouse. There are more than three million shells here on open display on the shelves — that is if you count all the tiny rice shells, too! There are shells for craft work, jewellery making, flower arranging and for beautiful ornaments.

'In the middle of all the shells we clear a space for our visitors. They can sit down and hear a delightful talk given by a professional speaker who will tell them all they wish to know about any and every aspect of shells and shellcraft. Visitors will also see jewellery designed by Millicent Rich, principal of the Millicent Rich School of Shellcraft, and she can give advice on shellcraft and jewellery design.

Practical details: Individuals may visit the shop only, on Mondays to Saturdays 9.30 am to 6.30 pm. They are free to wander into the warehouse if they wish. Groups of all ages are

A refuelling machine at Dungeness

welcome to the warehouse seven days a week throughout the year. The minimum size of group is twenty-five people, the maximum sixty.

Unfortunately, you will have to make your arrangements far in advance, as they are now fully booked for about two years for the talk. However, you can still go to just look around.

10   Amateur Winemaking Supplies

Southern Vineyards Limited
Nizells Avenue, Hove, East Sussex BN3 1PS
Tel: Brighton 779971

Home winemaking in Britain has been increasing over the past twenty years and inflation and taxation are encouraging many more people to make their own wines. Southern Vineyards also export widely, though a few foreign visitors raise their eyebrows because it is neither legal nor profitable for them to make wines at home. Southern Vineyards import grape juices from all over Europe, blending them in England to produce a range of eighteen types of wines.

Recent new products have been Ginora, Whiskora and Brandora, now pushing the frontiers of winemaking even further to include these spirit substitutes, or as some say, spirit extenders. It is recommended that a bottle of commercial equivalent be added to each gallon for the best results. By serving a double 'Ginora' with less tonic than usual, a similar alcoholic effect is achieved at far less cost.

Wine enthusiasts will also be interested in the wine filter to remove cloudiness, the agitator to speed fermentation and reduce the risk of stuck fermentation, the hydrometer to measure sugar content as fermentation progresses, and the heater with patented holder to fit the traditional gallon jar without need for a special cork.

Practical details: The factory itself is not open to the public but their latest equipment is on display in the showroom, the receptionist answers questions about

winemaking, and you can sample their wines. Open to individuals and groups without booking, Monday to Friday from 9 am to 12.30 pm and 1.30 pm to 5 pm.

11   Power Station

Brighton Power Station
Basin Road South, Portslade
Brighton BN4 1WG
Tel: Brighton 593131

The visit includes a short film on the generation of electricity followed by a conducted tour around the power station accompanied by a uniformed guide. Visitors see coal milling plant supplying pulverised fuel boilers, the steam driven turbo alternator generating electricity, and the central control room. The visit lasts about 1½ hours.

Practical details: The power station is open to the general public at dates and times advertised in the local press. These are usually Tuesday and Thursday afternoons during the months of July and August. Organised visits can be accepted by prior arrangement Monday to Friday at 10.30 am, 2.30 pm and 7.30 pm and four weeks' notice is requested.

The power station is at Southwick, three miles West of Brighton.

12   Lace Maker

Isobel Kennet
34 Rise Park Gardens
Eastbourne, Sussex BN23 7EY
Tel: Eastbourne 764717

Visitors can watch Isobel Kennet making various kinds of lace. She makes bobbin lace, torchon, point ground, beds Maltese and Honiton. She also makes crochet lace, hairpin lace and broomstick lace. A number of items including handkerchiefs, paperweight miniatures, brooches, pendants, boxes and tablemats are usually on sale.

Practical details: Visits must be arranged by

appointment, Monday to Friday between 9 am and 4.30 pm. Individuals or small parties are welcome.

13   Theatre Complex

The Congress Theatre
Eastbourne, Sussex
Tel: Eastbourne 36363

A senior member of staff takes visitors on a tour of the complex, giving them a background history. Technical stations throughout the building are visited and there is opportunity for visitors to ask questions. The theatre has been reseated, has a new computer lighting system and new stereo sound system and has one of the largest stages outside of London.
Practical details: Groups of ten to twenty people are welcomed by prior arrangement.

14   Pottery and Craftshop

The Craftsman Gallery
8 High Street, Ditchling, Sussex
Tel: Hassocks 5246

The Craftsman Gallery and Sussex Crafts Centre is a centre for the crafts made in East and West Sussex. There is a pottery workshop where Jill Pryke throws and decorates earthenware pottery. A craft gallery houses a wide range of craft work which may be bought or commissioned, including batik, weaving, engraved wood, glassware, corndollies, silver, jewellery and metalwork.
Exhibitions of work by Sussex craftsmen are held two or three times each year. There is also an information section with details for those wishing to track down local craftsmen whose varied crafts include enamelling, marquetry and hessian modelling.
Practical details: Opening times are Monday to Friday from 10 am to 1 pm and from 2 pm to 5 pm. The centre is closed Wednesday afternoon and the pottery is closed during

Jill Pryke at her wheel

school holidays. Parties of up to fifteen people are welcome during opening hours and at other times by appointment, including evenings. By making an appointment you can ensure that you will see Jill Pryke at work.

15   Hand-made Glass Figures

Beckhurst Glass Studio
The Pier, Eastbourne, Sussex

This is a studio where hand-made glass figures are produced using a gas and oxygen flame.

The figures are sculpted freehand using soda glass and are then mounted on teak bases. This is a small family business that began thirty years ago and has been resident on Eastbourne Pier for the past thirteen years.

Practical details: Work is in progress for most of the day and visitors are welcome to watch. The workshop and showroom are open from 10 am until 5.30 pm Monday to Saturday and from 11 am to 5.30 pm on Sundays. There is a small pier toll during the summer months but admission to the studio is free. Models may be purchased and are packed for travelling. There are full catering facilities for all visitors on the pier.

16   Trug Making

Thomas Smith (Herstmonceux) Ltd
Herstmonceux
East Sussex
Tel: Herstmonceux 2137

A trug is a boat-shaped basket which gets its name from the old English word 'trog' meaning boat-like. Thomas Smith, the founder of the firm, designed the original trug over 150 years ago, and Queen Victoria ordered several at the Hyde Park Exhibition in 1851. When they had been made, Mr Smith walked the 60 miles from Herstmonceux to London to deliver them to her personally. The modern-day trug has changed little. It is still hand-made from willow boards set in an ash, or chestnut frame. It is a light strong basket and the open shape makes it particularly useful in the garden. In addition to garden trugs with supporting feet, the firm manufactures fireside log trugs, square trugs, bowls, and oval trugs decorated with pokerwork. A guide explains the processes, and you will see the pieces of wood used for the frame being shaved to the correct thickness, the bending of the frame around the shaping box, and the overlapping leaves of willow being hammered to the frame. Several of the staff of nine work only part-time, and there is more to be seen in the mornings. Perfect quality trugs are on sale to visitors at special prices.

Practical details: Individuals are welcome to call without notice. The shop is open Monday to Friday from 9 am until 5 pm, and the works keep the same hours but close for lunch at 1 pm. Groups (maximum 15 people) please book. School children over 14 years are accepted. The half-hour tour is free.

17   Pottery and Sculpture

Hastings Pottery
West Hill Villa, Cobourg Place
Hastings, East Sussex TN34 3HY
Tel: Hastings 422229

This studio pottery is situated by St. Clement' Caves on the West Hill, above Hastings Old Town. It is set against a background of natural sandstone and caves and overlooks the fishing quarter. Mr Dennis Lucas, potter and sculptor, works here with two part-time assistants to produce a variety of stoneware

Mrs Winnie Smith making a trug

and earthenware pottery and some individually sculptured ceramics. Visitors are welcome to walk around the studio while work is in progress. An added attraction is the indoor garden — where one can see the work on display.
Practical details: The pottery is open seven days a week from 10.30 am to 5.30 pm March to October, and from 11 am to dusk November to February except in severe cold weather and snow. Special demonstrations may be arranged by contacting Mr. Lucas at his home at the above address.

18 Traditional American Rag Rugs

Dormer's Farmhouse
Windmill Hill, Herstmonceux
East Sussex BN27 4RY
Tel: Herstmonceux 2388

Mary Murphy is an American who makes rag rugs in the American tradition, woven on a large ash and walnut loom made by her English husband Barry. The rugs are in wool with either cotton or acrylic warp. Rugs are on sale and visitors can see procedures leading up to and including the finished item, depending on the work in progress.
Practical details: Visitors are welcome from Tuesday to Saturday between 9 am and 3 pm, and on Sundays from 2 pm to 4 pm. Appointments should be made for special demonstrations. Since the Murphys are restoring their 300-year-old farmhouse, parties of more than five cannot be accommodated at present.

19 Rye Pottery

Rye Pottery
Ferry Road, Rye, Sussex
Tel: Rye 3363

Rye Pottery is a small craft pottery making hand-thrown, cast and machined tableware, lamps and commemorative items. Each pot is decorated by hand using the 17th century Delft or majolica technique. All pottery is made to order, either for retail shops or directly for the customer.
Practical details: The seconds shop is open on Monday to Saturday from 9 am to 12.30 pm and 2 pm to 5 pm except bank holidays. Visitors may see the ware being made and decorated on Monday to Friday from 9 am to 12 noon and 2 pm to 5 pm. Conducted tours can be booked for a maximum of eight people.

20 Vineyard

Drusillas
Alfriston, Sussex
Tel: Alfriston 870234

Drusillas has a vineyard with winetasting and tours, wine cellars and an exhibition of cider making methods. In autumn they make cider using a 120-year-old cider press. Then you will also find them harvesting grapes — and you can have a go yourself. There is also a pottery, and a woodworker making country furniture, a leatherworker who produces bags, hats, belts, pouches, etc. He dyes the cured leather and tools it himself. Sussex trug- (boat-shaped basket) making will probably start in 1981. Flamingoes and farm animals can be seen, and there is a miniature railway and adventure playground. Sussex mead, trugs, English wine and bread and scones baked here are sold to take away. Phone first to avoid disappointment for vineyard tours.

21 Needlework Tapestries

Patricia Hecquet
Northfield House, Boreham Street
Hailsham, East Sussex BN27 4SF
Tel: Herstmonceux 2147

Patricia Hecquet is an artist and designer who specialises in handpainted needlework designs. These are used for cushions, or as chair sets, rugs and similar items. You can

watch the stages involved in transforming a rough sketch into a finished painting.
Practical details: The studio is open throughout the year on Tuesdays, Thursdays and Fridays from 10 am to 4.30 pm. Individuals and parties of up to six people are welcome to visit the studio but are advised to telephone. Tapestry materials are on sale. There is ample parking at the studio which is situated on the outskirts of the village of Boreham Street, on the A271.

22   Hessian Sculpture

Audrey Jarrett
Little Costley, Langham Road
Robertsbridge, East Sussex
Tel: Robertsbridge 880130

Audrey Jarrett specialises in Hessian sculpture, making figures and groups to her own design. These range in size from a small child of eight centimetres to an adult figure of twenty centimetres. She also makes traditional dolls including peg dolls, rag dolls, and floppy dolls. The floppy dolls are made from Sussex puffs which were originally used for patchwork.
Practical details: Audrey Jarrett's workshop is open by appointment, and visitors will always see her working. People wishing to see a particular skill being demonstrated can make an arrangement in advance. Six visitors at a time can be accommodated.

23   Batik Artist

Mary Potter Studio
Laughton, Lewes, Sussex BN8 6DE
Tel: Halland 438

The Mary Potter Studio is set in the countryside a few miles from Lewes. The house is surrounded by fields with a backcloth of woods. The studio is purpose-built for making and displaying batik pictures. Batik printing is a craft which originated in Java and is now very popular, and Mary Potter

has adapted it to our own cultural needs. She works mainly on silk, applying wax with a brush or the tjanting or by hand, then dipping the material into the dye bath or brushing dye on to the design according to its requirements. One of the attractions is the brilliant and subtle colours possible in dyes. At stages in the process the wax can be cracked so that the dye penetrates the cracks, giving the characteristic lined effect which a skilled artist incorporates into the design. The English countryside is the main source of inspiration for Mary Potter's designs and pictures. She sells batik pictures and wallhangings, batik silk scarves, and she undertakes commissions. You can also buy original silk screen prints — cards with Sussex themes, handprinted scarves and traditional prints of brasses and the Bayeux Tapestry.
Practical details: The studio is open every day including weekends and bank holidays, but as Mrs. Potter is not always at home a phone enquiry is advised. All visitors are welcome, including small parties. Groups are accepted by appointment only.

24   Hand-painted Porcelain

Sheila Southwell
7 West Street, Burgess Hill, Sussex
Tel: Burgess Hill 44307

The artist, Sheila Southwell, works from home, decorating many differently shaped pieces of porcelain and bone china. No two pieces are the same. Each piece is designed, decorated and fired, signed and dated by the artist. The range of articles includes large wall plates, vases, dishes, trinket boxes and children's wall and door plaques. Pieces may be commissioned to make a really personal gift commemorating a special occasion. Most of the designs have an 'olde worlde' effect.
Practical details: The workshop is open Monday to Friday from 10 am to 5 pm. Individual visitors and groups are welcome provided they telephone or write in advance.

Mary Potter — silk screen and batik work

Demonstrations and lectures can be arranged for organisations.

25   Church Decorations

The Guild of St. Dunstan
Mount House, Burwash
Etchingham, East Sussex TN19 7EH
Tel: Burwash 243

The Guild of St. Dunstan was founded in 1968

for Christian artists and is based on the Ditchling Community founded by Eric Gill. The Guild specialises in church decorations including wood and clay statues, crosses, embroidered banners and memorial books. The three founder members live on the premises working in the studio which was the original fifteenth century farmhouse kitchen. Jean Maude-Roxby makes animalia, signboards and wooden figures, Barbara Newton uses her skills in pottery, needlework and calligraphy, while Raymond Newton makes detailed plank and small decorative boxes, brooches and plaques.
Practical details: Visitors may make an appointment to view work in progress from Monday to Saturday. Up to six visitors can be accommodated.

26   Harpsichord Maker

Malcolm Rose, Harpsichord Maker
1 The Mount, Rotherfield Lane
Mayfield, Sussex
Tel: Mayfield 2268

Visitors are welcome at this workshop, where they can see early keyboard instruments, both completed and in various stages of production. The workshop specialises in faithful copies of seventeenth and eighteenth century French and Flemish harpsichords, as well as Italian virginals and spinets. The traditional woods used include lime, poplar, Swiss pine, beech, ebony, pear, holly, walnut and Italian cypress.
Time-honoured materials, tools and construction methods are used throughout. Restoration work is also undertaken.
Practical details: The workshop is open at any time by appointment, including weekends and bank holidays. Individuals and groups of up to ten people can be accommodated, and short demonstration recitals on finished instruments are given. Please telephone for an

Right: Tuning an Italian virginal
Below: Crucifix carved in holly

appointment. Mayfield is an outstanding Sussex hill-top village, and offers good facilities for refreshment.

27   Wine and Cider

Merrydown Wine Company Limited
Horam Manor, Horam
Heathfield, East Sussex TN21 0JA
Tel: Horam 2401

At Horam Mill visitors are given a comprehensive tour of the cider mill, the winery and the vineyard. You can see the acetators, the fermentation vats and watch as cider and wine are bottled. This is followed by an opportunity to sample English grape wines, fruit wines and cider.
Practical details: Tours take place from mid-April to the end of September. Individuals and parties of up to forty people are welcome and should book in advance. The tour is unsuitable for the disabled and children under twelve years cannot be accepted. There is an admission charge.

28   Simulated Fur Manufacturer

Richesse Furs
Industrial Estate, Chichester, Sussex
Tel: Chichester 783748

Light refreshments are served when visitors arrive and this is followed by an informal fashion show and a tour of the factory to see the manufacturing process involved in making simulated fur. The visit lasts about 1¾ hours and no charge is made. There is no pressure selling but any garment can be purchased at wholesale prices.
Practical details: The factory is open Monday to Friday and tours are held at 10.30 am and 2.30 pm, except on bank holidays.
Bookings need to be made about one month in advance. Visitors are accepted in groups of between twenty-five and forty-two people. Children are not accepted.

The factory car park has space for coaches, and anyone organising a day out for older people will be interested to learn that no stairs are involved.

29   16th Century Britain at Work

The Horsham Museum
Causeway House
9 The Causeway, Horsham, West Sussex
Tel: Horsham 4959

Part of a sixteenth century black-and-white timber-frame has been converted into old-time shops where one can see how a wheelwright, a saddler and a blacksmith used to work. Costume, pottery and toys are on display and exhibitions are also held.
Practical details: The museum is open from 1 pm to 5 pm Tuesday to Friday, and Saturday from 10 am to 5 pm. It is open at other times by arrangement, and closed on public holidays. School parties are always welcome. The ground floor only is suitable for the disabled. Admission to the museum is free.

30   Musical Instrument Makers

Arnold Dolmetsch Limited
Arnold Dolmetsch Workshops
Kings Road, Haslemere, Surrey
Tel: Haslemere 51432/3

Arnold Dolmetsch was a concert artist and a pioneer in the manufacture of musical instruments. His desire to play preclassical music on the proper instruments led him to make the first modern lutes, viols, harpsichords and recorders.
Arnold Dolmetsch was responsible for reviving recorder-playing, and his son developed the low cost plastic recorders which are now used by so many school children. The company makes and sells instruments, such as harpsichords, spinets, clavichords, viols, lutes, classical guitars and recorders. It also restores and services harpsichords,

Viol-maker at Arnold Dolmetsch Ltd.

square pianos and old stringed instruments.
Practical details: Individuals and groups of
up to twelve people are accepted for tours on
Thursday at 11 am or 2.30 pm by appointment.
A conducted tour of the workshops is given
and you can see the craftsmen making musical
instruments — spinets, harpsichords and viols,
all hand crafted. The woodworking is done by
hand — wooden recorders are hand-turned
and hand-cut.

31   Gatwick Airport

Gatwick Airport
Horley, Surrey RH6 0NP
Tel: Crawley 28822 or 01-668 4211

For security reasons there are no tours of the

airport, but spectators are welcome to watch
Britain's second busiest airport in operation
from the special area on the roof of the
international arrivals building.
Practical details: The airport is open every day
from 8 am to dusk. There is a small admission
charge. Refreshment facilities are available in
the area and there is a car park, again with a
charge.

32   Grayshott Pottery

Surrey Ceramic Company Limited
Grayshott Pottery, School Road
Grayshott, Hindhead, Surrey GU26 6LR
Tel: Hindhead 4404

A wide selection of products is manufactured,
ranging from those made on the potter's

wheel, to more intricate shapes cast in moulds, and other articles, particularly plates, which are suited to machine manufacture. Visitors can watch these processes at close quarters and where a guide is not available the members of staff are only too pleased to explain. Glazing and decorating can also be seen.

The large pottery shop sells products at reduced prices including seconds.

Practical details: The pottery shop and works are open Monday to Friday from 9 am to 5 pm. The pottery shop alone is open on Saturday from 9 am to 5 pm. Both are closed on bank holidays.

During opening hours (except lunch time 1 to 2 pm) visitors can go round the pottery. Small groups of up to twelve people may do so without notice, but no guide will be available. These visits are free of charge. For groups of twelve or more people the visit must be arranged in advance and a guide will be provided. These visits can be arranged on Monday to Friday mornings. A charge is made for party bookings. The numbers in a party can be up to fifty-four and children may be included. Morning visits can also be arranged for groups of children up to the age of twelve and there is no charge.

33   Theatre

The Redgrave Theatre
Brightwells, Farnham, Surrey GU9 7SB
Tel: Farnham 722790

The Redgrave Theatre is built on to a Georgian house providing a half Georgian-half modern structure which contributes greatly to the atmosphere of the building. Drama is presented for fifty-two weeks of the year in an informal and friendly atmosphere and plays run for either three or four weeks. Monday evenings bring a change from the plays when the Redgrave presents a variety of concerts and recitals with the best artistes available.

Practical details: Tours round the theatre and backstage are always possible (except

Sundays) if prior arrangements have been made with the House Manager. The theatre foyer has the main bar, box office, and a small shop selling sweets, books, souvenir tee-shirts, bookmarks, key rings, tankards, ties, bags, aprons, greetings cards and other gifts.

34   Poppy Factory

The Royal British Legion Poppy Factory
20 Petersham Road
Richmond, Surrey TW10 6UR
Tel: 01-940 3305

Until 1975 the Factory of Remembrance employed only ex-service men, with preference being given to those who are disabled. But now ex-service women, widows of ex-service men and their disabled dependents are also employed. Ninety-six per cent of the employees are disabled in one or several ways.

The making of poppies for remembrance was inspired by the poem by Colonel John McCrae who died in 1918.

'In Flanders fields the poppies
Between the crosses, row on row . . .'
'To you from failing hands we throw
The torch; be yours to hold it high,
If ye break faith with us who die
We shall not sleep, though poppies grow
In Flanders fields.'

In 1922 members of The Disabled Society started making poppies for the British Legion, and since then the factory has grown into 'a human war memorial' employing about 150 full-time people and another sixty or so who are part-time or obliged to work in their own homes.

The factory now produces about 45 million poppies a year, 184 thousand remembrance crosses, and 70.000 wreaths. The disabled employees also make rosettes and show badges, and do printing work for the British Legion and for commercial organisations.

Practical details: Townswomen's Guilds, members of the Round Table and other groups, as well as royalty, frequently visit the

Wreaths at the Poppy Factory

factory, which has an average of 300 visitors each week. Individuals can join a group tour provided they arrange this beforehand. A tour of the factory takes 1½ to 2 hours and tea and biscuits are provided. There is no charge.

35   Unique Pottery

Wharf Pottery
55 St. John's Street, Farncombe, Godalming
Surrey GU7 3EH
Tel: Godalming 4097

Visitors have the opportunity of watching potters at work — throwing on the wheel, turning and decorating. In addition, Mary Wondrausch writes, 'The work that we do here is unique. I believe that I am the only potter using the slip trail and sgraffito methods of decoration on earthenware, in the seventeenth century English tradition.

They specialise in making individual plates to commemorate births, anniversaries etc. These come in presentation boxes and are sent all over the world. Most of the work they do is for mail order.

Practical details: The pottery is open Monday to Friday from 9 am to 5 pm and on Saturday from 9 am to 12 noon. Visitors are most welcome but as it is a tiny workshop the maximum number of visitors at one time is eight, and a telephone call in advance is helpful.

36   Design Centre

Design Centre
28 Haymarket
London SW1Y 4SU
Tel: 01-839 8000

The Design Centre has displays of well-designed British consumer goods and thematic exhibitions. Also the Design Index — information cards with photographs of hundreds of British products.

The Design Council has its own magazines, 'Design' and 'Engineering'. There are three shops in The Design Centre, two selling gifts and items for the house and another selling books on subjects such as lighting, and bathroom and kitchen planning.

Practical details: Open to the public Monday to Saturday from 9.30 am to 5.30 pm, and until 9 pm Wednesday and Thursday. Groups please phone first. A talk and design quiz are given to school groups of 11-15 year olds. Disabled visitors welcome.

37   London Visits

The London Appreciation Society
17 Manson Mews, South Kensington
London SW7 5AE
Tel: 01-370 1100

Those who enjoy unusual visits, but would rather leave the organising to somebody else, may be interested in the London Appreciation Society. This society was started by Mr. Bryant Peers who, when he was a young teacher in 1932, used to take schoolboys out on Saturday afternoons around London. Many of the boys could not even afford the ½d. tram fare, but the outings were so popular that brothers and sisters, then mothers and fathers asked if they could join the groups. And so a society for the parents was started. Nowadays buildings and institutions are visited, with guide lecturers, and evening walks usually end in a friendly pub.

At the beginning of 1977 they visited the headquarters of the London Salvage Corps which salvages material from fires, toured the self-service Post House Hotel at Heathrow airport, the Reliance Security Services, which patrols factories and offices, the Greenwich District hospital, and Sanderson's fabric printing factory at Uxbridge.

Practical details: If you are interested in joining the London Appreciation Society the subscription is £3.15 per year, payable on January 1st. The society's programme is published twice a year and covers the periods January to April and October to December. Visits are limited in number, and places are allocated on a first booked first served basis, but often additional dates are arranged if there is heavy demand for a particular outing. Free copies of the programme can be obtained by sending a large s.a.e. to the Hon. Sec. Mr. Bryant Peers. Most events take place on Saturdays and in the evenings. Anyone is welcome.

38   Science Museum

Science Museum, Exhibition Road
London SW7 2DD
Tel: 01-589 3456

While strictly speaking there is nobody 'at work' here, the Science Museum is full of interesting pieces of equipment, including working models. A visit to the science museum will quite probably teach you as much about how scientific principles have been applied to industry, as several visits to small firms which can show you only their own activities.

As the science museum is so vast, teachers should look around before bringing groups along, or if distance prevents this, they should write stating which galleries or exhibits they would like the children to see. There is a special application form for teachers. The science museum has a free lecture service, too. Some of the lectures are for the general public (adults only), others are for specialists. There is a regular schedule of lectures for schoolchildren of various ages. Special arrangements are made for handicapped groups. Of special interest are the 'Joint Industrial Lectures' given by scientists and technologists working in industry. Details of all the facilities, and advice on planning a museum visit, are given in the 'Visit Planning Pack' available free to teachers from the museum's Education Service. Public lectures and films are listed in a separate two-monthly programme.

Practical details: The museum is open to casual visitors Monday to Saturday from 10 am to 6 pm, and on Sunday from 2.30 pm to 6 pm. It is closed on Christmas Eve and Christmas Day, New Year's Day and on Good Friday.

39   Diamond Cutting

The London Diamond Centre
10 Hanover Street, London W1R 9HF
Tel: 01-629 5511

A permanent exhibition shows visitors the entire production process from mining diamond-bearing rock to creating beautiful jewellery. Visitors enter the exhibition through a reproduction section of a diamond mine, recreating conditions 1,500 feet below the surface of an African diamond field. Experts explain how the rock is blasted, crushed and washed to expose the rough stones, and the craftsmen who are at work cutting, polishing and setting precious stones are happy to answer questions.
In the showroom visitors can see and buy brooches and other jewellery as well as unset diamonds. These can be set in stock mounts or specially designed settings. Visitors should prepare to be tempted by their unique Grow-a-diamond scheme whereby diamonds bought here can later be sold back for not less than the original price, and for an extra sum a larger diamond can be fixed in the original setting. Don't forget to bring jewellery you would like valued. The centre offers an on-the-spot valuation for which a flat fee is charged.
Practical details: The centre welcomes visitors

Diamond mining exhibition

singly or in organised groups Monday to Friday from 10 am to 5 pm. Parties should give 48 hours' notice. The admission charge which is over £1 per head includes a souvenir of the visit.

40   Independent Brewery

Fuller, Smith and Turner Limited
Griffin Brewery, Chiswick, London W4 2QB
Tel: 01-994 3691

Strong draught bitter and other traditional draught beers are brewed by Fullers. Here, at one of the two remaining independent breweries in London, you will be taken on a tour which will show you the processes for brewing beer.
Practical details: Groups may arrange visits and individuals can sometimes join one of these groups. It is advisable for individuals and groups to make applications in writing well in advance as there is usually a waiting list.

41   Dyes and Dye-craft Kits

Dylon International Limited
Worsley Bridge Road
Lower Sydenham, London SE26 5HD
Tel: 01-650 4801

In their theatre, Dylon demonstrate the art of home-dyeing, including tie-dyeing (creating patterns by sewing or knotting, pleating or folding the fabric and tying it with string before it is dyed to prevent the dye penetrating those areas) and batik (painting the fabric with hot wax to keep out the dye) and fabric painting.
Dyes can be used to change the colours of old (or new) clothes and accessories to make them match, or to give them the season's colours. Soft furnishings can also be colour co-ordinated with dyes. Dylon make dyes for fabrics, suede, leather and wood. There are also dye-craft kits, fabric paints, whiteners for

sports equipment, rain and stain repellants, and suede and leather cleaners.
Any member of the public can get individual advice and free leaflets on all aspects of home dyeing by writing to Miss Annette Stevens. She will also send free leaflets and instruction sheets on dye-crafts to teachers. A set of four colour posters illustrating home-dyeing using multi-purpose dyes, cold dyes, tie-dye and batik, is available at £1.25 including VAT and postage. Educational establishments can obtain a special price list.
Practical details: Demonstrations are given during the day, Monday to Friday by prior arrangement. Schools, women's clubs, youth clubs and so on are welcome, and should contact Mrs. Anne Turner. Individuals who have a special interest can also come to these demonstrations, but may have to fit in with times and dates of other parties.

42   Planning a New Town

Thamesmead Information Centre
Harrow Manor Way, London SE2 9SA
Tel: 01-310 5223

This large development will eventually be a new town which will house 45,000 people. Visitors will see examples of town planning and architecture which won the Abercrombie Architectural Award in 1961. There are also areas currently under construction and plans for future development.
Practical details: Film shows, talks and guided tours can be arranged by contacting the Centre.

43   The County Hall

Greater London Council
The County Hall, Westminster Bridge Road
London SE1 7PB
Tel: 01-633 5000

Visitors are given a short talk and are shown a film. Then they visit the council's permanent exhibition, and the Council Chamber if it is

from the Greater London Council Bookshop.
Practical details: Meetings of the Council,
when it is in session, are held on every
alternate Tuesday afternoon at 2.30 pm and
are open to the public.

Weekday visits can also be made for visitors to
attend committee meetings. Weekday visits to
The County Hall by parties, including school
groups, can be arranged by the information
officer. Applications should be made well in
advance because this is a very popular visit.

44   Maritime Museum

National Maritime Museum
(including the Old Royal Observatory)
Romney Road, London SE10 9NF
Tel: 01-858 4422

You could easily spend the whole day at
Greenwich. The museum has more than two
and a half miles of galleries showing British
maritime history using actual craft, paintings,
contemporary ship models, uniforms,
weapons, personal relics, photographs,
navigation and astronomy instruments, charts
and globes. More visitors come here than to
any other group of historic buildings in
London except the Tower of London.

The Half Deck (junior centre) can be booked
in advance by schools for practical work and
packed lunches can be eaten here. (The
museum threatens to throw children
overboard if they don't behave!) The boat
building shop can be booked for a series of
building sessions by senior classes, youth
groups and amateur builders who must use
traditional materials and methods.

Party visits can be arranged with the PR
officer, and school visits through the
Education Officer, both of whom require four
weeks' notice. The museum's three bookshops
stock souvenirs, posters, ship model kits and
books — and there is a licensed restaurant.
Admission is free and regular special
exhibitions are held.

One can approach Greenwich Park by
British Rail, by bus, or in summer by
passenger launch from Tower Pier. (Tel: 01-

*The New Neptune Hall, National Maritime
Museum*

858 3996 for details.)
Practical details: In winter, the museum is
open Monday to Friday from 10 am to 5 pm,
Saturday 10 am to 6 pm, and Sunday 2 pm to 5
pm; in summer, Monday to Saturday from 10
am to 6 pm, and Sunday 2 pm to 5.30 pm. It is
open on bank holidays with the exception of
Christmas Eve, Christmas Day, New Year's
Day, Good Friday and May Day bank holiday.

45   National Newspaper

Express Newspapers Limited
121 Fleet Street, London EC4P 4JT
Tel: 01-353 8000 Ext: 3596 (Daily
Express), Ext: 3113 (Sunday Express)

A guide takes you from the top of the building
at the editorial and news sections and works
down to the bottom where you can see
newspapers coming off the press.

Practical details: Tours of the Daily Express
offices, lasting two and a half hours, take place
on Sunday and Monday evenings, starting at
8.30 pm. At the Sunday Express a similar tour,
lasting two to two and a half hours, takes place
on Saturday evenings at 7.30 pm. The
maximum number of people on each tour is
twelve, with a minimum age of sixteen years.
There is no fee.

46   The Stock Exchange

Brokers at the London Stock Exchange

Offices of the Council
The Stock Exchange, London EC2N 1HP
Tel: 01-588 2355

Guides explain the activities on the busy
trading floor and colour films are shown in
the cinema to explain the work of the Stock
Exchange. This is where the fortunes of
companies, even the fortunes of countries, go
go up and down. It is an extremely popular
attraction with, sometimes, many thousands
of visitors in a week.
Practical details: The public viewing gallery is
open from 10 am to 3.15 pm Monday to Friday.
Individuals have no need to book. Groups of
up to a maximum of forty people should write
to the Public Relations Officer well in
advance. School parties are particularly
welcome and there is no charge.

47   The Guildhall

The Guildhall
Gresham Street, London EC2

This has been the centre of the City's
government for more than 1,000 years and the
present Guildhall dates from 1411. In the
Great Hall the Court of Common Council, the
Local Council for the square mile of the City,
meets on a Thursday lunchtime every three
weeks, except during the Christmas and
summer recessions. The Lord Mayor presides
and arrives 'in state' with his officers.
Practical details: Apply to the City
Information Centre, St. Paul's Churchyard,
London EC4, Tel: 01-606 3030, for dates of the
Court of Common Council. School groups
and tourists often wish to see the Guildhall.

48 Vegetable and Flower Market

Spitalfields Market
65 Brushfield Street, London E1 6AA
Tel: 01-247 7331

Spitalfields is a wholesale fruit, vegetable and flower market just outside the City of London, serving not only London and the home counties, but all parts of Britain.
During the night, lorries bring in home grown produce for sale when the market opens at 4 am. Imported produce from all parts of the world arrives by lorry from the docks, or comes direct from the Common Market.
Spitalfields Market includes the London Fruit Exchange which houses many firms distributing fruit nationally and internationally. About 1,600 people work there, including the 300 or so market porters. Trading takes place six days a week and lasts until 12 noon on weekdays and 9.30 am on Saturdays. It is here that your morning grapefruit arrives, long before you get up. The flower market houses wholesale flower distributors, many of whom have been in the flower business for generations. The building is specially designed to make sure that flowers are kept in the best possible condition. The lighting is arranged so that no direct sun rays wither the blooms. Beneath each stand are spacious cellars in which flowers can be stored at a cool, even temperature.
Practical details: Formal, conducted tours are restricted to people connected with horticultural or catering industries. Contact Mr. C. A. Lodemore, the superintendent, at the above address. There is no reason, however, why any early riser, or late night reveller, should not stroll through the market. There is no guarantee what you will see as a casual visitor, but at peak hours the comings and goings are very interesting.

49 Town Planning
The Barbican
London EC2

The Barbican is a residential and arts centre

Acres of fruit and flowers—Spitalfields

which is still under construction in the City of London. Built on a thirty-five acre site, it has more than 2,000 flats and maisonettes, and garaging for 2,000 vehicles. An arts centre, comprising a theatre, cinema, concert hall, art gallery and library, is due to open at the end of 1981.

Of course, the real test is, what is it like to live there? Some residents have reservations. They find it lonely at night and think it would be cheaper to shop in the East End.

Non-residents are usually full of praise. They bring children here on Sunday mornings to feed the fish in the ornamental lakes. They admire the tubs of unusual plants, and comment on the way that old-fashioned lamps and parts of old London Wall have been made part of modern surroundings.

Practical details: Individuals can walk through this development, and architects and planners will be particularly interested. Plans and models are on show in the Barbican Estate Office, Aldersgate Street, EC2Y 8AB, which is open Monday to Friday from 9.15 am to 5 pm.

Conducted tours can be arranged for specialist groups of up to twenty-five people with particular interests; write to public relations office, Corporation of London, Guildhall, London EC2.

50   City Farm

Kentish Town City Farm
Cressfield Close, Grafton Road
Kentish Town, London NW5
Tel: 01-485 4585

The farm is run by Inter-Action, a non-profit organisation which specialises in youth and community activities. Children taking the guided school tour are shown the horses, and the use of the bridle, harness and other equipment. In the farmyard, chickens run loose, and there are ponies, donkeys, rabbits, guinea pigs, ducks, geese, cows, goats, sheep, pigs and ferrets. Children on pre-arranged tours are allowed into the pens in small groups to handle the animals.

The eating habits of the animals are described

Children can touch animals at City Farm

and children can feed the animals if feeding time occurs during the visit.

Practical details: Adults and accompanied children are invited to walk around on their own at any time until the stables close at about 8.30 pm (earlier in winter). There is no charge for casual visitors. One-hour tours of the farm can be arranged for school parties, Monday to Friday. Groups usually arrive at 10.30 am, 1.30 pm or 3 pm. There is a small charge for children (no fee for adults). Within ten days of the proposed date of an organised visit, the farm sends a map and confirmation. After the tour children can eat sandwiches in a nearby picnic place.

51 Glassblowing Studio

The Glasshouse
65 Long Acre
London WC2
Tel: 01-836 9785

Five young artists make and sell glass at this groundfloor glassblowing studio and gallery. Glass objects on display include multi-coloured paperweights in numerous designs, goblets, bowls, perfume bottles, vases and plates. Prices range from £5 to £100. A weekend glassblowing introduction course is held here, and beginners can learn to blow glass and apply colour. Also evening courses.

Practical details: The Glasshouse is open Monday to Friday from 10 am to 5.30 pm and on Saturday from 11 am to 4 pm. Visitors are welcome to come here and watch glass being made. Groups of more than 5 people please telephone in advance.

52 National Newspaper

Daily Mail
Harmsworth Publishing
Carmelite House, London EC4Y 0JA
Tel: 01-353 6000 Ext: 872

The Daily Mail, founded in 1896 by Lord Northcliffe, has a circulation of almost two million copies. An official guide takes visitors through the editorial offices and production areas, including the composing department, the foundry, the press room and, finally, the warehouse, where copies of the Daily Mail are loaded on to vans for delivery to stations and wholesalers.

The various departments are situated on many floors of the building and this entails walking up and down staircases.

Practical details: Tours start at 9 pm and finish about 11.15 pm on Tuesdays, Wednesdays and Fridays all year round, apart from public and religious holidays. Groups of up to twelve people, over fourteen years of age, are accepted. Contact the Daily Mail production manager, Mr. J. L. Cooper, at least five months in advance as the tours are very popular. There are no parking facilities.

53 Criminal Courts

Central Criminal Court
Old Bailey
London EC4

Proceedings rarely take place with the speed of the television court case with which we are all so familiar. A major court case may take days, even weeks. So, if you are visiting the courts for no more than a day, the shorter cases will be equally interesting as you will be more likely to see the conclusion.

Children often find visiting courts while they are in session rather boring. You have to sit still and keep silent in the gallery, and even then you may have to strain to hear a nervous mumbling witness. The people who find our courts most interesting are the foreign visitors. Commonwealth citizens are delighted to see this bit of British pageantry carrying on just as they had imagined it; Europeans find the mode of dress quite amazing, and, if they speak good English, are often impressed by British justice.

Practical details: The public are admitted to the courts during sessions from 10.15 am to 1 pm and from 1.45 pm to 4 pm. Visits can be arranged by writing to the Keeper.

54   Musical Instruments

Boosey & Hawkes
Deansbrook Road, Edgware
Middlesex HA8 9BB
Tel: 01-952 7711

Boosey and Hawkes are the largest musical instrument manufacturers in Europe. Five hundred people are employed at this factory, where brass and woodwind instruments are made. The tour includes seeing the press shop where tubing is pressed into shape, a look at brass being polished, and a visit to the tuning room. The instruments made are trumpets, cornets, trombones, flugel horns, tenor horns, tubas, euphoniums, clarinets, oboes and flutes.

The tour ends with a visit to the museum which has brass and woodwind instruments dating back to 1750.

Practical details: Guided tours are given on Wednesdays only, at any time of year except during works' holidays. Tours start at 10 am and 2 pm and last two hours. They are intended for people with musical connections such as schoolchildren (aged over eleven), orchestras and musicians. Individuals and couples can usually get on a tour within a fortnight. Full groups of forty people (maximum) need to book a year in advance, groups of up to ten people two months in advance.

55   Musical Museum

The National Musical Museum
The British Piano Museum Charitable Trust
368 High Street, Brentford
Middlesex TW8 0BD
Tel: 01-560 8108

The National Musical Museum is one of the few museums where you can actually hear automatic musical instruments play. On a tour of the museum reproducing piano systems and reproducing pipe organ systems may be heard. Other instruments demonstrated include phonographs, orchestrions, barrel organs and a Race Horse piano. Some restoration work is also carried out and you can watch pianos with 'expression' systems being restored.

Practical details: The museum is open on Saturday and Sunday from 2 pm to 5 pm April to October. It is closed on bank holidays. Entrance is eighty pence for a tour lasting one and a half hours. Party visits can be arranged by sending a stamped addressed envelope for form PV15. The museum is situated by the giant gas holder near Kew Bridge.

56   Artists' Paints and Brushes

Winsor & Newton Limited
Wealdstone, Harrow HA3 5RH
Tel: 01-427 4343

Winsor & Newton's Wealdstone works is a vast site of several factories. Different workshops produce paints, inks, brushes, canvasses, not to mention aluminium tubes and a host of artists' accessories.

The artists' materials industry is too small to be able to afford special machinery, so machines for making tubes and containers are adapted from the cosmetics and grocery industries. In some cases the tubes are filled by sausage-making machinery, and labelled with beer labelling machines!

To make brushes, sable tails are imported from Russia and China. It takes four years to learn how to make a brush. For sable brushes the fluff is combed out, the hairs are graded for size, and given a point. For hog brushes the bristles are bleached, put in a ferrule, and attached to the wooden handle.

Practical details: Unfortunately school children under fourteen years of age are not admitted for safety reasons. Groups of up to twenty, art teachers, practising artists and professionals are accepted. Tours are arranged by appointment Monday to Thursday,

A big paint vat at Winsor & Newton

throughout the year. The usual starting times
are 10.15 am and 2.15 pm and tours normally
take two hours. A prompt start is appreciated
as tours have to be carefully timed to avoid
factory breaks.
For further information please telephone the
publicity department.

57   Steam Pumping Engine

Kew Bridge Engine Trust
Kew Bridge Road, Brentford
Middlesex
Tel: 01-568 4757

The Kew Bridge Engine Trust has a collection
of engines which supplied west London with
water until 1944. Here you can see the world's
largest Cornish beam pumping machine.
There is also a museum containing large
pumping engines which are in steam every
weekend.
Practical details: The Engine Trust is open
from 11 am to 5 pm at weekends. School visits
may be arranged by appointment. There is a
small admission charge.

58   Fabric Printing

Sanderson Fabrics
100 Acres, Oxford Road
Uxbridge, Middlesex
Tel: Uxbridge 38244

Sanderson's print over 2,000 colourful
material designs. Some of the fabric is
expensive, 'But it doesn't wear out — you get
tired of it first', jokes the guide. In fact, the
same patterns continue to be popular for
years. You may recognise a William Morris
design from the late 1800s on furniture in a
modern department store.
Customers often wish to re-order matching
material for curtains and upholstery months
or years after their first purchase. So
Sanderson's keep a record of every colour used
in a design. The squares of colour are printed
on a piece of material the size of a traycloth,

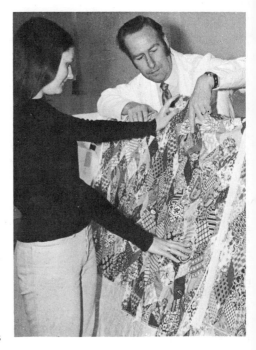

and it is locked away. Every time a new batch
of colour is mixed, an experienced person
compares the new squares with the old one
before printing can begin.
As the fabric is printed it is carried along under
a series of screens — one screen for each colour.
The fabric is printed either via the flat bed
screen printing method or on the more
modern and faster rotary screen printing
machine. Every piece of cloth now goes
through several processes including rinsing,
oxidising to fix the colour, soaping to make
sure the colours are fast and a final rinsing.
Overhead you can see the material running
over steam filled cylinders.
Finally the material is checked against an
illuminated screen. It is graded for colour, and
weaving faults are marked with tags so that the
cutter can cut up to the fault when
despatching orders. Thousands of metres of
bright, pretty material are despatched from
here every day.
At the end of the tour, groups have tea and
biscuits in the canteen and can ask the guide

questions. The processes are quite complicated and as there is a certain amount of noise in the factory, visitors usually take this opportunity to discuss some of the processes.

Practical details: The factory tour is popular with groups such as school-leavers, home economics students, art colleges and women's clubs. Each tour is for up to twenty people, aged sixteen or over. Tours take place at 2 pm prompt, on Tuesday and Wednesday throughout the year except during holiday periods. Write to the personnel department three months in advance. The nearest public transport is ten minutes away, so visitors come by coach or car. Allow extra time for finding the factory which covers a large area at the end of a long driveway.

59   Dairy and Sheep Farming

Park Lodge Farm Centre
Harvil Road, Harefield
Near Uxbridge, Middlesex

Park Lodge Farm Centre is a working commercial farm which aims at providing a means whereby visiting groups can observe and learn about farming. There are two main enterprises, a dairy unit producing milk, and a sheep unit producing fat lambs and wool. In addition to these units there are two trails through dairy/arable farmland.

Practical details: Bookings should be made through the Greater London Council, Department for Recreation and the Arts, 91 to

95 Uxbridge Road, Ealing. The farm caters specifically for school parties but other groups of up to fifty people can sometimes be accepted. There is an admission charge. The farm is open from 10.30 am to 4 pm with milking taking place between 2.30 pm and 4 pm and class teachers may conduct school visits after prior consultation with the farm manager.

60   Farm — Dairy, Pig and Arable

Oakridge Farms Limited
Blackbirds Farm
Aldenham, Near Watford, Hertfordshire
Tel: Radlett 6518

Cows and pigs are bred on the farm. Wheat, barley and oats are grown as fodder and seed. Grass is grown for seed and oil seed rape for its vegetable oil content. The farm rears its own pork and makes its own cream, yogurt and soft cheeses, which are sold through the farm shop. The farm also grows potatoes and a wide range of fruit and vegetables, sold through its Pick Your Own enterprise as well as the farm shop.

Practical details: School parties are accepted on Mondays to Fridays and should write to make arrangements. The public are welcome on the farm open days which are usually held biennially. A combine harvester is demonstrated and there are weaving and thatching displays. The *shop* is open Tuesday to Sunday from 9 am to 5 pm.

61   Woodturning

The Maltings
99 North End, Meldreth
Near Royston, Hertfordshire
Tel: Royston 61615

An old malthouse has been converted into a workshop where four woodturners, two men and two women, transform timber in its raw form into items of treen. Visitors can watch

pieces such as salad bowls, platters, spurtles and rolling pins being made. The Maltings also makes furniture to order using homegrown wood including ash, acacia, oak, hornbeam, elm and yew.

Practical details: Open from 9 am to 5.30 pm, Monday to Saturday. A prior appointment is essential. They can accommodate up to twenty people. There is no entrance fee.

62   Patchwork and Quilting

The Stables Studio
Dene Lane (by the church)
Aston, Near Stevenage, Hertfordshire
Tel: Shephall 271 and 308

In the rural setting of a pleasant Hertfordshire

village visitors can watch patchwork being made in its many shapes and colourings. They can see quilting in progress on a quilting frame and some historic examples of the two crafts.

A range of kits, materials, templates and aids to patchwork and quilting are on sale, together with quilts, coverlets, table cloths, cushions, bags, jackets, waistcoats, cosies and many smaller items. These are designed and made by Betty Randles.

Practical details: The studio is open from 11 am to 4 pm every day except Monday and bank holidays. Groups of less than twenty are welcome by arrangement.

63   International Airport

Luton International Airport
Luton, Bedfordshire LU2 9LY
Tel: Luton 36061 Ext: 223

At this international airport casual visitors in the spectators enclosure can watch the taking off, landing and taxying of aircraft. Groups may arrange to take a guided tour.

Practical details: One month's notice is required for the tour and groups should consist of twelve or more people. There is a car park and refreshments are available.

64   Small Weavers and Spinners

Joyce Coleman
Speen Weavers and Spinners
Speen, Aylesbury, Buckinghamshire
Tel: Hampden Row 303

'If you are enthusiastic about genuine handwoven fabrics, and would like to see some of the few remaining hand-looms still at work, you have only to come along to Speen and I will show you the whole operation,' says Joyce Coleman.

'Your interest may be in fine silks, curtains, or individual wall hangings; it may be in floor-

Hand-finishing a patchwork quilt

Aerial view of Didcot power station

mats; you may wish to indulge yourself in a once-in-a-lifetime luxury of a personal design which will be unique to yourself alone, and will never be repeated.

All goods are for sale.

A small charge is made for parties of visitors who like to be shown the work in progress. No catering facilities are available but on occasion and with plenty of notice the W.I. are willing to do teas in the village hall not five minutes' walking distance.

Practical details: Joyce Coleman writes, 'In normal circumstances I am available any afternoon but if you find it more convenient to make your call in the morning, it would be as well to telephone in advance. I might also be out and everything shut up if people arrive out of the blue so a fortnight's notice is a great help. People come as individuals or in parties — only about eight to twelve people can actually come in at a time but others wait in their coaches or cars till there is room for another batch.'

Follow the 333 or 334 bus route out of High Wycombe, up the Hughenden Valley for about five miles, into Speen.

65 Didcot Power Station

Central Electricity Generating Board
Didcot Power Station
Oxfordshire OX11 7HA
Tel: Didcot 813495

On arrival, visitors are shown a film about the power station. During the tour, which lasts for about 1½ hours, you see the boilers, steam turbines, generators, control room, gas turbines and coal unloading.

Power stations produce some staggering statistics. Didcot Power Station supplies 2,000 megawatts of electricity from 4 x 500 megawatt units — this is enough for ten cities the size of Oxford. Each of the boilers at full load burns 200 tons of coal and produces over 3¼ million pounds of steam per hour. There is a closed loop cooling water system which circulates a million gallons of water per minute. To re-cool this water there are six massive cooling towers, 375 feet high.

When you are standing outside you may be able to see the flue gases released from a 650 feet high chimney at 50 miles per hour.

Practical details: Tours of the power station are held Monday to Friday at 10.30 am and 2 pm, excluding bank holidays, and at 7 pm when lighter evenings make this possible. Requests for visits by individuals or groups should be made in writing to the station manager one month in advance. Up to thirty people can be accepted at one time. Restricted tours are given to children under fourteen.

The power station is not very easy to reach by public transport — go by car or arrange a coach or minibus for your group if you can.

66   Jewellery and Metalwork

The Old School
East Lockinge, Near Wantage, Oxfordshire
Tel: East Hendred 550

The Old School which is in the middle of an estate of 19th century timber and brick houses has been converted into a jewellery and metalsmith workshop. Craftsmen work here every day and the gallery has a display of their work, plus frequent one-man exhibitions. Jewellery and silversmith courses are planned at the Old School.

Practical details: Opening hours are Monday to Friday from 10.30 am to 6 pm and Saturday and Sunday from 12 noon to 6 pm.

67   Post Office

Reading Head Post Office
7–10 Friar Street, Reading
Berkshire RG1 1AA
Tel: Reading 55868 Ext: 249

Visitors see letters being sorted by the latest machinery which uses the Postcode system to sort mail electronically. They are also taken to the mechanised parcel sorting office and the delivery sections.

Practical details: Local groups and schools are welcome to make an appointment for a tour which takes place at 2 pm or 7 pm.

68   Working Horses

Courage Shire Horse Centre
Maidenhead Thicket
Maidenhead, Berkshire SL6 3QD
Tel: Littlewick Green 3917

The Shire Horse is known for its great strength and stamina, and has beautiful 'feathered' hair around the hooves. Some of the horses work on farms in winter and photographs show the history of Shire horses, pulling anything from ploughs to coal carts, railway or brewery delivery vans.

Harness is on display, plus photographs illustrating the history of the Shire Horse.

Practical details: Open daily from March to October except Monday, unless Monday is a bank holiday. Hours are 11 am to 5 pm (last admission 4 pm). Groups must pre-book for guided tours. The entry charge is reduced for booked groups of 20 or more. There is a pub, a tea room, pets' corner and a playground. Handicapped people are welcome.

69   Wine Making

Hambledon Vineyards Limited
Hambledon, Portsmouth
Hampshire PO7 6RY
Tel: Hambledon 475

This is an interesting visit for anyone who enjoys winemaking, wine drinking, or simply fresh air. Major-General Sir Guy and Lady Salisbury-Jones welcome visitors. They write, 'Visitors can see five acres of grapes growing on vines in the open. Notice boards explain the vineyard. Wine-making equipment can be seen in the press-house where a short tape-recorded talk explaining wine-making is given

Shire Horses at Courage

'We only make one wine and this is a dry white wine. It is not considered possible to make a good red wine in this northern climate, nor is it possible to make a natural sweet wine'. Most of the wine is sold to merchants and restaurants in the south of England but quite a lot is exported. All the wine is bottled here. It is drinkable after three months in the bottle, but it is at its best after about three years. You can buy wine at the vineyard (except when prohibited by Sunday licensing laws), and also from the local village grocers
Practical details: The vineyard is open to the public on certain days from the end of July to the beginning of October. For details contact the Secretary, Lady Salisbury-Jones. The admission charge includes a small wine sampling. A free car and coach park adjoins the vineyard.

70   Oil-fuelled Power Station

Fawley Power Station
Fawley, Southampton, Hampshire SO4 1TW
Tel: Southampton 893051

Fawley power station is one of the largest in

Europe, having an output of two million kilowatts. It is also the first station in this country to be under computer control.

The station was built to meet the rising demand for electricity in the south. It is on the western shores of Southampton Water — this site is convenient for the supply of fuel oil from the nearby refinery and because sea water is available for cooling. There is no need for cooling towers.

About ten thousand tons of oil are consumed in a day when the full load is required. Each of the four main boilers has thirty-two burners and consumes about 110 tons an hour. For the cooling process, eleven and a half million gallons of sea water are needed every hour for each of the four turbine condensers.

Four extra gas turbine-driven generators cope with peak loads and emergencies. They produce enough electrical power to run all the electrical equipment associated with each main boiler and turbine. So, in the event of disconnection from the grid, or at times of very high load demand, the station has its own internal electricity power supplies.

Practical details: For permission to visit write to the station manager. Individuals or groups of up to fifty people (aged over fourteen) can be accommodated at any time. Younger children are given a restricted tour by special arrangement. A guide accompanies the tour, which is free. Catering can be provided in special cases only. Parking is available.

71   Horse-drawn Waggons

Peter Ingram
Limes End Yard, High Street, Selborne
Near Alton, Hampshire GU34 3JW
Tel: Selborne 312

Mr. Ingram builds, paints and restores a variety of living-waggons. Restoring horse-drawn vehicles is one of his specialities, and building and repairing Gypsy caravans another. He has collected some items from Gypsy life which are displayed in his showroom.

Practical details: Visitors are welcome during the week but should make arrangements in advance. The workshop is usually open at weekends. There is a small admission charge and there are a number of items on sale.

72   Stoneware Pottery

Old Forge Pottery
37 Durrants Road, Rowlands Castle
Hampshire PO9 6BE
Tel: Rowlands Castle 2632

The Old Forge Pottery buildings date from the reign of Charles I. The workshop was built 150 years ago as a blacksmith's forge, and some of the smithy's tools are on display in the showroom.

In this unique setting Harry Clark and two other potters make hand-thrown stoneware in a simple, functional style using warm natural coloured glazes. Items include ashtrays, mugs, wine goblets, carafes, salt pots, coffee sets, table lamps, ovenware, large decorative platters and unusual clocks.

Practical details: Visitors are welcome seven days a week, from 9.30 am to 4.30 pm.

73   Art and Craft Centre

The Old Granary
Bank Street, Bishop's Waltham
Hampshire SO3 1AE
Tel: Bishop's Waltham 4700
(craftshop and restaurant)
Tel: Bishop's Waltham 4595 (workshop)

This two hundred year old granary, listed in Britain's archives as a building of architectural interest, has successively served as a wheelwright's shop, a wine cellar and a miller's store for threshed grain. Within the old brick walls a number of craftsmen may be seen at work. Their skills include the making of hand-dyed knitwear, fashion and textile design, silk screen printing, patchwork and macrame, picture framing, jewellery design in gold and silver, pottery, leatherwork, and the making of articles including toadstools in porcelain, dolls' clothes, dolls' food and dolls' houses.

The thatched craft shop sells a selection of traditional crafts from nearby cottage industries. The work includes crocheted bedspreads, patchwork quilts, hand-blocked fabrics, tapestry, hand-dipped candles, pottery, mohair rugs, Jacob's sheep rugs, ties and socks, hand-hewn walking sticks, shepherds' crooks, knitwear, rag dolls, lavender dolls, corndollies and baskets made from sedge found in local rivers.
Practical details: The Old Granary is open Tuesday to Saturday from 10 am to 5 pm. The restaurant serves home-cooked food. Parties are welcome but should make prior arrangements with the restaurant. There is no entrance fee and there is a large free car park opposite the building.

Rustic table at Barker & Geary

74 Specialist Bookbinding

Roger Powell
The Slade, Froxfield
Petersfield, Hampshire
Tel: Hawkley 229

Roger Powell is a bookbinder who specialises in conservation. He repairs and rebinds early manuscripts, printed books and documents and he also produces decorated bookbinding for collectors.
Practical details: Individuals and parties of up to ten people can watch work in progress by making arrangements in advance.

75 Forestry Products

Kings Somborne Craft Centre
Barker and Geary Limited
Romsey Road, Kings Somborne
Hampshire SO20 6PW
Tel: Kings Somborne 205

Barker and Geary manufacture and supply many unusual hand-made items, including rustic poles, hand-carved stools, wickerwork, coffee tables made to customers' requirements and canal painted ware. The shop has a display of old country tools and heavy horse harnesses.
Practical details: They are open six and a half days a week all year round.

76 Large Pottery

Denmead Pottery Limited
Forest Road, Denmead, Hampshire PO7 6TZ
Tel: Waterlooville 3017

Visitors can walk around the production area of this large pottery which produces modern pots and casseroles. The family can have a good day out as there is an adventure play area with scrambling nets, rope ladders and a zip wire to fly along, plus a duckpond, pet enclosures and wood grounds where you

Bald eagle handpainted on a plaque of
Brazilian agate

can picnic.

Practical details: On weekdays the production areas are usually working but phone first just in case they are not. The seconds shop is open seven days a week from 9.30 am to 5 pm.

---

77   Painting Miniatures

Anahid
164 Castle Street, Portchester
Fareham, Hampshire PO16 9QH
Tel: Cosham 376289

Anahid is an Armenian who paints miniatures, some measuring only half an inch by a quarter of an inch, on semi-precious gemstones. Among the items she produces are pendants, bracelets, earrings, hair combs, cuff links and tiepins, set in silver and gold. Anahid specialises in the detailed decoration of pill boxes and wall plaques. Visitors can watch her painting handmade jewellery and wall plaques and buy goods from stock or commission her to make a particular item.

Practical details: Visitors are welcome any time by appointment, either as individuals or in small parties, but large groups cannot be accommodated. There is no charge.

78   Unique Glassware

Michael Rayner Island Glass
London House, Queens Road
Freshwater, Isle of Wight PO40 9EP
Tel: Freshwater 3473

Free form hot glass sculpture and glassware decorated with enamel are among the unusual sorts of glassware Michael Rayner makes when he experiments with glassmaking. Most of his time, however, is devoted to producing a wide range of domestic glassware including jugs, vases, decanters, dishes and goblets — he also makes jewellery using glass.

Practical details: The showroom is open from 9 am to 1 pm and from 2 pm to 5.30 pm Monday to Saturday. Glassmaking may be viewed when in progress. There is a second showroom (but no studio) at The Broadway, Totland Bay, Isle of Wight (Tel: Freshwater 2116). It is advisable to telephone in advance before visits made out of season.

79   Mixed Craft Workshops

Viables Activities Trust Limited
Viables Centre, Harrow Way
Basingstoke, Hampshire RG22 4BJ
Tel: Basingstoke 3634

At the Viables Centre the visitor has a choice of crafts to see, with twelve men and women making their livelihood at the same location. In addition, there are various clubs, a miniature railway and a craftshop. Refreshments are available at weekends. The centre was previously a cattle breeding farm just outside Basingstoke, until the town spread out around it. Extensive renovation work has turned the bull pens and stables into individual craft workshops; the milking parlour has become the workshop for the disabled; the barn is now a community hall used by the clubs and one of the old farm cottages is a workshop. The rural character has been retained and the open space in the five acre tree-lined site retains a quiet, undisturbed

atmosphere — with the growing industrial town around it. The longest established craftsmen include a potter, a leatherworker, two silversmiths, a glass engraver, a wood turner and several ladies who knit woollen garments. More recent arrivals have been a wood carver, a pen-and-ink artist, a goldsmith, a painter and picture framer, and a furniture manufacturer.

Practical details: The general public can visit each unit and see the craftsmen at work. They are all open at the weekend and on the last few days of each week, with Monday and Tuesday being the days most craftsmen take as their days off. Visitors are free to wander around the centre.

The October Craft Fayre attracts thousands of visitors each year when all tenants as well as other visiting craftsmen have their work on display.

There is plenty of space for parking, although advance notice is preferred for coaches.

Groups wishing to have a conducted tour and those wanting evening visits should telephone to make arrangements.

80   Ceramics and Paintings

Ventnor Pottery Studio
10 Victoria Street
Ventnor, Isle of Wight PO38 1ET
Tel: Ventnor 852871

Kim Reilly makes hand-thrown pottery with a red body and a wide range of interesting coloured glazes but no decoration. Mugs, jugs, bowls, vases, flower pots, cheese dishes, preserve jars, storage jars and lamp bases are among the products. Paintings by her father, John Reilly, are displayed in the showroom.

Practical details: The pottery is open Monday to Saturday from 9 am to 1 pm and 2 pm to 6 pm. It is open on bank holidays but closed on Sundays, Christmas week, and possibly for one week at the end of October or early November.

Individuals are welcome at any time but there is only room for small groups of about ten people at a time. No warning is required but it is wise to telephone beforehand in winter in case John Reilly is out for a short while.

81   Award-winning Glass

Isle of Wight Studio Glass Limited
Old Park, St. Lawrence
Ventnor, Isle of Wight
Tel: Ventnor 853526

Vases, bottles, paperweights and bowls are among the items you can watch being made here. You can wander at leisure through the studio where the decorative glassware has earned its makers the Design Award in 1979 and the Gift Award in 1980.
Practical details: The studio is open from 8 am to 12 noon and from 1 pm to 4 pm Monday to Friday. The showroom is open from 9 am to 5 pm Monday to Friday and it is also open at weekends from June to September. Group visits can be arranged during spring and winter only. There is a small charge. The studio is situated off the A3055.

82   Vineyard and Vine Nursery

Cranmore Vineyard
Yarmouth, Isle of Wight PO41 0XY

The vineyard was started as a part-time venture in 1967 and is now a full-time business run by Bob Gibbons and Nick Poulter — enthusiasts who point out that southern England has similar temperatures to some of the German winegrowing regions and sometimes better sunshine. Winegrapes are sweet and as good to eat as dessert grapes, but only the winegrapes will produce a really good wine.
The vineyard produces high quality Estate Bottled Wine and vines from its own nursery. In 1979 60,000 plants were produced. Visitors are shown round the vineyard and see vines, from first year plants to those bearing mature crops. The cellar is included in the tour and the process of making wine is described. The grapemill, press, fermentation tanks and

bottling equipment can be seen. A tasting of the wine is given after the tour and questions are welcomed. Wine and books on vinegrowing and winemaking are on sale.
Practical details: Guided tours of the vineyard and cellar are given on Sunday at 3 pm and on Wednesday at 5.30 pm during August and September.
Visitors cannot be seen at other times because of a heavy work load and lack of free staff. Parties of more than ten should book in writing to avoid overcrowding. Up to sixty people can be accepted in a group. There is an admission charge.
Approach the vineyard from Cranmore Avenue, an unmetalled road leading north from the A3054, 2½ miles out of Yarmouth.

83   Restored Water Mill

Yafford Mill
Shorwell, Newport, Isle of Wight
PO30 3LH
Tel: Brightstone 740610

This beautifully restored eighteenth century water mill is in full working order and has a unique collection of carefully restored antique farm machinery and tools. The mill is surrounded by ponds and streams stocked with trout and teeming with wildlife.
Features include natural displays of waterfowl, rare cattle, sheep and pigs, and the Yafford seals.
Tours are not guided but all exhibits are clearly marked and staff are readily available to answer questions. Children in school groups are given a brochure and worksheet.

Working on the wheel, Jersey Pottery

There is a beautiful riverbank nature walk, a children's play area, refreshment bar, and well-stocked gift shop.
Practical details: The mill is open Easter to October from 10 am to 6 pm and on Sunday from 2 pm to 6 pm. There is no limit to the size of groups but as reception for coaches is limited, it is advisable to give advance notice. There is an admission charge, with reductions for children, o.a.ps and parties.

84   Large Modern Pottery

The Jersey Pottery Limited
Gorey Village, Jersey, Channel Islands
Tel: Channel Islands 51119

This large pottery is one of Jersey's major

industries and has been designed especially so that visitors can wander through each department following the process from the basic clay being thrown, cast, fettled and decorated to the final firing in the kilns. A craft and design studio adds further interest. Finished articles are on display in the showroom.
Practical details: The pottery is open all year round Monday to Friday from 9 am to 5.30 pm. It is closed on bank holidays. There is no admission charge and there is a large free car park. The Scandinavian-style cafeteria is noted for its food so arrive early in high season if you want to eat strawberries and avoid queueing.
The pottery is signposted from the main

Gorey road from St. Helier before the descent to the harbour.

85   Island Pottery

The Island Pottery
School Green Road, Freshwater
Isle of Wight
Tel: Freshwater 2356

This studio on the Isle of Wight was founded by the two Joes, father and son, and has retained its original concept of being the village craft pottery. It caters for the local folk, with bespoke articles such as commemorative plaques or mugs with individual lettering. Visitors may gather round the potter's wheel and watch a pot being thrown, or they may see the potter tending to the kiln. The various stages involved in producing a pot will be demonstrated.

Practical details: Visitors to the studio and showroom should phone a day or two in advance. Up to ten people can be accommodated and children must be accompanied. There is a car park.

Top: Handpainting at Jersey Pottery
Left: Joe Lester decorates a small pot

THE MIDLANDS
and East Anglia

Suffolk, Norfolk, Lincolnshire, Cambridgeshire, Northamptonshire, Leicestershire, Nottinghamshire, Derbyshire, Staffordshire, West Midlands, Warwickshire, Gloucestershire, Hereford and Worcester, Salop

1   Vineyard

Cavendish Manor Wines
Nether Hall, Cavendish
Sudbury, Suffolk
Tel: Glemsford 280221

Basil Ambrose of Nether Hall planted the first vines here in 1972 and produced a prize-winning wine three years later. Wines are on sale and there is a picnic site in the grounds.
Practical details: The house and grounds are open daily between 11 am and 5 pm (4 pm November to February). Coach parties should make prior bookings, and they can arrange for conducted tours with a lecture and winetasting. The price of admission to the house and gallery includes free parking, a complimentary glass of wine and access to the vineyards.

2   Rake Factory

The Rake Factory
Station Yard, Little Welnetham
Bury St. Edmunds, Suffolk
Tel: Cockfield Green 828630

They describe themselves as "a rural factory full of cranky machinery, driven by the original overhead shafts and belting from a 'pop pop' engine . . . a serious (though somewhat eccentric) factory", where craftsmen make useful things from local woods. You can see rakes being made, also scythe handles in five patterns, and mallets in all sizes up to the enormous 'try-your-strength' Beetles. Milking stools, rolling pins, bowls and kitchenware are also produced in English hardwoods such as Ash, Yew, Birch and Elm.
Practical details: The factory is open Monday to Friday from 7.30 am to 4.30 pm and during July and August it is also open on Sunday. Guided tours are provided without prior notice for two or more people, but large parties should make an appointment in advance. There is a small charge. A shop sells factory products, but refreshments are not available and there are no toilet facilities. Parking for cars and coaches is available. The factory is four miles south of Bury St. Edmunds on the A134 (turn left at the Eagle pub).

3   Pottery — Oven-to-table Ware

Henry Watson's Potteries Limited
Wattisfield
Diss, Suffolk IP22 1NH
Tel: Walsham-le-Willows 239

In front of this factory the remains of an old Roman kiln are displayed. Pottery-making has been carried out in Wattisfield since before

the age of recorded history.
By the factory door is a large beehive-shaped kiln, last used in 1961. It was fired by seven coal furnaces. Now the factory uses electric kilns. Inside you will see oblongs of mixed clay which have had air bubbles squeezed out of them, and these are then made into the rows of moulded teapots and crockery. One woman shows you how she sponges the lines where two halves of a pot are joined together, while another presses handles onto mugs.
Coloured glaze is then sprayed on by a group of girls in another area, and across the way, in the warehouse, finished articles are stacked high. Here you will find the seconds shop where you may buy a souvenir of your visit.
Practical details: Tours of the factory can be arranged by appointment Monday to Friday except for a fortnight in the July-August period when the annual holiday is taken. Times of arrival are 10.45 am, 2.15 or 3.15 pm and the visit takes about three-quarters of an hour. Groups may also visit the factory in the evening although there is no production in progress.
The shop, selling seconds, is normally open

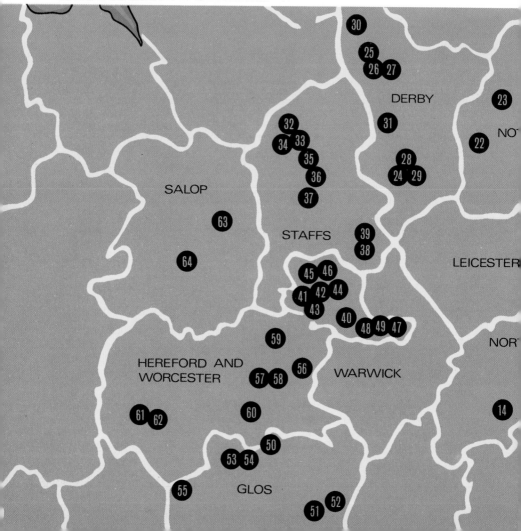

Monday to Saturday from 9.30 am to 5 pm, and remains open if there is a special evening tour.
No conducted tours can be arranged for individuals.

4 Food Manufacturers

Colman Foods
Carrow, Norwich NR1 2DD
Tel: Norwich 60166

The factory buildings are spread over a vast complex of sixty acres and you will see mustard flour being milled and packed: also many other products which are produced and packed here, such as barley waters, whole-fruit drinks, baby foods and honey.
Practical details: Conducted tours of some of the manufacturing departments of the factory are held from April to October, except during holiday periods at Easter, Whitsun and August when most of the factory is closed. Tours take place on Tuesday, Wednesday and Thursday afternoons starting at 2 pm prompt and lasting until 4 pm. Tea is then served and

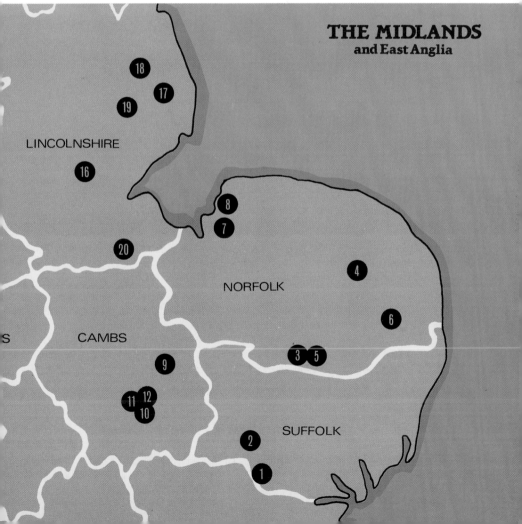

THE MIDLANDS
and East Anglia

visits usually finish about 4.30 pm.
The number of people in any party is limited to thirty-five. Children over the age of twelve are accepted provided they are accompanied by an adult. School groups are welcomed if the students are fourteen years old or over. As the tour involves a good deal of stair climbing it is not recommended for elderly people or those with heart troubles. Because of a heavy demand party visits need to be booked well in advance and this should be by letter to the Visits Organiser.

5   Steam Engines

Bressingham Gardens and Live Steam
Museum
Bressingham, Diss, Norfolk
Tel: Bressingham 386

Bressingham Gardens contain the largest collection in Britain of hardy plants, heathers and conifers — all displayed informally in a setting of mature trees and grassy walks. The gardens, hobby of the owner of a nearby nursery, were originally opened for charity, but public interest in them and the few steam engines caused the venture to grow.
Visitors can now see over fifty railway, road and other stationary steam engines plus steam driven threshing tackle in motion. They can take footplate rides on main line standard gauge engines and steam train rides on three narrow gauge railways.
The double attraction has made this outing very popular and there are often hundreds of visitors. A steam-powered roundabout, fair organ and street organ playing in the gardens are an added attraction.
The museum is a non-profit-making charity. Restoration of one engine can cost anything from 5,000 to 20,000 man hours and £10,000 to £17,000 for de-rusting, welding old and new parts and re-painting, not to mention continued maintenance and the cost of coal when the trains are run!
Practical details: Opening days are Sundays from early May to September, Thursdays from

late May to mid-September, Wednesdays in August, and spring and summer bank holiday Mondays. Opening hours are 1.30 pm to 5.30 pm and until 6 pm on Sundays.

6   Feathercraft and Taxidermy

Pettitts Rural Industries Limited
Reedham, Norwich
Norfolk NR13 3UA
Tel: Freethorpe 243/4

Pettitts Rural Industries include feathercraft and taxidermy. The products, which are on sale to visitors, include feather flowers, foliage, posies, quill pens, coffee tables, plaques with feather designs and many other feather products unobtainable elsewhere.
The feathers come from the main business of the company, which is table poultry and game.
Apart from making wedding bouquets to order (two months' notice needed) Pettitts hire out their stuffed animals. So if you want to hire a baby sea-lion for an exhibition, or perhaps a crocodile or python (coiled with head raised), this is where to get it. Some of the creatures are unnervingly realistic.
After you have seen the taxidermy you may also like to look at the collection of natural history specimens. Then, flocks of live peacocks and many ornamental birds, including waterfowl and black swans, can be seen in the attractive grounds, which include pools, bridges and summer-houses.

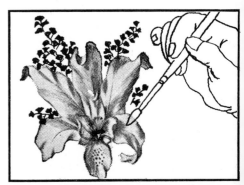

Pettitts were pioneers of oven-ready game and poultry, and produce is sold from the freezer in their showroom. Take a freezer bag along if you are likely to want to buy something.
Practical details: Pettitts Rural Industries are open throughout the year, Monday to Friday from 9 am to 5 pm, and on Sunday from 12 noon to 5 pm, also on bank holidays, except for Good Friday, Christmas Day and Boxing Day.
Individuals and groups are welcomed, including children and school parties. Large groups should get in touch with the company a week in advance. There is an admission charge. Refreshments are available from Easter to October.
Pettitts is near Reedham's fine thatched church. Approaching Reedham from the South you must cross the river Yare by chain ferry, which cannot carry coaches. Allow about 20 minutes extra for travelling.

7 Hand-blown Glassware

Wedgwood Glass
Oldmeadow Road, King's Lynn, Norfolk
Tel: King's Lynn 65111-6

King's Lynn was a glass-making centre from the seventeenth to the nineteenth centuries. But when the Wedgwood glass factory was opened in 1967 glass-blowers had to be brought from abroad — mainly Sweden — before local people could be trained. Now about one hundred are employed here making hand-blown glass-ware, including full lead cut crystal.
Glasses, decanters and candlesticks are made, and paperweights in apple, pear and mushroom shapes. There are also glass animals — seals, whales, snails, polar bears, mice, birds, ducks, penguins and owls.
Practical details: Guided tours of the factory are given Monday to Friday from 10 am to 2 pm. Write for an appointment, giving at least two dates, and as much advance notice as possible. All are welcome. The factory is closed on bank holidays. There is a small admission charge. The souvenir shop is open Monday to Saturday.

8 Lavender Harvesting

Norfolk Lavender Limited
Caley Mill, Heacham
King's Lynn, Norfolk PE31 7JE
Tel: Heacham 70384

Norfolk Lavender are the largest growers and distillers of lavender in Britain. Linn Chilvers, whose name appears on all Norfolk Lavender products, started growing Norfolk Lavender for distillation in 1932 with two acres of fields. Now nearly one hundred acres of lavender are harvested each summer and six varieties are distilled. Lavender used to be cut by hand, but today the flowers are harvested by the company's specially designed cutters.
The perfumer's art lies in blending the different oils. The formulae are based on an eighteenth-century recipe, when lavender was a favourite with both sexes. Until recently, flower perfumes have been more popular amongst the older generation, but nowadays flower fragrances are back in fashion.
If you wish to take home a little of 'the scent of English summer' you may buy lavender perfume, talcum powder, bath cubes, travel soap, mini soap tablets for guests, hand-made sachets containing dried lavender flowers, after-shave or talc for men — all dried by the company's new drying plant which you may see in operation. You may also purchase lavender seedlings in pots for your garden.
Practical details: Visitors are welcome during the period when the lavender is in full bloom and being harvested and distilled. This takes place every year from early July to mid-August.
Visits for coach parties may be booked in advance and a guided tour will be arranged for them, if they write for a list of suitable dates. These start at 10.30 am, 12 noon, 2 pm and 3.30 pm when the company's representative will join your coach for the drive to the field where harvesting is in progress, then to the distillery and back.

Norfolk Lavender—harvesting in July

The round trip involves about fifteen miles and takes around one and a half hours. There are also tours outside the harvest for coach parties only. Car parties can be shown through the distillery for a small charge. Please note that on Sundays, no coach parties are accepted and that the distillery's operations are also dependent on weather. Please write for details. Naturally the company hopes that after you have enjoyed the lavender's colour and scent out in the fields you will buy some of their unique products. There is a tearoom and a herb garden in the mill grounds.

Caley Mill is on the A149 two miles south of Hunstanton.

9   Rural Weaving Workshop

Fenweave
37 Main Street
Witchford, Ely, Cambridgeshire
Tel: Ely 2150

All-wool tweeds, linens and many other kinds of woven goods are made in this rural workshop. Interested visitors will be shown power looms at work and the processes will be explained to them. There is a shop where goods may be bought, and groups are entertained with coffee and tea.

Practical details: Individuals are welcome from 9 am to 5.30 pm, and in the evenings by appointment. Closed on Sunday, Monday and all bank holidays. Telephone Mrs. I. F. Allen. Parties of ten or more should give one month's notice and are accepted only in the evenings. No small children.

The workshop is at the east end of the village.

10 Newspaper Production and Journalism

Cambridge Evening News
Cambridge Newspapers Limited
51 Newmarket Road, Cambridge CB5 8EJ
Tel: Cambridge 358877

Visitors are given a slide presentation and a tour, and a local school reports that they had a most enjoyable visit. The Cambridge Evening News is a large and well-known provincial paper, and the printing and production processes make this a worthwhile and exciting outing.
Practical details: The newspaper welcomes groups of up to fourteen people. Bookings are handled by the circulation department.

11 Doll Houses

Den Young
63 Earith Road
Willingham, Cambridgeshire CB4 5LS
Tel: Willingham 60015

Den Young makes all types of model and dolls' houses from 16th century Tudor manors to Victorian stately homes. Complete ranges of furniture in an inch to one foot scale can be made from your own diagram or design. Custom built 'one off' items are a speciality.

Practical details: Visits can be made by telephone appointment only. For collectors and really interested individuals. Sorry no large parties. Den Young's workshop is open seven days a week.

12 Sculptor in Stone

Keith Bailey
63 Eden Street, Cambridge CB1 1EL
Tel: Cambridge 311870

Keith Bailey designs and carves architectural and memorial plaques, headstones and heraldry. Visitors are shown current work in progress, which may include restoration carving or garden sculpture. There is a display of photographs and drawings of previous commissions and sculptures.
Practical details: It is advisable to telephone before calling on Keith Bailey as he may be away fixing his work on a site. Owing to limited access only individuals and small parties can be accommodated.

13 Large Modern Brewery

Carlsberg Brewery Limited
140 Bridge Street
Northampton NN1 1PZ
Tel: Northampton 21621

'You wouldn't necessarily expect a brewery to be a beautiful building,' say the company, 'but with our Scandinavian background we felt we had a certain design reputation to maintain. So Knud Munk, an award-winning Danish architect, was commissioned to design the brewery. The result, we like to think, demonstrates quite clearly that industrial design can be beautiful as well as functional.' Carlsberg Brewery spent over £20 million on designing and building this brewery and claim that it is one of the most beautiful lager breweries in the world.
The brewery has all the latest equipment, including a computer, and the control panel in the brewhouse controls the brewing process

Above: Keith Bailey carves Welsh slate
Right: High-speed bottling at Carlsberg

from the silo to the fermenting vessels. The process begins with the steeping vats and mills, then during the mashing process the crushed malt is mixed with water and heated in giant coppers.

Eventually the high-speed bottling section automatically fills, caps and labels every bottle. This is one of the most fascinating sights, just like one of those films where bottles on an assembly line go jerking away to jangly modern music.

The output is about 54 million gallons a year. They make sure that the 'Carlsberg taste' is maintained by bringing over the strain of yeast developed way back in 1883. Samples of the brew are constantly sent across to

Denmark where they are matched with the original brews.
Practical details: The brewery welcomes everyone except small children throughout the whole year, from Monday to Friday at 9.30 am and 2.30 pm.

14 Canal Boats

The Waterways Museum
Stoke Bruerne, Near Towcester
Northamptonshire
Tel: Northampton 862229

Comprehensive collection of relics from canal life and industry, including a full size reconstruction of a butty boat cabin fitted out and decorated traditionally, brasses, traditional clothing and cabinware. Boat models and diesel engines show the craft of the inland waterways and a restored narrowboat is on display outside the museum. Recent displays show the tools and skills needed for canal maintenance and include a reconstruction of a workshop and blacksmith's forge.
Practical details: Open daily in summer from 10 am to 6 pm, and in winter 10 am to 4 pm (except Mondays). The last admissions are half an hour before closing. Closed on Christmas and Boxing Day. Groups by arrangement. There is a small charge.

15 Glass Modelling

The Glass Workshop
(The Rear of) 1 Bridge Street
Rothwell, Kettering, Northants.
Tel: Kettering 760165

Mr. Martin makes glass animals, birds, flowers and trees from glass rods and strips in thirty different colours. The figures take from five minutes to half an hour to make, depending on their size. He uses an oxy-butane lamp, which mixes one jet of oxygen and eight of gas. The oxygen makes the flame

Glass-modelling with an oxy-butane lamp

hotter. Most of the shaping is done with glass rods but he sometimes squeezes an ear or wing into shape with 'flappers'. These are strips of metal with U or V shaped or flat ends.
Mr. Martin makes a range of about seventy items, from galloping horses carrying miniature jockeys, to cartoon-like elephants, galleons, birds in cages, lace bobbins and lace spangles. All items are on sale. There are no seconds. 'Anything with a crack in it would eventually fall to pieces,' he explains.
Practical details: The workshop is open most times but phone to fix a definite time as Bob Martin does many shows and demonstrations to clubs. Individuals and small groups are most welcome to visit. Arrangements for larger groups can be made.

16 Pumping Station

Dogdyke Pumping Station Preservation Trust
Bridge Farm, Tattershall
Lincoln LN4 4G

The Dogdyke Pumping Station serves to drain water off low-lying land where, because of peat shrinkage, the land falls below the level of the rivers. At the station visitors may view the restored 1856 cast iron beam engine which drives a 28-foot diameter scoop wheel, capable of lifting about twenty-five tons of water per minute. The diesel engine and centrifugal pump, which replaced it in 1940, can also be seen. This pump moves forty tons of water per minute and was used until 1980 when an electric pump half a mile down river took over.
A small museum of fenland drainage is in the nearby engineman's house.
Practical details: The pumping station is open on the first Sunday in the month from Easter to October between 1.30 pm and 5 pm. Groups can arrange visits by contacting Mr. W. Edgar, 69 High Street, Tattershall, Lincoln LN4 4NN. Access is off the A153 Sleaford–Skegness road at Bridge Farm, Tattershall, one mile west of Tattershall Castle.

17 Pottery Animals

Ark Pottery
Hedgetoft, Maltby-le-Marsh
Near Alford, Lincolnshire LN13 0JP
Tel: Withern 543

The Ark Pottery is situated in a converted barn and, in keeping with its name, makes hand-modelled animals. Other novelty items, including cottages, are made here, and the pottery also produces domestic and garden earthenware. Visitors may look around the workshop and view work in progress.
Practical details: The pottery is open every day during summer and on weekdays during winter. Coach parties may arrange to watch a pottery demonstration and listen to a talk.

There is no admission charge. The showroom is unsuitable for the disabled.

ALVINGHAM WATER MILL

18 Water Mill

Alvingham Water Corn Mill
Church Lane, Alvingham
Near Louth, Lincolnshire
Tel: South Cockerington 544

There has been a water mill at Alvingham for at least 900 years. The mill, which was rebuilt in 1782, is in full working order and run as a working museum. Visitors can see meal and flour being ground by the power of the waterwheel.
Practical details: The mill is open to the public in August and September on the 2nd and 4th Sunday from 2 pm to 5.30 pm and every Monday and Thursday from 2 to 5 pm. Also Easter, May Day, Spring and Summer bank holidays 11 am to 5.30 pm. Groups can have guided tours by appointment.
Alvingham is three miles north east of Louth. In Alvingham there is also a traditional working forge and a pottery.

19 Cabinet Makers/Antique Restorers

Edmund Czajkowski and Son
96 Tor O'Moor Road, Woodhall Spa
Lincolnshire LN10 6SB
Tel: Woodhall Spa 52895

The workshops are run by Edmund Czajkowski and his son Michael who make and restore furniture. As cabinet-makers the Czajkowskis specialise in reproducing the

furniture of earlier periods. The special needs of each customer are taken into account in designing a piece of furniture which may be made of an exotic wood such as ebony and which may involve the special techniques of marquetry, gilding or carving. The restoration of antique clocks, barometers and furniture is also carried out in the workshops.
Practical details: The workshops are open from 9 am to 5 pm and appointments may be made for evening or weekend visits.

20 Saddlers and Harness Makers

S. W. Halford and Son
10 South Street, Crowland, Peterborough
Lincolnshire PE6 0EN
Tel: Peterborough 210605

Halford and Son specialise in leather goods and they are always making some type of harness in their small workshop. They make racing, hunting and riding harness or those suitable for Shetland ride and drive or heavy Shire show horses.
Practical details: Opening hours are Monday to Friday 7 am to 7 pm and Saturday 7 until noon. Everyone is welcome.

21 Power Stations

Staythorpe 'A' & 'B' Power Stations
Near Newark, Nottinghamshire
Tel: Newark 70331

The tour lasts approximately two hours. It begins with a short film about how electricity is made, followed by a tour of the plant, which is steam plant using pulverised (coal) fuel. The tour also includes a visit to the coal and ash plant, the boiler house and the turbine hall.
The Central Electricity Generating Board produces helpful booklets explaining how power stations work. An electric current is made when you turn a loop of wire in a magnetic field. You can try this yourself in a small way using a small horseshoe magnet and a paperclip. The dynamo of a bicycle or car makes power in the same way. So does the power station, but on a very large scale.
Here you will see the people and the machinery who make it possible for you to turn on the lights and use electrical appliances every day of your life.
Practical details: The power station is open from 10 am to 5 pm Monday to Friday. Applications should be made in writing to the station manager, giving at least three weeks' notice. Children under fourteen years are not eligible. Parties up to twenty-five in number can be accommodated. Sensible footwear should be worn at the station as it is an industrial site.
There are several other power stations in the Nottingham district which may be visited, so choose whichever one is the most convenient for you. All have similar facilities for visitors, and all provide a tour. We suggest that perhaps you select one of these three: West Burton power station near Retford; Ratcliffe-on-Soar power station; or High Marnham power station near Newark.
Write to individual station manager for appointments.

22 Pottery Demonstrations

Wood End Pottery
Near Cuckney, Mansfield, Nottinghamshire
Tel: Mansfield 842599

One-week residential courses and day courses in pottery-making using electric wheels take up about 60% of the time at this pottery overlooking Sherwood Forest. However the workshops and sales shop are always open and visitors are likely to see demonstrations of throwing on the wheel. Glazes made from local clays and wood ash are used. Domestic utilitarian ware is produced as well as copies of Greek and Roman pottery.
Practical details: The pottery is open for most of the year on seven days a week, usually 9 am to 6 pm (later in summer), but visitors travelling a long way are advised to phone

first. Admission is free. Home-made scones and cakes are available for evening parties.

23   Cabinet Makers

Hamlyn Lodge Cottage Industry
Welbeck, Worksop
Nottinghamshire S80 3LR
Tel: Worksop 85252

The Barrow family have converted a large house into a home workshop and showroom. They make reproduction furniture and restore antiques and they also make stoneware domestic pottery. Their work, as well as that of other craftsmen, is on display in the gallery and showroom.
Practical details: The Lodge is open seven days a week from 10 am to 6 pm. Parties can be shown around in the evenings by appointment. Admission is free and there is plenty of parking space.

24   Industrial Museum

The Silk Mill
Silk Mill Lane, Off Full Street
Derby DE1 3AR
Tel: Derby 31111 Ext: 740

The first-floor gallery has the theme 'An Introduction to Derbyshire Industries'. Displays show how the county's geology has determined its industries including lead mining, coal mining, iron founding, limestone quarrying, ceramics and brick making. The textile industries are introduced with displays of handframe and machine knitting and narrow tape weaving. More sections are planned to show the rapid growth of railways and other engineering in the nineteenth and twentieth centuries.
The Rolls Royce aero engine collection shows the development of aero engines over the past sixty years, plus the history of flying and aircraft, from the brilliant successes of the Wright brothers in 1903 with 'Flyer No 1' to the VTOL (vertical take-off and landing)

aircraft of today.
Practical details: The museum is open for all members of the public on Tuesday to Friday from 10 am to 5.45 pm, and on Saturday from 10 am to 4.45 pm. It is closed on Sundays, Mondays, Good Friday, Christmas Day, Boxing Day and New Year's Day. There is shop where goods may be purchased but no catering facilities are offered.
Admission is free and the nearest car park is in Full Street. Lessons offered in term-time include subjects like 'How aircraft fly' and 'Coal mining'. Teachers should contact the museum's education officer on extension 79

25   Pottery

The Derbyshire Craft Centre
Calver Bridge, Calver, Near Baslow
Derbyshire S30 1XA
Tel: Hope Valley 31231

In the Derbyshire Craft Centre in the Peak District National Park visitors will find a working pottery, a playroom for the children an eating house serving home baked food and a shop.
Practical details: The centre is open from 1 am to 6 pm seven days a week between March and December. It opens at weekends only during January and February. It is closed on Christmas Day and Boxing Day.

26   Folk Museum

The Old House Museum
Cunningham Place, off Church Lane
Bakewell, Derbyshire

The museum has a collection of leadminers saddlers', wheelwrights' and cobblers' tools There is also farming equipment and farmhouse utensils on display.
A Victorian kitchen has been recreated and Victorian costumes, lacework and old children's toys can be seen.
Practical details: The museum is open daily

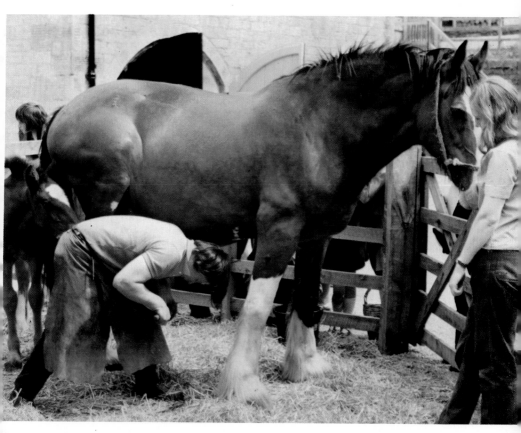

for individuals from Good Friday to October 31, from 2.30 pm to 5 pm. Groups must make an appointment, and the number for this is Bakewell 3647 (out of working hours).

27 Farming Demonstrations

The Farmyard at Chatsworth
Chatsworth, Bakewell
Derbyshire DE4 1PJ
Tel: Baslow 2242

The live farming and forestry exhibitions show visitors how the farms and woods on the Chatsworth Estate are managed. A milking demonstration takes place in a modern milking parlour every afternoon. Other

The Shire horse in Chatsworth farmyard

demonstrations of farming and forestry activities are shown from time to time in summer.

The livestock on view include beef and dairy cattle and their calves, sheep of several different breeds, pigs (both sows with litters and fattening pigs), poultry of old-fashioned breeds and modern egg-producing birds. A number of working horses including a Shire, Haflinger, and Shetland ponies are also on view. The life-cycles of the animals are described and an explanation is given of their use on a farm.

There is plenty to see and do, even on wet days, as there are several undercover exhibitions on farming and forestry. You can also take lovely walks through the woods or visit Chatsworth House, with its palatial apartments and frescoed ceilings. The house is closed on Mondays.

Practical details: The farmyard is open to the public every day from the beginning of April to mid-October, Monday to Friday from 10.30 am to 4.30 pm. It is also open Saturdays and Sundays from 11.30 am to 4.30 pm, and bank holiday Mondays and Tuesdays from 10.30 am to 4.30 pm. There is no guided tour of the farmyard, but school parties are catered for, and two-thirds of the visitors are children. School parties should write to the manager. Tea, coffee and biscuits are available in the Stables Tea Room (no need to book) and good catering facilities are available in Bakewell — famous for its tarts.

28   Porcelain Factory

Royal Crown Derby Porcelain Co. Limited
Osmaston Road, Derby DE3 8JZ
Tel: Derby 47051

Visitors are taken round the factory, where they may see fine bone-china tableware, figurines, china-handled cutlery, china brooches and ear-rings being made, and the final stage of the whole process, which is painting the china by hand.

The factory has a museum and visitors learn something of the factory's history. China has been made in Derby since 1748. The owner of the factory, William Duesbury, later bought the Chelsea works and moved some of its artists and workmen up to Derby. King George III gave his permission for the crown to be incorporated into the backstamp in 1775, and in 1890 Queen Victoria agreed that the word 'Royal' could be added to the title.

A museum open day is held on the first Tuesday of every month (except on bank holidays) when members of the public may bring pieces of old Derby ware to be identified. If you have a well-cluttered attic, it might be worth checking to see if you have any old china.

Practical details: Morning tours are mainly reserved for overseas visitors. They start at 11 am on Monday, Wednesday and Thursday, and at 10.30 am on Friday. Up to fifteen people can be accepted on a tour. Afternoon tours are held Monday to Friday at 2 pm for up to thirty people. Individuals and groups should contact the Visits Organiser in advance. The admission charge covers the cost of a booklet on the history of the Derby factory. Refreshments are available for organised parties if requested in advance.

29   Airport

East Midlands Airport
Castle Donington, Derby DE7 2SA
Tel: Derby 810621

This international airport deals with a variety of types of aircraft from the most modern jet to the smallest private aircraft. Services include scheduled flights to the Continent and holiday flights to the majority of popular resorts. The airport has a spectators' area which provides a picnic place and a children's playground. You will also find a restaurant, buffet and car parks.

A popular attraction is the airport's aircraft museum where you can see such aircraft as the Sabre, Vampire, Hunter, Whirlwind helicopter, Varsity, Harvard and Anson.

Practical details: The airport is conveniently near to the M1 motorway — take turn-off 24. For further details write to, or telephone, the Airport Director.

30   Stilton Cheese

J. M. Nuttall & Company
Dove Dairy, Hartington
Buxton, Derbyshire
Tel: Hartington 496

Here you can see Stilton cheese being made and stored in a modern factory — and rounds of cheese are on sale. The tour is free and, if the sight of all that food makes you hungry, there are several places where you may eat afterwards in Hartington village. These are open mainly in the summer months.

Practical details: Contact the manager of the dairy, Mr. I. C. Millward, to make an appointment. Factory tours are arranged from April to August, but are booked up well in advance. Groups of up to twenty-five or thirty people are welcome, though the tour is not suitable for small children or the elderly. During August smaller groups can see the process provided they apply in advance.

31 Engine House of Inclined Railway

Middleton Top Engine House
High Peak Trail
Middleton-by-Wirksworth, Derbyshire
Tel: Matlock 3411 Ext: 7165 (Derbyshire County Council)

The engine house contains steam-winding equipment which was built in 1829 and hauled wagons up the Middleton slope. The incline is one in eight feet, and 708 yards long. The Derbyshire Industrial Archaeological Society has restored the engine house and a member of this society, or the countryside ranger, will explain the history of the railway and how the machinery works. There is a small entrance charge.

The Middleton incline is part of the Cromford and High Peak Railway which linked the Cromford and Peak Forest canals.

It ran for thirty-three miles, carrying coal, iron, lime, corn and minerals to the main towns.

Practical details: The engine house is open on Sunday from 10.30 am to 5 pm and on the first Saturday of each month when the engine can be seen in motion. Everyone is welcome and groups may take mid-week visits by arrangement with the countryside ranger. He is Mr. K. Harwood, Rangers House,

Testing blue Stilton cheeses

Middleton Top Picnic Area, Middleton-by-Wirksworth, Derbyshire. Tel: Wirksworth 3204. Motorists may leave cars in the car parks at Middleton Top Engine House or Black Rocks picnic site. Both have picnic areas and toilets.

32   Coal Mining Museum

Chatterley Whitfield Mining Museum
Chatterley Whitfield Colliery
Tunstall, Stoke-on-Trent
Staffordshire ST6 8UN
Tel: Stoke-on-Trent 813337

The colliery, which was the first in Britain to win one million tons of coal a year, closed in 1977. It is now a uniquely exciting mining museum where visitors are taken 700 feet underground on guided tours, conducted by experienced local miners. Protective helmets, caplamps and belts are provided and visitors are advised to wear warm clothes and stout shoes. Past and present methods of coal mining are shown, also cutting machinery and exhibitions on safety, technology and geology, plus the lamproom, colliery canteen, boiler house and railway sidings.
Practical details: The museum is open from Tuesday to Friday 9.30 am to 4.30 pm and at weekends and bank holidays from 10 am to 5 pm. The last trip underground leaves at about 3.30 pm. On Mondays it is closed, except for bank holiday Mondays. The admission charge is reduced for booked parties. Children under 10 are not accepted. Parking is free, there is a museum shop, and refreshments are available.

33   Fine Bone China Factory

The Minton Factory, London Road
Stoke-on-Trent, Staffordshire
Tel: Stoke-on-Trent 47771

The Minton Factory is a modern two-storey building and it produces fine bone china tableware and fancy items such as vases, jugs and boxes. Downstairs you will see the raw materials and the making departments. Cups and plates are cast in moulds and handles are put on by hand. The china is fired in the biscuit kiln, dipped into glaze and fired a second time ready for decorating.
Upstairs you will see painting, decorating, lithography and gilding. One of the most interesting processes is gold acid work. This produces a design that is in relief by acid etching. Before immersion in the acid the areas of the plate where a relief design is not wanted are protected by a resistive material applied by a print and hand painting. After etching the resistive material is washed off and then gold in liquid form is applied to the etched areas and then fired. After firing the gold must be burnished.

A skilled engraver cuts the pattern for gold decoration of a Minton plate

A printed transfer for a Spode plate

On the ground floor is the works museum and people who cannot manage stairs, or antique collectors with a particular interest in old china can opt to spend their time in the museum instead of following the tour upstairs.

The shop has a stock of gift ware. Articles on sale include ashtrays, coasters, marmalade pots, cruet sets, cachepots for plants, oblong sandwich trays and pairs of candlesticks.

Practical details: Morning tours are held on Tuesday, Wednesday and Thursday starting at 10.30 am and lasting one to one-and-a-half hours. These are for up to ten people. Afternoon tours for up to twenty people are held on Tuesday, Wednesday and Thursday starting at 2 pm. Individuals can sometimes join small groups which do not reach these numbers. Contact the Personnel Department. Tours take place all year except on bank holidays.

34 Spode Bone China

Spode Limited
Stoke-on-Trent, Staffordshire ST4 1BX
Tel: Stoke-on-Trent 46011

The first Josiah Spode founded the Spode factory in 1770. He perfected the method of printing in blue underglaze and discovered the correct formula for bone china, fifty per cent of which consists of calcined cattle bone. Spode issue a booklet (price 50p including postage), which tells you a great deal about the history and manufacture of Spode wares. This information is very useful if you are interested in pottery making in general, as, for example, they list the main ceramic colour groups. The factory stands on its original site and some of the first buildings are still standing. Several of the manufacturing processes which you will see on the tour have changed little since the earliest times.

Practical details: Guided tours of the Spode factory are arranged from Monday to Friday each working week, and start at 10.15 am and

2.15 pm. The maximum number of people acceptable is forty and because of factory regulations children are only accepted if they are aged twelve or over. Individuals and groups must write in advance — people who 'pop in' are not catered for. Groups should try to arrive promptly so that there is time to visit all the processes which are normally seen on the tour, which lasts 1¼ hours. There is a small charge but you may redeem some of this charge on a minimum purchase in the Spode gift shop, where ware is sold at greatly reduced prices.

35   Earthenware Factory

Royal Doulton Tableware Ltd (Beswick)
Gold Street, Longton
Stoke-on-Trent, Staffordshire
Tel: Stoke-on-Trent 313041

This factory specialises in animal and character studies.
On the tour you see the clay department, where the figures are made, sponging to remove the seams on moulded items, the decorating department where hand painting takes place, aerographing (colour spraying) before glazing, the kilns, and decorating on the glaze.
The shop sells seconds only. You will not find items from the connoisseur range here but there are many tempting and attractive items which would make ideal gifts for children and animal lovers. There are Beatrix Potter figurines, Winnie-the-Pooh, Kittie McBride characters such as the Family Mouse, Alice in Wonderland, foals, cattle, cats and dogs.
Practical details: Tours are held from March to October excepting bank holidays on Tuesday, Wednesday and Thursday afternoons for groups of up to twenty-four people. The minimum party booking is twelve, but individuals or couples could probably manage to join a group which was slightly smaller than the maximum accepted number. Children aged 16 and over are accepted. People who cannot climb stairs would not find this visit suitable. No charge is

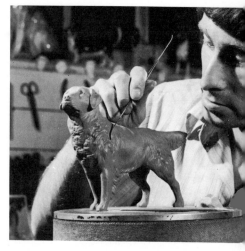

Beswick—modelling a dog study

made for the tour. Contact Mrs. I. Underwood well in advance to make arrangements.

36   Pottery Museum

Gladstone Pottery Museum
Uttoxeter Road, Longton
Stoke-on-Trent, Staffordshire ST3 1PQ
Tel: Stoke-on-Trent 319232

A living and working museum of the British pottery industry, which won the museum of the year award in 1976. Named after Gladstone in the late 19th century, it is an original and typical early Victorian 'potbank', with four spectacular bottle ovens, cobbled yard, engine house (steam power once drove clay mixing machinery) and workshops. Craftsmen and women are working and demonstrating pottery skills.
Practical details: From April to September the museum is open Monday to Friday from 10.30 am to 5.30 pm and on Sundays and bank holidays 2 to 6 pm. Also Wednesday evenings 6.30 to 9 pm for booked parties only. From October to March the times are as above but it is closed on Mondays. All visitors are welcome but groups of 10 or more should book in

advance. Guides are available (maximum 20 persons per guide) at a fixed cost for a 1½ hour session. Admission charges for individuals are reduced for children, students and senior citizens. A family ticket is available for two parents and up to four children. Write enclosing an sae for party booking forms, publications lists, etc. There is a teashop.

37   Wedgwood China

Josiah Wedgwood and Sons Limited
Barlaston, Stoke-on-Trent
Staffordshire ST12 9ES
Tel: Barlaston 3218

In 1759 Josiah Wedgwood — the 'Father of English Potters' — founded his company. Now in its third century, Wedgwood manufactures a wide range of traditional and modern ornamental and tableware in fine bone china, Queen's Ware (fine earthenware), oven-to-tableware, Jasper and Black Basalt at this extensive modern factory near Stoke. Recently Wedgwood has expanded more than at any time in its 218-year history, acquiring famous, long-established and large tableware manufacturers. Wedgwood employed 2,400 people in 1966 and grew to a group of companies with over 9,000 employees in the UK by 1977. Its 20 factories produce a fifth of the British ceramic industry's output and a quarter of its exports.

Visitors touring the Wedgwood factory

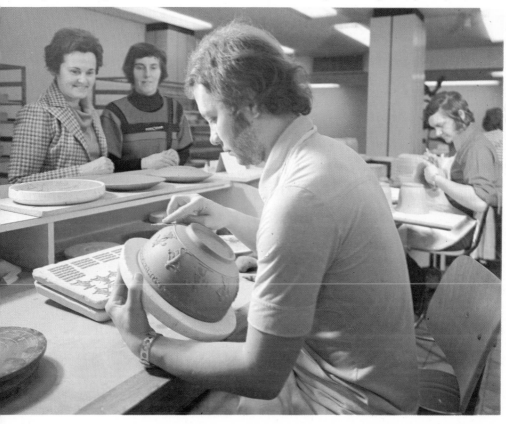

Visitors see an award-winning film and tour the museum and craft demonstration area. You will learn about Wedgwood's invention of Queen's Ware, Jasper and Black Basalt, and the development of fine bone china in the early 19th century. Examples of almost all the ceramic wares made by the first Josiah and his successors are displayed, with trials, early moulds, original wax models and documents. Full-length cases re-create parts of an 18th century pottery factory, such as a mouldmaker's workshop and a modelling studio. In the demonstration hall visitors see the traditional hand processes, many unchanged since Josiah's time, used to make Wedgwood today. For Jasper ware — throwing on the wheel, turning, figure-making and ornamenting. Also the casting of busts, figures and other ornamental items — mainly in Black Basalt, Josiah's first ornamental ware. Traditional and modern techniques for decorating fine bone china are usually also shown, including hand-lining, raised enamelling or colour transfer applications.
Practical details: The Wedgwood museum and visitor centre is open Monday to Friday 9 am to 4 pm except in certain holiday periods. An appointment is advisable. Parties up to 250 can be accommodated in a single visit. Children under 5 are not admitted and 5 to 15 years olds must be accompanied. Special arrangements can be made for schools.

38   Brewery Museum

The Bass Museum
Horninglow Street, Burton-on-Trent
Staffordshire
Tel: Burton 42031

The Bass Museum is Britain's first open brewery museum. It concentrates on the 900-year history of brewing in Burton-on-Trent with extensive use being made of dioramas, reconstructed workshops and offices and two audiovisual presentations. A new section shows visitors the history of the transport of beer. There are external exhibits, including a railway siding with two locomotives, several vintage vehicles, such as a 1916 Sentinel Steam Dray, and a 1905 Robey Compound Stationary Steam Engine. The brewery still maintain shire horses, and these are frequent visitors to the museum.
Practical details: The Bass Museum is open to the general public from 10.30 am to 4.30 pm Monday to Friday, and from 11 am to 5 pm, Saturday and Sunday. Refreshments are available, and there is a shop selling a wide range of items connected with brewing, including many reprints of early publications and postcards.

Left: An early horse-drawn beer cart
Below: Beer casks in an 18th century ship's hold

Engraving of a sixteenth century glasshouse

39 Coal-fired Power Stations

Drakelow 'A', 'B' and 'C' Power Stations
Near Burton-on-Trent, Staffordshire
Tel: Burton-on-Trent 63341

The tour lasts approximately two hours. It begins with a short film about how electricity is made, followed by a tour of the plant, which is steam plant using pulverised (coal) fuel. The tour also includes a visit to the coal and ash plant, the boiler house and the turbine hall. There are also the Rugeley 'A' and 'B' power stations at Armitage Road, Rugeley, which may be visited. Write to the individual station managers for details.
Practical details: The power station is open from 10 am to 5 pm Monday to Friday. Applications should be made in writing to the station manager, stating the time and dates preferred and the number in the party, giving at least three weeks' notice. Children under fourteen years are not eligible. Parties up to twenty-five in number can be accommodated. Individuals can arrange to visit on days when a small party is booked.
Sensible footwear should be worn at the station as it is an industrial site.

40 Exhibition Centre

National Exhibition Centre
Birmingham B40 1NT
Tel: 021-780 4141

The International Furniture Show and The Boat and Leisure Life Show are two of the exhibitions which are open to the public. Trade shows are also held here and cover such fields as Communications Equipment, Printing Machinery, Environmental Pollution Control and Building and Construction.
Practical details: Contact the Information Bureau at the above address for dates and times of forthcoming exhibitions.

41 Hand-made Crystal Glassware

Thomas Webb & Sons
Dennis Hall, King William Street
Amblecote, Stourbridge
West Midlands DY8 4EZ
Tel: Stourbridge 2521

The Dennis Glassworks produces crystal glassware including stemware, salad bowls, decanters and vases. On a tour of the factory visitors see various aspects of producing crystal: the raw materials, glassmaking, cracking off, marking, cutting, washing and

acid polishing. They will also see the warehouse and packing room, and they will learn something about the company's history by visiting the Thomas Webb Museum.
Practical details: Small parties of ten or under and casual visitors need not make an appointment for the factory tours, which take place Monday to Friday, from 10 am to 3 pm. Larger parties are advised to contact the Tours Supervisor to avoid disappointment. The museum is open Monday to Friday from 9.30 am to 4.30 pm and the shop is open Monday to Friday from 9.15 am to 4.30 pm, and Saturday from 9.30 am to 1 pm. There is an admission charge.

42 Large Brewery

Ansells Brewery Limited
Aston Brewery, Aston Cross
Birmingham B6 5PP
Tel: 021-327 4747

Five thousand years before Christ, beer was popular in the harems of Babylon and the Druids were brewing beer in England before the Roman invasion. In the thirteenth century children drank beer because it was less likely to harbour infection than milk or water. At the time when Anne Boleyn was a maid of honour, Henry VIII allowed her and her companions a gallon of ale a day, and men-at-arms received double that quantity!
Beer is made from germinated barley (called malt), mashed and brewed like tea with hot water. Brewing sugars and yeast are added to ferment it and to produce that creamy head. Hops, introduced to Britain from the Low Countries in the fifteenth century, are used to give that distinctive bitter flavour.
Ansells was founded in 1857 and has expanded steadily, to become a familiar landmark. Their trading area covers the Midlands and Wales —

in all eleven million people.
Beers brewed at the Birmingham brewery ar Ansells Mild, Ansells Bitter and Ansells Astor Ale.
Practical details: Organised groups of fifteer to thirty people, including school parties ove fifteen years, are accepted by arrangement, fo Tuesday, Wednesday and Thursday at 2.15 pr and 7.30 pm. Contact the marketing department for an appointment. There are n tours on public holidays. Individuals and small parties can join larger groups as long a they write in advance.
This is the only Midlands brewery belonging to the Allied Breweries group which accepts other than trade visits. Admission is free and refreshments are served.

43 Traditional Cut Crystal

Webb Corbett Limited
Coalbournhill Glassworks, Amblecote
Stourbridge, West Midlands DY8 4HF
Tel: Stourbridge 5281

Their range covers stemware (wine glasses with stems), bowls, vases and dishes.
The factory specialises in cased glass — crystal glass dipped in glowing colours. Stunning effects are created when the decorator cuts through the colour — perhaps ruby or cobalt blue — so that patterned gleams of crystal show through. The technique is used mainly for vases. It was originally pioneered at this factory for decorating paperweights, which you will see here, but it is now also used on hock glasses which are made in ruby, amethyst, cobalt blue and yellow. The person who runs the shop, says that sherry glasses sell more than anything else. She also tries to make sure that there are also some inexpensive small items available for children and students to buy as a souvenir of their visit. Favourites for children are the glass animals in varying sizes — a swan, penguin, horse, duck, owl, or a family of three bears. On the tour you learn how all these popular

Cask-filling at Ansells Brewery

point etching.

Practical details: The factory is open Monday to Friday throughout the working year. Tours are held in the mornings on Monday, Wednesday and Friday for up to twenty people. Individuals and groups are welcome and should telephone or write to the tour organiser in advance. The factory shop is open Monday to Friday from 10 am to 5 pm, also Saturday 10 am to 12 noon, and it sells first quality goods at normal retail prices and seconds and discontinued lines at reduced prices. The small admission charge is waived in the case of students and schoolchildren.

44   Newspaper Production

Birmingham Post and Mail Limited
28 Colmore Circus
Birmingham BA 6AX
Tel: 021-236 3366 Ext: 402

The tour of the Post and Mail building covers various stages in the production of a newspaper and culminates in the excitement of watching the paper being printed and then despatched to newsagents.

Practical details: Tours take place at 2 pm Monday to Friday and at 10 am on Saturday mornings.

Groups of up to twelve people can be given a one and a half hour tour, and the minimum age limit is twelve years. Parties should apply in writing well in advance.

45   Lead Crystal Glassworks

Stuart and Sons Limited
Redhouse Glassworks, Wordsley
Stourbridge, West Midlands DY8 4AA
Tel: Brierley Hill 71161

Visitors are met by guides and parties are divided into groups of eight to ten people. During the one-and-a-half-hour tour visitors learn a great deal of interesting information about Stuart and Sons as well as glassmaking in general.

objects are made.

Crystal occurs naturally in the form of quartz or silica. The basic ingredient is sand, so it is not surprising that the secret of making glass came to the Mediterranean countries from the Middle East. The Egyptians were making pressed or cast glass objects as long ago as 1500 years BC. The technique of blowing was not discovered until the first century BC.

On the tour you will see the traditional English techniques of glass blowing and hand cutting, together with the more sophisticated methods of decoration such as intaglio cutting, copper wheel engraving and diamond

The glass is made by heating it in pots which are placed inside the furnace. Pots take about two months to build and three months to dry — but once in the furnace they last a mere six months. The pots are heated up to about 1000°C before being transferred to the furnace. Each pot holds about fifteen cwt of glass, the same weight as a small car. It takes about thirty hours for the glass to melt or 'found'. A furnace remains lit year after year. It is never put out.

Glass cracks if it is cooled too quickly so the glass is cooled or 'annealed' very slowly by passing it through electrically heated lehrs on a conveyor belt. The longest lehr here is seventy feet and a glass takes between three and four hours to pass through.

The fact that glass cracks at a point of strain can be turned to the glassmaker's advantage. In order to cut off surplus glass, a line is marked round the article with a hard tungsten carbide point. The glass is heated along the line with a propane gas air flame, and it cracks. The cut edge is rubbed smooth and then reglazed by melting in a flame.

Now the glass is ready to be decorated. Patterns are cut using carborundum wheels (containing carbon again), and stone wheels. Cutting brings out the full beauty of the lead crystal. The glass is engraved by using copper wheels. Finally, the name Stuart is stamped on with a rubber stamp using an acid etch solution instead of ink.

Five hundred and ten people are employed by the company. The firm's designers have included Graham Sutherland and Dame Laura Knight. The old Redhouse works is now used as a showroom, and at the end of your tour you can buy reject glassware in the factory shop.

Copper-wheel engraving at Stuart & Sons

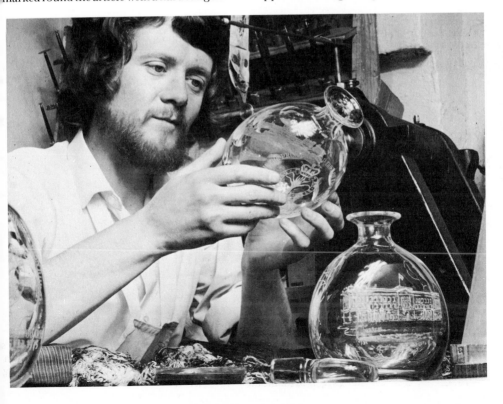

Practical details: The glassworks is open all year except for bank holidays, spring bank holiday week, the last week in July and the first week in August. An appointment must be made to join factory tours which take place Monday to Friday at 10 am and 2 pm.
The morning tour is for small groups of up to thirty-five people. The afternoon tour, intended for group bookings, is often booked a year ahead.
But individuals could possibly join one of the afternoon groups by arrangement. School parties are accepted only if the children are aged fourteen years and over, but children accompanied by parents are accepted if they are eight years of age or older.
Contact Mrs. V. Hayward to make arrangements. There is no charge for the tour.

46   Full Lead Crystal Glass

Royal Brierley Crystal
Stevens and Williams Limited
North Street, Brierley Hill
West Midlands DY5 3SJ
Tel: Brierley Hill 77054

Royal Brierley Crystal is full lead crystal — which has to contain at least thirty per cent lead oxide. The company makes utilitarian glassware, meaning that it is useful as well as beautiful. Their range includes decanters and wine suites. Each suite has a range of seven or eight shapes — liqueur glass, sherry glass, tumbler and so on. Suites are made in about twenty different patterns. They also make holloware, such as salad bowls and rose bowls — with flower arranging wire added in the packing department. Their vases range from three and a half inches to twelve inches high
On the tour you see the raw materials being mixed, the craftsmen forming molten glass into beautiful shapes and the skilled cutters creating designs on the glass by hand.
Though the actual making of glass is the thing which impresses most first-time visitor to a glassworks, the decorating is just as fascinating. In addition to the straight cuts made with carborundum and stone wheels, yo will see intaglio work. The glass is held and manoeuvred under a small stone wheel, as water drips on to it. This enables more elaborate patterns to be made — floral shapes and freely curving designs.
There are bargains in the Brierley shop which offers visitors good export rejects and discontinued lines at about a third under recommended retail prices.
Practical details: Individuals and groups of up to fifty-five are welcome — to book a place on a tour contact the visits organiser well in advance. Morning tours are held at 10.30 am Monday to Friday and afternoon tours at 2 pm from Monday to Thursday. Allow about two hours for the tour. It is not suitable for the elderly or infirm and no children under sixteen are admitted.
Small charges are made for the tour and for afternoon tea and biscuits.

47   Fork-lift Trucks

Coventry Climax Limited
Sandy Lane
Coventry CV1 4DX
Tel: Coventry 555355

Coventry Climax manufactures a wide range of industrial fork-lift trucks which can lift loads from 1 to 25 tonne. They are powered by electricity, diesel, petrol or liquefied

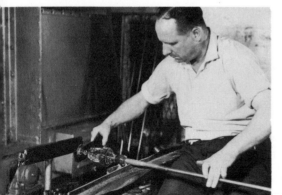

Shaping a wine glass at Brierley

A newspaper in production

petroleum gas. Visitors can be shown various stages in the manufacture of some of these trucks, including the basic machining of metal components, the assembly of electronic control systems, the assembly of the trucks themselves, the painting and finishing operations.

Practical details: The normal working hours of the company are 8.30 am to 4.30 pm Monday to Friday, excluding public holidays. As there are no full-time guides, individuals and groups are accepted by prior appointment only. Give at least one month's notice of your intention to visit. Educational or industrially-oriented groups are preferred.

48   Newspaper Printers

Coventry Newspapers Limited
Corporation Street, Coventry CV1 1FP
Tel: Coventry 25588

The Coventry Evening Telegraph sells about 110,000 copies a day, and as two or more people read each copy, the estimated readership is 275,000. The newspaper was founded by the late W. I. Iliffe in 1891 as the Midland Daily Telegraph, a four-page broadsheet newspaper selling for a halfpenny. The first editions of the Evening Telegraph appear on the streets before lunch. By tea-time, when visitors leave, the presses have printed the last edition of the day, and work has already begun on the next day's issue. This award-winning newspaper was the first one in the country to print a full-colour news picture of a man on the moon.

Practical details: Visits are arranged on Monday and Tuesday afternoons by prior appointment, starting at 2 pm and continuing until about 4 pm. The visits are very popular with local schools so it is advisable to book as far as possible in advance. Individuals are welcome if they are prepared to join groups — so they should book in advance. Numbers are

restricted to a maximum of fifteen, and children under twelve years of age are not allowed for safety reasons.
There is no charge for the tour and free light refreshments are provided.

cannot be accepted.
Admission is free and the estimated duration, including time for a cup of tea, is two hours. A wide range of the company's products will be available for purchase.

49   Specialised Weaving

J. & J. Cash Limited
Kingfield Road, Coventry CV1 4DU
Tel: Coventry 555222

Cash's most famous product is their woven name-tapes, used to identify the owners of items of school uniforms and other such clothing. The firm was started by the brothers John and Joseph Cash in 1846, at which time the weaving of small items was one of the main industries of the Midlands.
In the 1860s the lifting of restrictions on imported silk goods caused many of the Coventry weaving firms to go out of business. J. and J. Cash, however, widened their activities and started making woven pictures and bookmarks — still one of their lines — then cotton frilling which was popular with the Victorians. After this came labels, and then the famous name-tapes.
In the weaving department you will see the Jacquard weaving machines (invented in 1790 by Jacquard), which use punched cards to direct the loom to intersect threads, producing intricate patterns and woven pictures. In the printing department three types of printing processes are to be seen. Cash's factory, sole survivor of the old Coventry weaving firms, is now up to date with computer and electronic controls, making iron-on patches and promotional items, badges for scouts, guides, clubs and schools.
Practical details: Individuals and groups can make an appointment to tour this fascinating factory on Tuesday or Thursday at 2 pm. Organised groups of up to twenty people are accepted for the tour, but smaller groups or individuals can often be accommodated. Regretfully, the tour is not suitable for the elderly or those who have difficulty in walking, and children under the age of 14

50   Silk Printing

Beckford Silk
The Old Vicarage, Beckford
Near Tewkesbury, Gloucestershire
Tel: Eversham 881507

Beckford Silk design and make silk scarves. In their studios scarves are designed in a variety of styles which sometimes incorporate a motif suitable for a particular organisation such as an airline company or the National Trust. The scarves are hand-printed, each scarf having up to five screen printings. Both square and long scarves are made, and the edges are hand-rolled.
Practical details: Workshops and showroom open from 9.30 am to 1 pm and from 2 pm to 6 pm, Monday to Friday. Handprinting can be seen on Wednesday and Thursday afternoons. Parties of more than ten should telephone in advance.

51   Craft Workshops

The Cirencester Workshops
Cricklade Street, Cirencester
Gloucestershire
Tel: Cirencester 61566

The Cirencester Workshops are a group of Victorian buildings in the centre of Cirencester. Originally a brewery, there are now eleven workshops, an arts centre, a gallery, a craft shop and a coffee house. Twenty-five full-time professional craftsmen work here and every workshop is open a minimum of 8 hours a week so that visitors can expect to see at least one or two different

Specialist at J. & J. Cash

naturalist Arthur Severn and its main purpose is breeding and rearing Rainbow trout to restock angling waters throughout the country. In the farm's eight acres there are over forty ponds of different sizes containing trout in their various stages of development.

The farm is a great attraction for young and old alike and a visit offers a peaceful, relaxing interlude. You can buy food and watch the fish feeding on it. Anyone who has ever kept an aquarium will be interested to learn that the fish here are fed on floating pellets of food, which helps prevent under- and overfeeding.

Practical details: The farm is opened to visitors from the middle of March and closes at the end of October each year. During the visitors' season, the farm is open on every day of the week from 2 pm to 6 pm. The small entrance charge is halved for organised parties, for which prior bookings can be made. Advance bookings are not necessary, although they are helpful. Although guided tours are not given, many school parties ask for a talk on the aims of the farm, and a brief introduction to its work is often given. Fresh trout are on sale to visitors at the entrance kiosk.

crafts being practised during working hours. The resident craftworkers restore antique vehicles, make cane chairs, willow baskets and furniture, paint and restore clock dials, design knitwear and jewellery, bake, weave and produce pottery.

Practical details: Open Monday to Saturday from 10 am to 5.30 pm. Admission is free. The coffee house, which serves coffee and home-made cakes and soup, is open all day. Large parties should come early or telephone to make a booking.

52 Trout Farm

Bibury Trout Farm
Bibury, Cirencester
Gloucestershire
GL7 5ND
Tel: Bibury 215

The farm was founded in 1902 by the famous

53 Contemporary Glass

Cowdy Glass Workshops Limited
27 Culver Street, Newent
Gloucestershire GL18 1DB
Tel: Newent 821173

Cowdy Glass Workshop specialises in functional glass with colour. The glass is made by a small team of craftsmen and designed by artists. The positive use of colour which distinguishes Cowdy Glass is popular among many people who up to now have appreciated only clear glass.

The young craftsmen, trained either at art college or at the workshop, fashion the molten glass combining the traditional skills of the glassmaker with the new techniques of studio glass. The material is a lead crystal with characteristic ring and brilliance made from raw materials mixed and melted on the

remises.
ractical details: The workshop is open
Monday to Friday from 9 am to 12.30 pm and
from 1.30 pm to 5 pm. In December it is open
n Saturdays from 10 am to 12.30 pm and from
pm to 4 pm.

4   Falconry Centre

The Falconry Centre
Newent
Gloucestershire GL18 1JJ
Tel: Newent 820286

The Falconry Centre is one of the largest
collections of birds of prey in the world.
Weather permitting, visitors can see a bird
flown to exercise within an hour of arriving at
the centre. They may also visit the Hawk
Walk, a weathering ground for all the trained
birds. In the Brooder Room young chicks may
be viewed during the breeding season, and
breeding pairs tending to their young are in
the aviaries. There is also a museum of
falconiana.
Practical details: The centre is open daily
except Tuesday from 10.30 am to 5.30 pm (or
dusk, if earlier) all year, but it is closed during
December and January. Parties are welcome
but should book in advance. There is an
admission charge with reductions for
children. Cameras may be used in certain
areas, but not for commercial use except by
prior arrangement. There is a free car park.
The Falconry Centre is one and a half miles
south of Newent and eleven miles west of
Gloucester.

5   Nuclear Power Station

Berkeley Nuclear Power Station
Berkeley, Gloucestershire GL13 9PA
Tel: Dursley 810431 Ext: 38

This power station was Britain's first
commercial nuclear power station and
commenced supplying electricity to the
National Grid in 1962. It has a net output of
276 megawatts. Its two 'Magnox' reactors are
fuelled with natural uranium and are graphite
moderated and gas-cooled.
Practical details: Visitors over fourteen years
of age are welcome to visit the station by
appointment on weekdays. Telephone the
station warden, or write to the station
manager for full details. The power station is
on the east bank of the River Severn midway
between Bristol and Gloucester.

56   Artists and Craftsmen

Worcestershire Guild of Artist-Craftsmen
20 Vine Street,
Evesham, Worcester
Tel: Evesham 2895

The guild is an association of independent
professional craftsmen formed over twenty-
five years ago to link together people who by
the nature of their craft tend to be isolated. The
crafts include glass and slate engraving,
miniature painting, batik painting,
silversmithing, jewellery-making, wood
carving and turning, rush weaving, potting
and so on.
Practical details: Contact Ray Key at
the above address for a list of craftsmen, most
of whom will show their work by
appointment.

57   Worcester Royal Porcelain

The Worcester Royal Porcelain Co. Limited
Severn Street, Worcester WR1 2NE
Tel: Worcester 23221 Ext: 255

The Worcester Royal Porcelain has been in
continuous production since 1751 — a record
that cannot be matched by any other British
china factory. Today it manufactures top-
quality tableware and decorative china which
is exported all over the world.
Visitors gather in the Dyson Perrins Museum
which houses the finest collection of Royal

Compositors pasting up pages at the Worcester Evening News

Worcester porcelain in the world. Among the items on display are pieces of famous Blue and White, First Period, or Dr. Wall Period porcelain, manufactured when the factory first started.
Practical details: Factory tours take place Monday to Friday from 10 am to 1 pm and 2 pm to 5 pm; they last about 1¼ hours, and to avoid disappointment you are advised to book in advance. Individuals and groups of up to forty people will be accepted. A small charge is made, with half price for school children. Children under eight are not admitted on factory tours. No tours take place during the company's holiday period. For details of these dates and to make a booking contact Mr. Henry Sandon at the above address.
The museum, which is next to the factory, is open during the same hours and in addition on Saturday through April to the end of September.
In addition to the factory tour and the

museum there are a superb retail shop and showroom with a complete range of contemporary Royal Worcester items, and two 'seconds' shops where the visitor may pick up a worthwhile bargain.
The factory tour includes a number of staircases so it is not possible to accommodate visitors in wheelchairs.

58   Newspaper Printing

Berrow's Newspapers Limited
Berrow's House, Hylton Road
Worcester WR2 5JX
Tel: Worcester 423434

Visitors see how the Worcester Evening News is printed by the web-offset process, and a first visit to a newspaper press is always an exciting and worthwhile experience.
Practical details: Tours take place on Wednesday and Thursday evenings between 5.30 pm and 7 pm by arrangement, and last

about one hour. Groups of between four and sixteen people are acceptable (children aged eight and over). Contact them at least two months in advance.

59   Open Air Museum

The Avoncroft Museum of Buildings
Stoke Heath, Bromsgrove
Tel: Bromsgrove 31363

This is an open-air museum where a number of buildings have been rescued and re-erected on a fifteen-acre rural site. These include a fully operational windmill, various forges, a 15th century merchant's house and a number of agricultural buildings.
Practical details: The museum is open daily from March to November inclusive, from 10.30 am to 5.30 pm or dusk. There is an admission charge and groups have a reduction by arrangement. There is a shop and refreshments, also a free car park and a picnic site.

A working windmill at Avoncroft

60   Weaving Workshop

Malvern Weavers Limited
The Country Weaving Workshop
Stone Hall, Stone Drive, Colwall
Worcestershire WR13 6QJ
Tel: Colwall 40660

Members of this small company use hand and power-operated looms to make woven goods which include headsquares, ties, shawls, fabric lengths and clothes. Smaller items are produced on the hand looms — shoulder bags in intricate weaves and lampshades incorporating all sorts of materials. The shop sells craftwork gifts, pottery, spinning and weaving equipment and fleeces, which are hand-picked for the benefit of hand-spinners.
Practical details: They are open all year from 9 am to 5.30 pm Tuesday to Saturday and on Sunday afternoons. Coach parties please phone first.

61   Cider-making

H. P. Bulmer Limited
Plough Lane, Hereford
Tel: Hereford 6411

Visitors see a film about cider-making, tour the cider-processing and bottling factory, and the vat-house. The tour includes cider-tasting and a variety of ciders may be purchased. Bulmers use 50,000 tons of apples per year. These are unloaded into concrete silos at the factory and carried by water to the pressing mill. The pressing season lasts from October until December. Bulmer's underground vat-house at Hereford has 236 vats varying in size from 60,000 to 100,000 gallons. One vat named Strongbow holds 1.6 million gallons and is the largest container of alcoholic drink in the world.
Practical details: Groups of up to forty people may visit the factory from April to December, by making arrangements with the public relations manager twelve months in advance. Children over fourteen years are accepted. The

tour is not suitable for the elderly or infirm
There is an admission charge.
Individuals and small parties are welcome
provided notice is given. They are normally
attached to groups.

62   Waterworks Museum

Herefordshire Waterworks Museum
Broomy Hill, Hereford
Tel: Hereford 2487

This unique museum is intended to show not
only the complete Victorian waterworks but
also a large collection of pumping engines
and other fascinating items connected with
the history of water supply.
Practical details: The museum is open every
day during July and August from 2 pm to 5
pm. It is also open on the first Sunday in each
month in April, May, June and September,
and on the Easter, spring and late summer
bank holidays when the engines are in steam.
Parties may visit at other times by special
arrangement. There is a small charge. Further
information is available from the Secretary, 87
Ledbury Road, Hereford. Tel: Hereford 4104.

63   Open Air Industrial Museum

Ironbridge Gorge Museum
Ironbridge, Telford
Shropshire TF8 7AW
Tel: Ironbridge 3522 (at weekends call Blists
Hill Open Air Museum, Tel: Telford 586309)

The museum is spread over a number of sites
within Ironbridge Gorge. In the Severn
Warehouse a slide and tape show, and
exhibitions, outline the industrial
developments in the Gorge between 1700 and
1900. The Coalbrookdale Museum contains
the furnace where iron was first smelted using
coke as a fuel. Walk on around Coalbrookdale
to the Coalbrookdale Forge Workshop at Rose
Cottage where wrought iron is sold.

Massive cider vats at Bulmers

Next see the Iron Bridge, cast here in 1779 — the first iron bridge in the world. It has an information centre in the old tollhouse at one end.

The Blists Hill Open Air Museum is a forty-two acre woodland site where local industries are re-created. There are working exhibits, and iron, coal, clay and early transport scenes. The museum also has a completely furnished cottage in the Shelton Toll House, which has a pig sty complete with pigs. Two blast furnace beam blowing engines called David and Samson stand at the museum entrance.

The Coalport China Works Museum contains exhibitions on the crafts of the Coalport Works and a magnificent display of porcelain.

Practical details: The museum is open to the public every day of the year from 10 am, closing at 5 pm November to March and 6 pm April to October. Special arrangements, including a guide, are made for booked parties. Organisers write for party booking form. Free car parking. Admission charge covers the four major museum sites and the free exhibition centre. Small extra charge to enter the 100 metre long 18th century mining tunnel (Tar Tunnel) under Blists Hill.

Above: Hand-throwing at Ironbridge
Below: Corn stooked by hand to ripen

64   Working Farm Museum

Acton Scott Working Farm Museum
Wenlock Lodge, Acton Scott
Near Church Stretton, Salop SY6 6QN
Tel: Marshbrook 306/307

Acton Scott Working Farm Museum demonstrates life on a Shropshire upland farm before the introduction of the petrol engine. Working with Shire horses and skilled manpower, the farm demonstrates nineteenth century arable techniques and is stocked as a mixed farm of that period. The stock includes horses, cows, sheep, pigs and poultry of breeds rarely seen today.

Throughout the season visitors can watch butter being made in the dairy and a number of traditional crafts are demonstrated at weekends. The museum is situated on 22 acres

of the Home Farm of a country estate within sight of Wenlock Edge.

Practical details: There is a car park, toilets, a picnic area and shops which sell local craft material, local produce and refreshments. There is also a snack bar/cafe selling cold meals and home produced foodstuffs. Guides for parties can be booked in advance. There is a charge for guides. Disabled visitors should speak to the car park attendant, who will advise them of the facilities available. Open April to mid-October, every Sunday and bank holiday from 10 am to 6 pm. Open afternoons only, 1 pm to 5 pm, on Monday to Saturday in April, May, September and October. Open 10 am to 5 pm Monday to Saturday during June, July and August. A leaflet with more details and teachers notes is available on request. Visitors wishing to see a particular activity should telephone in advance as farm work can be affected by the weather.

Acton Scott is about seventeen miles south of Shrewsbury on the A49.

Threshing corn as it was done in the nineteenth century

WALES

Gwent, South Glamorgan, Mid Glamorgan, West Glamorgan, Dyfed, Powys, Clwyd, Gwynedd

1 Rumney Pottery

Rumney Pottery
Rumney, Cardiff
South Glamorgan CF3 7AE
Tel: Cardiff 78096

The pottery was started in the late 1400's, using the local red terracotta clay, but now imports white clay for making earthenware and other pottery. Most of the pottery is made to order for commemorative items. It specialises in large plates with golf and yachting club symbols, and dinner services with special designs. So, if you wanted to order a christening plate with your child's name or godchild's name, or if you'd always hankered after a coffee set carrying your coat of arms, this would be a good place to visit.
Practical details: The pottery is open to visitors all year Monday to Saturday from 9 am to 12 noon and 1 pm to 5 pm, and on Sunday from 9 am to noon. For further details contact Robert Giles.

2 Newspaper Production

Western Mail and Echo Limited
Thomson House, Cardiff CF1 1WR
Tel: Cardiff 33022 Ext: 290

Thomson House is the home of two newspapers, the Western Mail, the national morning newspaper of Wales, and the South Wales Echo, the largest circulation evening newspaper in Wales — both are part of Thomson Regional Newspapers Limited. Visitors are shown editorial and production departments and see the processes involved in planning and producing a newspaper. By the end of the tour visitors have a good idea of how the news and pictures are received, and how type is set and blocks are made before the papers are actually printed.
Practical details: Tours are conducted by prior arrangement only, Monday to Friday at 2.15 pm and 8 pm, with the exception of Thursday afternoon and bank holidays. The minimum number for groups is six, the maximum is twenty-four and the minimum age limit is eleven years. Because there is a heavy demand for tours the promotions department requires two to three weeks' notice.
Tours are free, and last about one and a half hours, including time for tea or coffee and biscuits.

3 Television Studio

HTV Cymru/Wales
Television Centre, Pontcanna
Cardiff CF1 9XL
Tel: Cardiff 21021

The IBA (Independent Broadcasting

Authority) publishes a handbook which includes a chapter on each of its fifteen television companies (and independent radio companies). This gives addresses which you should contact for studio tickets.
Members of the public from the HTV Wales area, are invited to see behind the scenes, usually in the evening. They are given a guided tour during which they learn how the company fits into the independent broadcasting network. HTV broadcasts between seven and seven and a half hours of Welsh language programmes each week, and three and a half hours in English — these are locally produced programmes. Viewers from the HTV Wales area can also appear on television in one of the programmes requiring an audience. There are entertainment programmes and discussion programmes.

Practical details: Write to the above address to request a tour or programme tickets. Try to give a choice of dates and also mention the

TV stations often take local visitors.

kind of programme you'd like to see. Groups are welcome to take the tour; individuals are also welcome, provided they write in advance.

4 Photographic Products

Gnome Photographic Products Limited
Gnome Corner, Caerphilly Road
Cardiff, South Glamorgan
Tel: Cardiff 63201

Visitors see lens grinding, press work, capstan and lathe work, painting, electro-plating and final assembly work. The firm makes slide projectors, enlargers and visual aids. There is very careful quality control, which perhaps explains why Gnome products sell well throughout the United Kingdom and in many

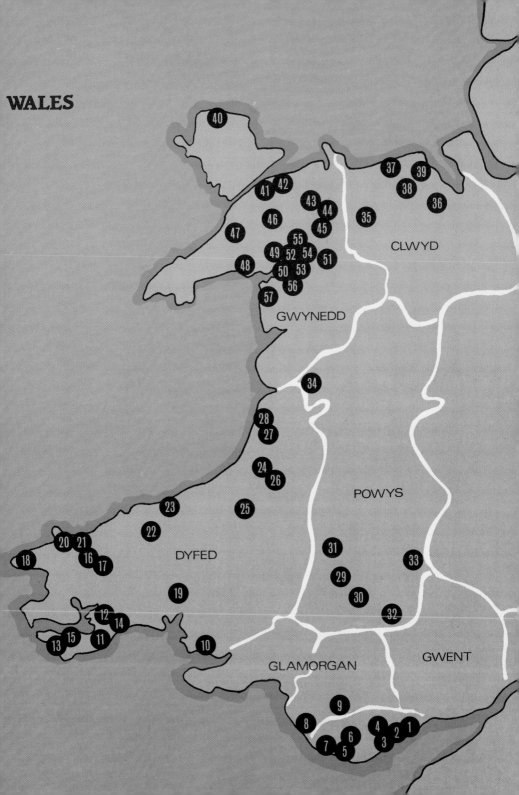

Lens grinding shop at Gnome Photographic

overseas countries.

Practical details: Visits to the works take place on Wednesdays at 2.45 pm and last about one and a half hours. A written request is required at least three weeks in advance. Write to Mr. J. Hallsworth, joint managing director. Groups of twenty to twenty-five persons can be shown around the factory. Interested individuals may also make an appointment to join a group.

5 Royal Air Force

Royal Air Force St. Athan
Barry, South Glamorgan
Tel: Llantwit Major 3131 Ext: 3062

This is the largest multi-role engineering station in the RAF. It covers an area of about two thousand acres in the Vale of Glamorgan and employs more than three thousand people. The station opened in 1938 and was originally a large wartime training school. Nowadays, though training still goes on here, the main role of the station is effecting major servicing and reconditioning of front-line aircraft for operational squadrons throughout the RAF. During a two to three hour tour visitors can see inside the service hangars, where aircraft such as the Vulcan or Victor are being stripped down and reconditioned.

Visitors also see the workshop facilities and the aircraft museum, which has a unique collection of aircraft from the world wars.

Practical details: Visits can be arranged for groups of up to twenty people. Interested individuals are also accepted. You must apply in writing to the community relations officer.

6 Coal-fired Power Stations

Aberthaw 'A' and 'B' Power Stations
Near Barry, Glamorgan
Tel: St. Athan 750271

At these power stations members of the public can see coal pulverised in mills which grind the coal finer than face powder. The Aberthaw B power station building consists of a coal bunker, boiler house and turbine hall. The single multi-flue chimney is five hundred feet high. A sea wall one and a quarter miles long was built to protect the site against flooding and erosion from the fast running tides of the Bristol Channel.

Practical details: Visits can be arranged by contacting the administration officer.

7 Cardiff-Wales Airport

Cardiff–Wales Airport
Near Cardiff, South Glamorgan CF6 9BD
Tel: Rhoose 710296

This is Wales' premier airport and one of the best provincial airports in Britain. On the technical and operational side, it is fully equipped to international standards with the latest navigational aids and Instrument Landing Systems.

Regular scheduled services on international routes are operated to Amsterdam, Paris, Cork and Dublin. By commencing the journey at

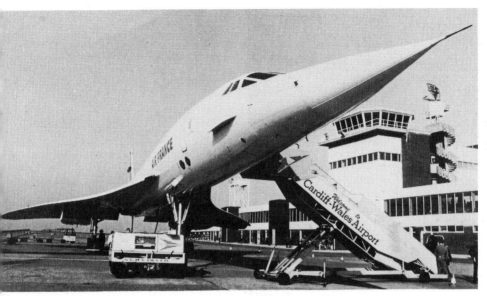

Concorde at Cardiff–Wales Airport

Cardiff–Wales Airport, the long and tedious journey to London's Heathrow Airport can often be avoided.

There are regular scheduled services from the airport to many cities in Britain, and Cardiff also handles a busy traffic in private business and executive aircraft. More than a million people live within a twenty-five mile radius of the airport and it is ideal for holiday flights both summer and winter. Some sixteen tour operators offer holiday charter flights to twenty-one overseas destinations.

First class comfort for passengers is provided in the terminal building which includes a spectators' terrace and in the first floor Concourse there is a spacious observation lounge, flight information board, restaurant, self-service buffet, licensed bar, duty free shop for international passengers and a shop selling newspapers, magazines, tobacco and souvenirs.

Practical details: All visitors are welcome to see the airport's activities and use its amenities and there are special facilities for the disabled. There is a large car park near the main terminal with cheap rates for spectators.

8 Ewenny Pottery

Ewenny Pottery
Ewenny, Near Bridgend, Mid Glamorgan
Tel: Bridgend 3020

The local rich brown glacial clay has been used for making clay for several centuries and Ewenny pottery was started in 1610. In those days clay was prepared by treading it with bare feet, in much the same way as grapes are trodden by winemakers. The feet of the person who was 'puddling' would become so sensitive that they could feel the tiniest stone in the mixture.

In our antiseptic twentieth century, the idea of treading wet clay seems rather strange, although the idea of getting one's hands covered in clay is still quite appealing. Anyway, this old-fashioned method was replaced by using a roller pulled by two men, then the roller was pulled by donkeys, then by horsepower, and today modern machinery is used.

The earliest potters would have made bread pans, water pitchers, drinking mugs and crock jugs. Nowadays you can see ashtrays, tankards and decorative mugs being made.

Practical details: The pottery is open all year Monday to Saturday, 9.30 am to 5.30 pm, except for Saturdays in winter, when it closes at 12.30 pm.

The potters here say they are only too happy to show their methods to children, so families will be sure of a welcome.

9 Welsh Characters

John Hughes Gallery
Broadway
Pontypridd
Glamorgan
Tel: Pontypridd 405001

'Visitors from all over the world call here,' says John Hughes, 'mainly because we are Welsh, working in Wales, making identifiably Welsh objects in a personal, slightly "primitive" style, probably also thought of as being Welsh'.

The shelves of the gallery are filled with Welsh miners (as befits Pontypridd on the South Wales coalfield), plus hill farmers and coracle men as well as mythological figures.

Visitors see sculptured figures from Welsh folk lore (the Mabinogion), Rugby rogues, and amusing animals (Groggs) made in unglazed, highly textured stoneware clay. John Hughes' amusing Welsh rugby characters include such figures as Push-over Pugh, Blind Side Bevan — a freelance Dutch Elm Disease Carrier, Davie the Dash — who got his blue at the open university, and Lewis the Leap — who has been asked to go North many times — by the Welsh Rugby Union! The Celtic creatures, individually handmade in light buff stoneware, have their texture emphasised in black. They rejoice in such names as Happy Hedgehogs and Welsh Love Birds. Cast and hand finished dogs are described as 'very friendly to burglars and no use at all as guard dogs'. Some of them resemble Welsh mountain cow terriers. Others are foreign, such as the Irish Bogghound, and they keep company with Scruffy pups, Lolloping Lion and Welsh Patchwork cows whose tails are the nesting place of the lesser fluffy lovebird.

For some reason lions sell well to Scandinavians and dogs are the firm favourites among the Japanese.

Visitors wander in informally to watch the team of five — John Hughes, daughter Kim, son Richard, plus Susan Liveridge, a friend of Kim, and Robert Osborne, a caster-modeller-salesman. There is always a variety of figures being made, some as small as three inches high and others weighing up to a hundredweight.

Practical details: The workshop is open 9 am to 6 pm including bank holidays and all visitors are welcome. You will receive a cordial and if necessary informed welcome. It is difficult for them to deal with large numbers (more than twenty) but an informal conducted explanatory tour can be given to groups, and evening visits can be made by appointment. By telephoning in advance, groups can ensure that members of the team are working on things of visual interest.

10 Coal-fired Power Station

Carmarthen Bay Power Station
Burry Port, Dyfed
Tel: Burry Port 3491

Carmarthen Bay, known locally as CarBay, is not as modern as other power stations we have described in south Wales. CarBay station's capacity, for example, is 240 megawatts while Pembroke power station's is 2,000 megawatt. Electricity is generated when a loop of wire is rotated in the magnetic field created by a magnet. In a power station it is the wire loop which is kept stationary and the magnet which is rotated, but the principle is the same. Tremendous force is needed to turn the shaft against the resistance of the magnetic field but this energy is converted into an electric current in the coils. The source of the original energy is steam, which can be created by burning coal or oil to raise the temperature of water. The Central Electricity Generating Board

John Hughes making one of his characters

issues booklets which explain the general principles fully, as well as booklets and leaflets on many individual power stations. For South Wales, contact the Public Relations Officer, CEGB South Western Region, Bedminster Down, Bridgewater Road, Bristol BS13 8AN.
Practical details: To arrange a visit to CarBay power station contact the station manager. Individuals and groups of up to thirty people can visit the station at mutually agreed times. Larger groups are accepted by special arrangement. Children under eleven years old cannot be admitted.

11 Hand-made Pottery

Tenby Pottery
Upper Frog Street, Tenby, Dyfed
Tel: Tenby 2890

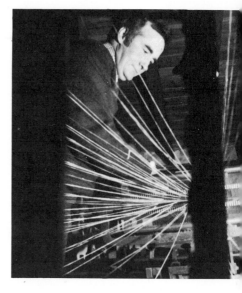

At work on a hand-loom

Anthony and Mary Markes produce hand-made pottery here in Tenby. All processes in the workshop can be seen from the showroom — throwing, firing, decorating, glazing and kiln-packing. There is always something to watch except during coffee break!
The Markes make honey-glazed brush painted earthenware, some slip-decorated dishes, and black-and-white, wax-resist pots.
Practical details: The pottery is open all year, Monday to Friday from 10.15 am to 1 pm and 2.15 pm to 5.30 pm. On Saturday it is open until 1 pm. All visitors are welcome.

12 Small Hand-loom Weavers

Stoney Park Weavers
Stepaside, Narbeth, Dyfed SA67 8JJ
Tel: Saundersfoot 813868

The weavers' loft is a small stone converted grain store, on a lonely country lane. The weavers work on domestic hand looms converted from foot pedal to power. They produce ties and rugs. The looms are normally working, but not always, because of pattern changes. Similarly the warping process can usually be seen, though there is no guarantee The raw material is, of course, wool, which is bought in from all over the country. As a hobby, Linda and David Noon also hand-spin the fleece of their two tame sheep 'Lamb Chop' and 'Midge'.
The Noons have one and a half acres of land. When they came here five years ago from the industrial Midlands, wanting to get out of the rat race and work for themselves, Stoney Park was a small farm which had been empty for twelve years. Their dream home and workplace had no water or electricity, and the privy was in the garden. However, they set to work, and two years later had managed to convert the farm cottage, grain loft and outbuildings.
Practical details: Individuals are welcome without notice Monday to Friday from 10 am to 6 pm between Easter and October, including bank holidays. They do open in winter but telephone first to avoid disappointment. The approach roads to Stoney Park are very narrow and therefore they cannot take coaches.

3 Cabinet and Furniture Maker

J. Owen Hughes Workshop
Building 69, Llanion Park
Pembroke Dock, Dyfed
Tel: Pembroke 4360, evenings

Mr. John Owen Hughes makes traditional
and contemporary furniture and woodcraft
products, such as tables, chairs, Welsh
dressers, settles, coffee tables and corner
cabinets. The woods he works with are
chestnut, ash, elm, mahogany and pine. He
also makes turned woodware and cabinets to
customers' own specifications. Visitors are
welcome, by arrangement.
Practical details: The workshop is open on
normal working days, by prior arrangement.
There is no charge. Up to five people can be
'entertained' by Mr. Hughes, and he will allow
children in provided they are supervised by an
adult. The workshop is not very easy to find. It
is within the area of the 'Old Barracks' close to
the Borough Offices.
If you wish to write to Mr. Hughes, his postal
address is 1 Beach Road, Llanreath, Pembroke
Dock, Dyfed SA72 6TP. Tel: Pembroke 4360.

4 Popular Pottery

Saundersfoot Pottery
Wogan Terrace, Saundersfoot, Dyfed
Tel: Saundersfoot 812406

The hand-made earthenware pottery made in
Saundersfoot by Carol Brinton has been
designed for both modern and traditional
settings. Care has been taken to preserve the
warmth and texture of the natural clay. The
glazes have been carefully chosen to offer a
range of colours which blend with the red
earthenware clay itself — an important part of
the decorated pots.
Visitors to this studio may see all the stages in
the making of the ware and there are frequent
demonstrations of all processes. It is visited by
thousands of holidaymakers every summer. As
well as a wide range of table and domestic ware
the pottery produces a number of limited

edition and individual pieces from time to
time — these may be seen here at the studio.
Practical details: Saundersfoot Pottery is open
from April to September, Tuesday to
Saturday, from 10 am to 6 pm. Viewing is by
appointment in winter. On some summer
evenings the studio is re-opened from 7.30 pm
until 9 pm for demonstrations. All visitors are
welcome.

15 Oil-fired Power Station

Pembroke Power Station
West Pennar, Pembroke, Dyfed
Tel: Angle 321

Pembroke is one of the largest oil-fired power
stations in Europe. It is comparatively new,

having opened in 1971. Nearby Milford Haven was a naval base until after the last war, and its deep waters are ideal for oil tankers.
Visitors see most areas including the computer control room. A surprisingly small number of staff control this large industrial complex with the aid of automatic processes. If the computer breaks down, the station continues working as safety devices are independent and engineers do the computer's work.
Practical details: From June to September tours are held on Tuesday, Wednesday and Thursday afternoons. Individuals and small groups are welcome but, regretfully, children under the age of twelve are not admitted. Larger groups should write to the station manager. Arrive early, as the guides leave the Visitors' Reception Centre promptly at 2 pm and 3 pm. In winter there are no regular tours but guides can be called in specially to take round large groups. Individuals can sometimes join one of these tours.

16   Textile Manufacturers

Wallis Woollen Mill
Haverfordwest, Pembrokeshire
Tel: Clarbeston 297

Wallis Woollen Mill, established in 1812, is situated in a quiet rural valley, eight miles north of Haverfordwest. In earlier times, the mill supplied yarns for handweaving, but nowadays it specialises in weaving cloth from pure new wool. In the early 1970s, the mill introduced a lightweight tapestry suitable for clothes — the first mill in Wales to do so. This was displayed at the Design Centre in 1971. Today, the mill specialises in carpet rugs and fine worsted flannel.
During the summer months, visitors can see a fascinating and colourful twenty minute audio visual show, in a specially designed studio, adjacent to the mill. The show describes the various stages of producing cloth from lambing and shearing to the making up of the final garment. It clearly explains the

various processes at the mill. The handweaving studio, well equipped with a variety of looms, produces a range of individual items, incorporating handweaving, spinning and natural dyeing. I offers day courses for those interested in these crafts.
Practical details: The mill, shop and studio are open from Monday to Friday from 10 am to 6 pm. Visitors are welcome to visit the mill and view the weaving during working hours. There is no charge to see around the mill. A small charge is made to cover the running costs of the audio visual show. Bookings must be made at least two days in advance for the handweaving and spinning courses. The mil is small and cannot accept large coach parties. There is a small tea room, open all year round

17   Woollen Mill

Tregwynt Woollen Mill
(Henry Griffiths & Son)
Letterston, Haverfordwest, Dyfed
Tel: St. Nicholas 225

The mill building dates back to the mid-eighteenth century and woollen yarns have been made here since that time. The site was chosen because water power was available. For many years Welsh mills such as Tregwynt have been famous for flannel and blankets woven by hand. The arrival of the power loom, and changes in fashion, have resulted in a greater variety of goods being produced. Tapestry bed covers are woven in various designs. The mill shop sells tweed clothes, tweed and flannel, skirt and dress lengths, blankets, travelling rugs, scarves, stoles and ties. Their speciality is knitting wools in two three and four-ply; the two-ply is roughly equivalent to English three-ply in thickness Welsh wool softens with washing and does no shrink, they tell us.

Practical details: Tregwynt Mill can be seen in operation Monday to Friday from 9 am to 5 pm. The shop is open at the same times and also on Saturday. Coach parties, supervised

chool parties and all visitors are welcome.
There are no conducted tours because of the
noise of the mill working. There is plenty of
car-parking space.
The mill is five miles south of Fishguard,
approached by turning west off the
Goodwick-St. Davids A487.

18 Cottage-style Furniture

Hugh Loughborough
The Craftsman, Solva
Haverfordwest, Pembrokeshire, Dyfed
Tel: St. David's 721294

Hugh Loughborough is a countryman who
worked for the Forestry Commission and on a
dairy farm for many years. He made furniture
as a hobby, before taking it up full-time.
The workshop is a small concern, making
cottage furniture from homegrown
hardwoods. Visitors will see small furniture
and old-fashioned kitchen utensils being
made in the workshop. Dining tables and
dressers and other furniture are made to
customers' orders. He also specialises in rush-
seated ladderback and rocking chairs.
Visitors can buy at ex-workshop prices —
paying no more than they would for mass-
produced items.
Practical details: The workshop is open from
April to September, 11 am to 5 pm Monday to
Friday, and from October to March, Monday
to Saturday. Groups of up to twenty people are
accepted by arrangement and should give two
weeks' notice. Young people are welcome so
long as they are under supervision. The shop
stays open on Easter Monday, Spring bank
holiday and Autumn bank holiday.

19 Pine Craft

Cwmduad Woollen Mill Shop
Cwmduad, Near Carmarthen, Dyfed
Tel: Cynwyl Elfed 337

Cwmduad Mill is no longer a working
woollen mill but is now a retail craft shop and
picturesque country workshop. It is run by
Fred and Chris Jennings who sell all varieties
of Welsh woollen goods.
Fred Jennings makes pine shelf units, bookcases and Welsh dressers and he makes them to
order.
The mill has one of the few turning waterwheels left in Wales today.
Practical details: The centre is open May to
September from 9 am to 7 pm and October to
April from 10 am to 5.30 pm. The tea rooms
are open during the summer season only and
the shop is closed on Sunday in the winter
months.
All members of the public, including coach
and organised parties are welcome to visit
Cwmduad.
Situated on the A484, nine miles north of
Carmarthen, the centre is well signposted and
has a large parking area.

20 Leatherwork

Inskin Leather
West Street, Fishguard, Pembrokeshire
Tel: Fishguard 872510

Ben and Elizabeth Morris have been
established in the manufacture of
leathergoods since 1971. Elizabeth studied at
Manchester and is mainly responsible for
design and Ben, a mechanical engineer, is
mainly responsible for manufacture.

Inskin produces handbags in soft leather and suede with celtic appliqué designs. There is a range of embossed hide products including belts and wine mats, of which three designs have been accepted by the Design Centre. **Practical details:** The shop is open Monday to Saturday from 9 am to 5.30 pm all year, and on Sundays and bank holidays during the summer season. Their workshop can accommodate only three or four visitors at a time although larger parties can be fitted in by arrangement. Visitors are restricted to times when the pressure of work permits.

21 Craft Workshop Complex

Workshop Wales
Lower Town, Fishguard
Dyfed SA65 9LY
Tel: Fishguard 2261

Workshop Wales is on the edge of Lower Town fishing village. The six-acre site includes the outbuildings of a mansion estate used as small individual workshops. The main craft activities are wood-turning, screen-printing, bellows-making, wood-carving, pottery, toy-making, clothes-making, leatherwork, and harness-work. The complex is not a commune. Each person is responsible for making his or her own workshop pay it way. The retail craft shop also operates independently, ordering only those goods which it believes it can sell — but it does help the workshops by paying for goods on delivery, not on a sale or return basis. Craftsmen have to prove the quality and saleability of their work by selling it through the shop for a year before joining the complex Products include leather-faced clocks, tables stools, kists, hand-carved wooden panels, bedheads, lamps, doors and clocks. Traditional wooden cawl (broth) bowls and bara (bread) boards are made. Clothes sold here include fishermen's woollen jumpers, fishermen's smocks in denim with matching caps, work shirts and work aprons. **Practical details:** The shop and workshop complex are open seven days a week from two

Just one of the crafts at Workshop Wales

veeks before Easter until the middle of
October. In winter, hours are sporadic, but
there is always someone on hand to help
isitors, and workshops will open on request.

2   Tweed Manufacturers

Cambrian Mills (Velindre) Limited
Drefach, Velindre
Near Newcastle Emlyn, Dyfed
Tel: Velindre 370209

Visitors can see the weavers at work and buy
tweed, flannel cloth, tapestry, flannel shirts,
rugs and blankets. A textile museum has been
opened next door with the help of the
National Museum of Wales.
Practical details: The mill is open to the
public all year round on Monday to Friday
from 9 am to 4.30 pm, and in summer on bank
holidays from 10 am to 4.30 pm.

3   Pokerwork

The Studio Craft-workshop
Tresaith, Near Cardigan
Dyfed, Wales SA43 2JL
Tel: Aberporth 810512

All year round Trevor and Valerie Green
produce pyrography or pokerwork on wood
and visitors can see them working in the
studio overlooking Tresaith beach. Their
pyroworked chopping boards, bread boards,
tools and spoons have wildlife themes and
Celtic designs. The work can be personalised
with the customer's name or message while
they wait. Enamelled jewellery, clothes,
paintings, ceramics and painted tiles are also
made here. Most of the craftwork is produced
in winter, because of the danger involved with
the use of kilns and other equipment.
Practical details: The studio cum workshop is
open all day in summer and as the Greens live
on the premises simply ring the doorbell at
other times of year. There is a shop which sells
the Greens' crafts.

24   Blacksmith and Welder

The Smithy
Penpompren, Ystrad Meurig, Dyfed
Tel: Pontrhydfendigaid 248

Mr. T. D. Davies does agricultural repairs and
wrought-iron work to order in this village
smithy. This is a one-man business and as
such is a fascinating place to visit. Visitors
take pot luck when they go to the Smithy, for
Mr. Davies may simply be repairing a piece of
machinery or he may be shaping a piece of
wrought iron into a balustrade or decorative
grate.
Practical details: As this is very much an
individual operation visitors are welcome
daily from 9 am to 5 pm.

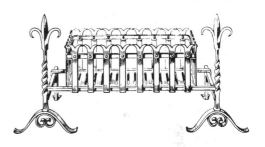

25   Wrought Ironwork

John M. Price & Son
Forge Works, Talsarn
Near Lampeter, Dyfed SA48 8QB
Tel: Aeron 565

The title John M. Price & Son should really be
John M. Price, Son & Daughter. Gwyneth
Price is the only girl in the country to have
undertaken a full-time apprenticeship. In the
old smithy she practises firework, forging, and
welding, acquiring the ancient skills from her
father, a master smith. She works on a
hundred year old iron anvil and her father
insists that she must make all her own tools. In
the forge, old bellows made in 1851 are used to
heat coal, so that the iron is at just the right,
malleable temperature.

At one time smiths would do all the ironwork and repairs for a village community, shoeing horses, re-rimming wagonwheels, and fixing machinery. Nowadays they make ornamental work such as house names, fire irons, bed-heads, balconies and gates. Mr. Price still does some farriery — making horse-shoes, and some industrial work (profile cutting) but most of the work is on articles for the home which are designed and forged on the premises.
Practical details: The workshop is open Monday to Friday from 8.30 am to 5 pm and at weekends by appointment.

26 Hand-thrown Pottery

Abaty Pottery
Pontrhydfendigaid
Ystrad Meurig, Dyfed
Tel: Pontrhydfendigaid 667

The pottery produces hand-thrown stoneware tableware including mugs, jugs, casseroles, coffee sets, plates, plant pots and salt kits.
Practical details: The pottery is open all year round Monday to Friday, from 7.30 am to 1 pm and 2 pm to 4 pm, and at other times by appointment. Individuals and parties of not more than fifty may visit the pottery and see the processes. Parties should advise them beforehand. No charge is made — 'We prefer to sell you a pot'.

27 Silver-lead Mine Museum

Llywernog Silver-lead Mine Museum
Ponterwyd, Near Aberystwyth, Dyfed
Tel: Ponterwyd 620

In the restored buildings of this Victorian silver-lead mine, you can discover the fascinating history of metal mining in Wales. An audio-visual programme introduces a

J. Price's daughter— smithy

Hand-shaping the clay at Abaty Pottery

series of authentic exhibits displayed in a traditional underground setting, re-created in the large museum building. This shows how the ores of silver and lead were mined, and explains the techniques of gold and slate mining.

Practical details: The mine is open to all visitors every day, Easter to September, from 10 am to 5.30 pm and at other times by arrangement. Please write or telephone for bookings and information on special facilities.

The mine has a bookshop, a craft centre — with a large selection of silver jewellery, lapidary and other local craft items — a tourist information centre, picnic site and a large free car park. There is a small admission charge.

28   Hydro-electric Power Station

Rheidol Power Station
Cwm Rheidol, Bangor
Aberystwyth SY23 3NF
Tel: Capel Bangor 667

At Rheidol you can see a picturesque and award-winning hydro-electric scheme. Hydro-electric power can only be produced in areas where there is sufficient rainfall and

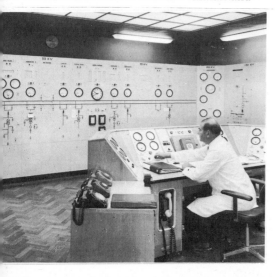

suitable, normally hilly land. The classic hydro-electric power station is built by collecting water behind a dam and allowing it to flow through turbines (electric power generators) on its way downhill.

Rheidol power station is situated in the valley of the river Rheidol. The scheme was completed in 1963 and has a generating capacity of fifty-six megawatts. The dams and lakes are open to the public and a nature trail has been established along the river bank.

Practical details: At Rheidol guided tours leave the Information Centre, a mile from the station, at intervals from 11 am to 4.30 pm each day from the Easter holiday to the end of September. Individuals and small groups may come along without notice. There is a small charge.

29   Salmon Hatchery

Cynrig Salmon Hatchery
Near Brecon, Powys
Tel: Llanfrynach 212

Cynrig Salmon Hatchery is on the Cynrig, a tributary of the river Usk. The hatchery is run by the Central Electricity Generating Board which is very concerned with protecting the environment around its power stations. It takes care that as few fish as possible are harmed when they accidentally get into the water cooling systems, by using special screening chambers. What is more, positive action is taken to breed fish at this hatchery. In the salmon hatchery adult female salmon are milked of their eggs. The salmon hatchery can cope with 250,000 eggs, which are incubated until they hatch. When the fish are ready to start feeding they are transferred outside to a series of tanks and ponds where they are kept in fresh, running, unheated water — just as in their natural conditions. The smolt are usually about two years old when they are ready to be set free — up to five thousand smolt are released every year. Every

Left: The control room at Rheidol
Right: Young parr at the Salmon Hatchery

third year the entire stock is anaesthetised and numbered tags are attached so that they can later be traced. The young salmon make their way to sea and two years later they find their way back to their home river — nobody quite knows how. Fishermen have co-operated in the experiment by sending salmon tags back to the hatchery from as far away as Greenland. An illustrated booklet about the hatchery is available from the Public Relations Office, CEGB, Bedminster Down, Bridgwater Road, Bristol BS13 8AN.

Practical details: Casual visitors can usually call at the hatchery between 10 am and 12 noon and from 2 pm to 4 pm without notice. Groups should definitely make an appointment in writing. A film is shown to school parties and other groups visiting by prior arrangement.

30 Welsh Whisky

Brecon Brewery Limited
Watton, Brecon, Powys
Tel: Brecon 2926

The Welsh Chwisgi (whisky) compoundery is located at the back of the Camden Arms Hotel. It was opened in 1979 after renovating an old brewery which dates back to 1778. Production is approximately one thousand gallons each month — which is small compared to the world renowned whiskies.

Practical details: Visits are strictly limited and can be arranged by contacting Dafydd Gittens.

31 Sheltered Weaving Workshop

The Royal British Legion
Cambrian Factory Limited
Llanwrtyd Wells
Powys LD5 4SD
Tel: Llanwrtyd Wells 211

The main purpose of this factory is to act as a sheltered workshop employing disabled people.

All the processes carried out here can be seen in

logical sequence: wool sorting, dyeing, blending, willeying, carding, spinning, warping, winding and weaving. Knitting, doubling the yarn, hanking, rug fringing and other activities can also be seen.

All the products are made to Woolmark and Welsh Woolmark standard from wool grown, spun, woven or knitted in Wales. Much of the tweed is now turned into garments by outside workers for sale in the factory shop. Bed covers are made as well as clothing — including made-to-measure suits and sports jackets, tweed caps, trilby and deerstalker hats, capes, car coats, socks, ties, scarves, purses, handbags and spectacle cases.

Practical details: The factory is open the whole year on Monday to Thursday 8.15 am to 5 pm and Friday, 8.15 am to 3.45 pm, and on all bank holidays except Christmas. The shop is open Monday to Friday 8.15 am to 5.30 pm the whole year. On Saturday it is open 9 am to 4.30 pm May to September and 9 am to 12 noon all other months except December and January when it is closed.

Individuals are welcome to arrive without prior notice and walk round the works. Groups of more than fifteen should make an appointment, as much in advance as possible, but sometimes a day's notice will be adequate. The factory sells by mail order as well as through its shop on the premises. The tea room serves refreshments from May to September and there is a picnic area on the factory site. The mill is on the main A483.

32 Furniture Craftsmen

Grahame Amey Limited
The Granary, Standard Street
Crickhowell, Powys
Tel: Crickhowell 810540

A tour of the works includes brief details about the manufacture of furniture, its history and the processes involved. Visitors are shown the whole sequence from rough sawn timber to assembly and polishing. There are five people employed.

They say, 'Come and see craftsmen making

Skilled craftsmen at Grahame Amey Ltd.

beautiful furniture in the heart of the Brecon Beacons National Park. We work in solid hardwoods — mainly ash or oak. If oak is the king of British hardwoods, then ash is the queen. It is a light and beautifully grained wood, not unlike pine in colour, but with all the strength, durability and resistance to bruising of oak.'

They take as much care with what is normally out of sight as with what is on show. For example, cupboard units are backed in solid timber, not cheap plywood, and are fixed by means of brass screws. Their standard finish is a matt, heat and stain-resistant polish which is then hand-waxed to perfection.

Lord Snowdon, honorary adviser to the Design Council, apparently visited the workshop and said, 'It is perfection in craftsmanship and woodwork'.

From the attached showrooms you can buy not only furniture but small items such as breadboards, kneeling stools or bookstands. Or, you can talk about the piece of furniture you want but have not been able to find, and they will send you a design and quotation. Finally you can walk across the road and see more handmade furniture, craft goods and locally produced knitwear in their craftshop, Hurdy Gurdy.

Practical details: The showroom and workshop are open Monday to Friday from 8 am to 5.30 pm and on Saturday from 9 am to 5 pm.

Individuals are welcome to arrive without

prior notice and walk around the works.
Groups of up to ten people should telephone
for an appointment.
The workshops are in a thirteenth century
granary, forty yards from the centre of town.

33 Distinctive Pottery

Wye Pottery
Clyro, Near Hay-on-Wye
Via Hereford, Powys HR3 5LB
Tel: Hay-on-Wye 510

In 1956 Adam Dworski, an ex-lawyer from
Yugoslavia, came to Clyro with his wife and
family and started the Clyro Pottery. He makes
a distinctive type of earthenware pottery using
majolica glazes and brushwork decoration. He
also produces figures, plaques and pots in
oxidised stoneware and has recently started to
work in porcelain.
Although Mr. Dworski does work on
commission and exports to Europe and
America, he prefers to work on his own and
most of his work is sold direct to people
visiting his studio, where he can be seen
working on most days.
Practical details: The pottery is open to the
public daily from 9 am to 1 and 2.30 to 6 pm,
all year. Also on Sunday by appointment.
Mrs Dworski also has a studio nearby, where
blanket chests, stools, spoonboxes and egg-
cups are painted in traditional designs.
Visitors by appointment — telephone number
as above.
Clyro is on the A438 between Hereford and
Brecon — a mile from Hay-on-Wye.

34 Self-Sufficiency Centre

National Centre for Alternative Technology
Llwyngwern Quarry, Machynlleth, Powys
Tel: Machynlleth 2400

A disused slate quarry overlooking
Snowdonia National Park has been turned
into a demonstration of 'how to live happily
on limited resources, causing a minimum of

pollution and waste without returning to the
Hardships of the past'. Here they practise what
they preach. Not only are there exhibitions of
machinery and systems, but the exhibition
hall itself is heated by a solar roof and the
guide booklets are printed on re-cycled paper.
They have installed their own energy systems
housing and horticulture. They re-cycle their
rubbish and have an electric truck and other
transport powered by electricity produced on
site from natural resources. Exhibits show
how you can produce your own energy from
sun, wind and water and grow your own food.
As you walk around you pass cottages built for
and by the staff, using re-cycled materials,
incorporating solar panels and heat
conserving techniques. You see vegetable
plots showing the results of different methods
of organic cultivation, and learn how
domestic sewage can be used to provide
compost and bio-gas for cooking in the home.
If all these new ideas make you want to learn
more, you'll be pleased to find the bookshop at
the end of the tour. It stocks DIY plans and
information sheets, magazines and books.
Practical details: The centre is open to all
every day of the year except over the Christmas
holiday, from 10 am to 5 pm (dusk in winter).
Parties and coaches are welcome but they
must make arrangements with the centre in
advance. Children must be accompanied by
adult as some of the exhibits could be
dangerous. There is a three hundred yard walk
up a seventy foot hill from the free car park to
the centre. Invalids may drive up. There is an
admission charge. No pets are allowed as this
is a nature reserve. Most of the exhibits are out
of doors so take rainproof clothing just in case.
The centre is three miles north of
Machynlleth, just off the A487.

35 Handcrafted Leather

Candles in the Rain
Ty'r Efail, Nantglyn
Near Denbigh, Clwyd
Tel: Nantglyn 389

The smell of leather hits you when you enter

his eighteenth century Welsh smithy which serves as workshop and showroom for the Jorringtons' leather goods. The Norringtons re a husband and wife team who design and andcraft a wide range of leather goods — rom keyfobs and belts to cowboy hats and andbags. They use only top quality British ridle hide which is treated to ensure that the products won't dry, crack or 'spot' in the rain. Hand-carved designs and monograms are a peciality and custom orders are welcome.

The Norringtons have won several awards for their workmanship, have sold goods to Heals and Liberty's of London and have done special commissions for members of the Welsh and Irish National operas.

Practical details: The smithy is open to the public from 10 am to 5 pm daily including weekends and bank holidays. Their shop on the A5 at The Coach House, Pentrefoeas near Betws-y-Coed, carries more stock and also serves as a workshop where demonstrations can be seen. It is open seven days a week but only during the tourist season (April to October).

36   Woollen Tweeds

Afonwen Woollen Company
Afonwen, Near Mold, Clwyd
Tel: Caerwys 427

At the mill, situated in picturesque scenery, visitors can watch woollen tweeds being woven. Skirts are made to order and there is a shop selling tweed garments, hand-knitted Aran socks, hats, skirt lengths and travel rugs, as well as other local crafts.

Practical details: The mill is open from 9 am to 5 pm Monday to Friday and from 11 am to 4 pm on Saturday and Sunday. There is a free car park and coaches are welcome. The mill is off the A541 Denbigh–Mold road.

37   Life-boat Station

The Life-boat Station
East Parade, Rhyl, Clwyd

The life-boat in use here at Rhyl is a self-righting life-boat called Har-Lil after Harry and Lilly, parents of the donor. You will probably not see the life-boat going out unless there is an emergency, though the crew of seven sometimes do exercises. Every six weeks they go out on a practice run. Every six months they have bad weather practice, and

Leathercraft at Candles in the Rain

every six months they have a 'black-out' practice on a moonless, starless night.

The life-boat most likely to be called out to rescue holiday makers — children floating out to sea on airbeds, picnickers cut off by the tide, and capsized boats—is the inshore life-boat. The full size life-boats are more often launched in bad weather. When you hear your radio programme interrupted by the announcement, 'Attention all shipping . . .' you can be sure that small fishing boats and pleasure craft in stormy areas will head straight for the nearest harbour. But it is just then that the life-boat crew are likely to be called out. They must be ready to put to sea at a moment's notice, day or night, summer or winter.

The people who man these life-boats are not full time crews. An RNLI life-boat station normally has only one full-time paid employee. The coxswain at St. David's in South Wales is a verger at the cathedral and other life-boat crew members have included a farmer, a power station worker, the manager of a building firm and a printer.

You can't miss the life-boat station at Rhyl because it is on the Parade with the Coastguard's look-out on top and a slipway running down from it. The life-boat house contains a display of life-boat pictures and a range of model life-boats.

Practical details: The Rhyl life-boat station is open in summer (Easter to the end of September) seven days a week, from 9 am to 9 pm and in winter a mechanic is on duty from 10 am to lunch time (12.30 pm). There is no charge and individual members of the public can walk in. School parties, rotary clubs and other groups who wish to receive a talk and guided tour should write to the Honorary Secretary, 7 Wayside Acres, Bodelwyddan, Rhyl. Tel: Rhyl 582725.

There are about 250 RNLI stations around the coasts of Great Britain and Ireland. If you would like to visit another one, write, enclosing a stamped addressed envelope, to Mrs Heather Deane, RNLI, West Quay Road, Poole, Dorset (Tel: Poole 71133). Mrs Deane will send you the address of your nearest life-boat station. No charge is made but donations are always welcome as the RNLI rescues people without charge.

8 Hand Weavers

Dyserth Hand Weavers
Netherton, Elwy Avenue, Dyserth, Rhyl
Clwyd LL18 6HW
Tel: Dyserth 570256

Three foot looms are in daily use here, and, as weaving classes are held, there are usually various sizes of table looms set up for teaching purposes. Visitors can watch hand weaving. Hand-woven materials such as dress lengths are on sale, and there are finished goods such as skirts, stoles, neck-ties, aprons, table mats, tray cloths, cushion covers and antimacassars. Articles are available for sale and others can be ordered.

Practical details: Mr. Cecil Rhodes and his nephew, Mr. Donald Lander, welcome individuals and small groups of interested people to their workshop at all reasonable times throughout the year. No advance notice is necessary.

9 Textile Mill

Holywell Textile Mills Limited
Holywell, Clwyd CH8 7NU
Tel: Holywell 712022

Spinning and weaving have been carried out in this valley since the late eighteenth century and Holywell Mills became an established limited company in 1874. The mill specialises in making tweeds from the wool of Jacob sheep. These sheep are named after the ones mentioned in the Bible, in the story of Jacob's

Learning about hand-weaving at Dyserth

courtship of Rebecca.

Visitors to the mill are taken on a conducted tour and the processes of spinning and weaving are explained. Besides Jacob tweeds, visitors see the making of Welsh tapestry tweeds, Welsh tapestry bed covers, blankets, travel rugs and Welsh flannels. 'Welsh tapestry' does not only mean 'made in Wales': it is also a cloth which had been traditionally made in Wales from Welsh wool.

Practical details: The mill is open for previously arranged visits Monday to Friday all year, including some bank holidays. Tours take place at 10.30 am and 3.15 pm. Evening visits can also be arranged, and for these a small fee is charged to cover the cost of reopening the mill. Individuals and parties welcomed.

The mill is next to St. Winifred's Well on the B5121.

40 Nuclear Power Station

Wylfa Power Station
Cemaes Bay, Anglesey, Gwynedd
Tel: Cemaes Bay 710471

Wylfa's output of 1000 megawatts makes it

one of the largest nuclear power stations in the world. It is situated on the rugged north west coast of Anglesey. There is a nature trail and an observation tower from which visitors can view the power station and surrounding countryside. (Open from 10 am daily.)
Practical details: Organised parties may tour the power station by prior arrangement with the station manager. There is a charge, but school parties are free. The minimum age is fourteen years.

41 Plastics Manufacturers

Hi-Speed Plastics Limited
Llandegai, Bangor, Gwynedd
Tel: Bangor 4281

On one side of this modern factory you can see men making watering cans, washing machine components, wheels for trundle toys, screen wash bottles for motorcars, and other hollow components. There is a long line of blow-moulding machines, each of which produces a continuous tube of hot plastic which is clamped into a mould and then automatically inflated.
The women work on the other side of the factory making articles which go into motor cars .
Practical details: Visits are arranged by the personnel officer and educational and other restricted groups are accepted. Individuals are welcome provided they write for an appointment.

42 Boat Builders

Denis Ferranti Laminations Ltd
Caernarvon Road, Bangor, Gwynedd
Tel: Bangor 53232 Ext 59

Makers of plastic moulded products, including a range of boats. Also electro-mechanical equipment made, including telephones, coin boxes and aircraft headgear.
Visitors may go to the engineering workshop

or the component assembly lines and they can watch workers in the boat–building and glass reinforced plastic moulding sections.
Practical details: Visitors must be over the age of fourteen years and may visit the works on weekdays by writing well in advance. Only four to ten people can be accommodated and priority is given to educational and overseas visitors.

43 Woollen Mill

Trefriw Woollen Mills
Vale of Conway Mills
Trefriw, Gwynedd
Tel: Llanrwst 640462

'Y DdRAIG GOCH'

Trefriw Woollen Mill was built on the banks of the River Crafnant in order to use the river water to drive the water wheels, and for washing wool and cloth.
Visitors can still see all the processes in the manufacture of wool — carding, spinning, dyeing, warping and weaving.
For more than one hundred years wool has been spun here and tapestry quilts, blankets and tweeds have been woven.
Practical details: The mill is open to all visitors Monday to Friday from 8 am to 12 noon and 1 pm to 4.45 pm. The mill shop is open Monday to Friday from 8 am to 4.45 pm on Saturday from 10 am to 4 pm; in July and August it is also open on Sunday from 2 pm to 5 pm.

44 Taxidermy

Snowdonia Taxidermy Studios
Fron Ganol, Llanwrst
Gwynedd LL26 0HU
Tel: Llanrwst 640664

The taxidermists make models and reproductions of animals and birds for museums, schools and home decoration. The models are hired for window displays, exhibitions, photographic work and theatricals.
The skins are prepared and tanned so that they

can be made to fit accurately reproduced models of the anatomy of the subject being prepared. A small exhibit shows photographs of the various stages of the work and moulds, casts and so on.
The taxidermy workshop is within Encounter! The North Wales Museum of Wild Life, so visitors would normally visit both. Encounter! has a wildlife museum and nature walk. There is an admission charge. Light refreshments and souvenirs are sold in summer.
Practical details: The studios are open all the year round and visitors are accepted by appointment between 9 am and 6 pm.

45   Pottery and Hand-Weaving

Pennant Crafts
Betws-y-Coed Potters and Weavers
The Pottery, Betws-y-Coed, Gwynedd
Tel: Betws-y-Coed 224

This is a small family business run by T. A. and M. G. Edward, producing earthenware pottery and small woven goods in wool, mohair and acrylic. Visitors can see all the pottery processes and weaving on single width power looms. The shop sells their own products and those of other craftsmen.
Practical details: The shop is open Monday to Friday from 9.30 am to 6 pm and Saturday 9.30 am to 5 pm. Organised parties cannot be catered for, due to the size of the premises, but other visitors are welcome without prior notice.
The pottery is on the A5 to Capel Curig.

46   Slate Quarrying Museum

Dinorwic Quarry Museum
Llanberis, Caernarvon, Gwynedd
Tel: Llanberis 630

Slate quarrying has been described as the most Welsh of Welsh industries, but for a number of years the slate quarries of North Wales have been closing down. Among the most recent of

these is the Dinorwic Quarry, near Llanberis, which closed in 1969 after nearly two hundred years of working.
It was once the biggest slate quarry in the world. Three thousand men were employed in the great quarry, which rises in steplike terraces for 1,400 feet above the waters of Llyn Peris.
The workshops and their contents have been developed into a slate industry museum, and a new Museum Bookshop has also been opened recently.
Four of the original ten blacksmiths' hearths have been retained to make up one smithy, which contains many tongs and shaping tools. In the fitting shops machine tools are displayed, including different kinds of lathes, slotting machines, and drilling machines.
Slate dressing is featured in a section containing slate-sawing tables, slate-dressing machines and hand tools.
One of the museum's chief attractions is the waterwheel — over fifty feet in diameter, eighty horse-power and installed in 1870
A film called 'Craftsmen of Dinorwic' is shown at regular intervals throughout the day.
Practical details: The museum is open every day, including Saturdays and Sundays, between 9.30 am and 6.30 pm, from Easter to September.
It is closed from October to March. Visitors can walk round freely on their own or take a guided tour. No advance notice is needed. There is a small admission charge.

47   Hand-built Pottery

Bryn Coch Pottery
Near Penygroes, Nebo
Caernarvon, Gwynedd
Tel: Penygroes 367

The emphasis at this small pottery, situated in the mountains of Snowdonia, is on hand-built pottery — although some wheelthrown pots are produced. Mugs, with handles in the shape of fish or seals, are among the unusual pieces made and there are also many one-off items which reflect the mood and mind of the potter. Animal studies and woodland and nature items are popular pieces.

Practical details: The pottery is open daily, except Saturday, from 11 am to 6.30 pm.

48 Welsh Love Spoons

Charles Jones Woodcarving Workshop
Criccieth
Tel: Criccieth 2833

Mr. Jones is a carver of the traditional Welsh

love-spoon, which used to be carved on long winter evenings by poor young men who wanted to create a love token which cost nothing. The intricacy of the carving indicated the degree of devotion of the young man.

Mr. Jones is self-taught. He turned his hobby into a business to supplement his income when pensioned off from the GPO, after injuring his back. He carves from hardwoods of fruit-bearing trees such as pear, lime, apple, elm and sycamore. He still carves the traditional symbols, the wheel meaning 'I work for you', the heart meaning 'I love you', the bells symbolising marriage, and the links indicating the number of children the couple hope to have. There are over sixty different designs on display in the workshops.

He describes his work as a 'hobby gone mad'. Orders are received from all over the world, and Mr. Jones' wife and son are pressed into helping with polishing the finished spoons with beeswax.

Should you buy a spoon from Wales you have a truly Welsh souvenir. And even if you cannot carve yourself, but want initials and date added so that you can present a spoon to your sweetheart, you are following a time-honoured Welsh tradition.

Mr. Jones also carves Welsh spinning and prayer stools to customers' own designs.

Practical details: The workshop is open seven days a week at most times of year except the occasional day off. The workshop is adjacent to the East Promenade car park.

49 Participate in Pottery

Porthmadog Pottery
The Mill, Snowdon Street
Porthmadog, Gwynedd
Tel: Porthmadog 2785

Visitors are welcome to walk around this pottery where brilliantly coloured pots, cruet and sandwich trays are made. Those who fancy having a go can try one of the potter's wheels. An added attraction is the weekly competition: the best pot of the week is fired

decorated and sent to the maker as a lasting memento of the visit.
Practical details: The pottery is open from 10 am to 5.30 pm on weekdays. It is also open at weekends during high summer. Admission is free. There is a seconds shop. Groups should book in advance.

50 Jewellery Workshop

Michael Rainger Jewellery
Cynfal House, Ffestiniog
Gwynedd LL41 4ND
Tel: Ffestiniog 2675

Michael Rainger Jewellery is a workshop which produces modern gold jewellery, as well as a wide range of traditional gold and silver jewellery, including charms, earstuds, pendants and rings. Some of these incorporate Celtic designs. They make jewellery to customers' requirements.
In front of the workshop there is a showroom, from which visitors can look through a glass partition into the main workshop. Most of the jewellery is made by the lost wax casting process, details of which can be explained to visitors, with the aid of demonstration models.
Practical details: The workshop is open Monday to Friday from 9 am to 5.30 pm. Visitors are welcomed at any time during opening hours.

51 Woollen Mill

Penmachno Woollen Mill
Betws-y-Coed, Gwynedd
Tel: Betws-y-Coed 545

Penmachno Woollen Mill is a historic mill situated in the Snowdonia National Park and the intricate 19th century machinery still produces woollen cloths which are made into products for sale in the mill shop. You may take a guided tour of the mill or just browse.
Practical details: The mill can be seen in operation Monday to Friday from 9 am to 5.30

pm in the tourist season. It is closed in winter. The shop is open seven days a week from 9.30 am to 5.30 pm in spring, early summer and autumn, and until 6.30 pm in July and August. Admission is free and so is parking.

52 Stoneware Pottery

Trefor and Gillian Owen
Crochendy Twrog
Maentwrog
Near Blaenau Ffestiniog, Gwynedd

The pottery produced is wheel-thrown domestic stoneware. Many individual pieces are made by resident and visiting craftsmen. All are fired in the wood kiln. Many local materials are used in the glazes, such as pine ash from the kiln and Criccieth clay. Although the work follows the Chinese tradition, many Celtic forms are used.
There is a showroom where pots and books can be bought.
Practical details: The pottery, showroom and shop are open to visitors seven days a week from 10 am to 7 pm. A pottery demonstration and talk is given on Saturday morning at 10 am, 11 am and 12 noon to a maximum of twenty people. The charge is 50p per person. You will find the pottery one mile from Maentwrog on the A487.

53 Slate Caverns

Quarry Tours Limited
Llechwedd Slate Caverns
Blaenau Ffestiniog, Gwynedd LL41 3NB
Tel: Blaenau Ffestiniog 306

'Thought provoking ... educational ... unique ...' say the advertisements. 'Take a tram-ride into a bygone age, and the vast underground slate quarries of Llechwedd.' At the quarries visitors climb aboard four-seater passenger cars, pulled by battery-driven locomotives, to tour the network of tunnels and caverns built in 1846. The tram takes you past the first abortive trial excavations to the new vein, stopping several times by tableaux of mining activities with the original machinery, or to admire vast caverns.

The guide accompanying the tram has worked in the slate mines and he explains what you see. One of the highlights of the tour are the spectacular cathedral-like caverns, where the guide turns off the lights, so that you can imagine how it felt to be a miner working by candlelight.

Using pillaring techniques pioneered three thousand years earlier in King Solomon's mines beneath Jerusalem, the miners made tier upon tier of these caverns. Visitors see only one of the sixteen floors — real mining takes place two floors below. Incidentally, the underground temperature stays constant at about 50°F (10°C) so take a cardigan or jacket with you in summer.

Demonstrations of slate cutting are often given to visitors and your guide explains the

techniques. The word slate comes from the old French word *esclater*, meaning to split, and the blue-grey slate can be split into as many as thirty-six to forty sheets per inch. Slate was used for roofing tiles in every continent until the first world war when cement took over much of the market.

When the mine was opened to visitors in 1972 it was awarded both the Welsh Tourist Board's Festival of Wales Trophy and the British Tourist Board's Come to Britain Trophy — a unique double for a tourist attraction.

Practical details: In the summer season, March to October, the caverns are open seven days a week from 10 am to 6 pm. The last tram into the mines leaves at 5.15 pm. During winter the caverns can be opened for booked parties by prior arrangement only.

Morning visits usually offer the advantage of lighter traffic.

There is an admission charge, which includes tramway fares, with reductions for pensioners and children under fourteen. Special rates apply to booked groups.

Down into the Llechwedd Slate Caverns

Slate-splitting at Gloddfa Ganol

The Llechwedd Slate Caverns are by the A470, half a mile north of Blaenau Ffestiniog. A free car park, cafe and gift shop are on the site.

54   Slate Mine

Gloddfa Ganol Slate Mine
(Ffestiniog Mountain Tourist Centre Ltd.)
Blaenau Ffestiniog, Gwynedd LL41 3NB
Tel: Blaenau Ffestiniog 664

At one time this was the world's largest slate mine. In the museum you can learn about the history of slate extraction, transport (from pack mules to steam locomotives), and a miner will describe mining of the past, comparing it with today's methods. Then visitors go to the picture windows to look down at the quarry hole 350 feet below.

At the beginning of this century the industry employed over three thousand men but nowadays only one hundred and twenty men work in the four local quarries and, over the past ten years, underground mines have been replaced by open-cast quarries.
In the Slab Mill you can see slabs of slate being sawn by diamond saws before being split, planed, drilled, cored, sanded and polished. The final products are roofing slates, monumental slabs, ornamental fireplaces and other craft goods which are on sale.

Quarrymen's cottages nearby have been furnished in styles covering a period of more than a century. You should also walk across to the viewpoints to see the panoramic view of the town of Blaenau Ffestiniog below.

You can take children to see the Grotto, a tunnel decorated with fairytale characters, or leave them in the supervised play area while you take a Land-Rover safari or a specialised tour of the old mine workings wearing a miner's lamp and helmet.

Practical details: The mountain centre is open daily Easter to October from 10 am to 5.30 pm. There is an admission charge. There are special admission rates for booked parties and reductions are made for block bookings in the restaurant. Teachers and party organisers can obtain an educational questionnaire or guide book in advance.

Gloddfa Ganol Slate Mine is on the A470 between Blaenau Ffestiniog and Betws-y-Coed.

55   Nuclear Power Station

Trawsfynydd Power Station
Trawsfynydd
Blaenau Ffestiniog, Gwynedd LL41 4DT
Tel: Trawsfynydd 331

This was the first nuclear power station to be built inland. It was designed by Sir Basil Spence and is situated in Snowdonia National Park. The Trawsfynydd Lake water is used for cooling. Visitors can follow a nature trail and from it they can view the Central Electricity Generating Board's trout farm.

Practical details: Visitors over the age of fourteen are welcome to visit the station by appointment with the station manager. Parties are restricted to thirty-six people. There is a charge.

56   Beddgelert Pottery

Beddgelert Pottery
Cae Ddafydd
Penrhyndeudraeth, Gwynedd
Tel: Beddgelert 213

The pottery was originally made in Beddgelert, hence the name. The pottery's main product is pomanders, which contain home-grown and blended pot pourri. In fact the making of the pottery containers came about as a means of marketing the pot pourri. Attractive domestic ware, including coffee sets, jugs, mugs and butter dishes are also made in a variety of beautiful glazes, and all items are replaceable if they get broken.

Ornamental poultry is kept, including pheasants, and there are peacocks which wander about among the visitors. Children enjoy the rabbits, guinea pigs, siamese cat, the sheep dog, sheep, goats, ponies and donkeys. The aviaries house doves, finches and cockatiels, and a Mynah bird and an African Grey Parrot which talk back at you.

Practical details: The pottery is open daily between 10 am and 6 pm from Easter to the end of August, after which time the coffee bar is closed. From September visitors can still watch the potters working and see their animals, but the place is occasionally closed completely during the winter. There is no guided tour. Visitors are welcome to wander about so long as they keep an eye on their children. No admission price is charged but collecting boxes for the World Wildlife Fund and North Wales Naturalist Trust are on display. The coffee bar sells simple snacks like hot scones.

Beddgelert pottery is off the main road between Llanfrothen and the famous Aberglaslyn bridge. Do not go through Nantmor village — it is a very hair-raising road.

57   Animal Pottery

Harlech Pottery
'Briws', Dyffryn
Ardudwy, Gwynedd
Tel: Dyffryn 397

A wide range of domestic and studio pottery is made at the Harlech Pottery. Individually modelled and hand-thrown animals, mainly sheep, cattle and badgers are made.

Practical details: Visitors are welcome to attend demonstrations by appointment. There is a small charge. Holiday and weekend courses can also be arranged. Pottery is on sale at a shop elsewhere in Harlech which is open daily for most of the year.

THE NORTH

Cheshire, Greater Manchester, Lancashire, West Yorkshire, South Yorkshire, Humberside, North Yorkshire, Cleveland, Durham, Tyne and Wear, Northumberland, Cumbria, Isle of Man

Pottery

Three Kings Studios
0-92 Lower Bridge Street, Chester
Tel: Chester 317717

In a restored Tudor building, given a conservation award in 1979, visitors can gaze through a glazed wall in the showroom and watch craftsmen at work in the pottery and toy workshop. Goods made by numerous local craftspeople are on sale.
Practical details: Opening times are 10 am to 6 pm Tuesday to Saturday and 2.30 pm to 6 pm on Sunday, from April to December. It is also open on bank holidays and until 8 pm on Thursday, Friday and Saturday evenings in August and December. There is no charge.

Craft Workshops

Abbey Green Studios
Abbey Green
Off Northgate Street, Chester
Tel: Chester 319413

At the Abbey Green Studios there are showrooms and workshops where craftsmen can be seen at work. Ceramics, silversmithing, embroidery, weaving and painting on silk are among the crafts carried out here.
Practical details: The workshops are open all day Saturday and visits can also be arranged on weekdays by appointment. There is no charge. Individuals and small parties are welcome.

3   Coal-fired Power Station

Central Electricity Generating Board
Fiddler's Ferry Power Station
Widnes Road, Cuerdley
Near Warrington, Cheshire WA5 2UT
Tel: 051-424 2020

Fiddler's Ferry is the largest power station in the North West Region of the CEGB and has an output of 2,000 megawatts. The striking features of the station include the 650 foot high chimney, the eight massive cooling towers, the eighty-nine foot high turbine hall and the two hundred foot boiler house. Electricity is made by burning coal to produce steam to power turbo-generators. Some stations use oil or a nuclear reaction to produce the steam.
Coal is delivered to Fiddler's Ferry by British Rail. Approximately twenty trains per day, which carry 1,000 tons, are received. The coal is discharged whilst the train is travelling at half a mile per hour over the track hoppers. Some of the coal is then transferred to stock by conveyor belts and the coal needed immediately is fed to the boiler house.

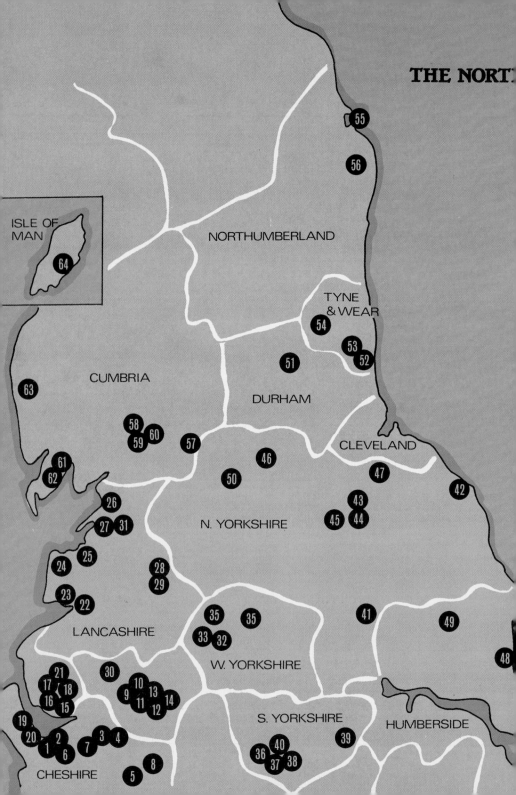

THE NORT

ISLE OF
MAN
64

NORTHUMBERLAND

55
56

TYNE
& WEAR
54

CUMBRIA

51

DURHAM

53
52

63

58
59 60

57

46

CLEVELAND

47

42

50

61
62

26

N. YORKSHIRE

43
45 44

27 31

24

25

28
29

41

49

48

23

22

LANCASHIRE

35
35

33 32

W. YORKSHIRE

21
17 18
16 15

30

10
9 13
11 12 14

S. YORKSHIRE

39

HUMBERSIDE

19
20 2
1 6

7
3 4

8

36
40
37 38

CHESHIRE

5

n the boiler house the coal is ground to a
owder in pulverising mills. It is then mixed
ith air and blown into boilers where it burns
n a similar manner to gas. The heat given off
s used to turn the pure water which is
irculating in tubes lining the boilers into
igh pressure steam.

here are four independent boilers at the
tation, each of which is capable of providing
ufficient steam for one of the 500 megawatt
urbo-generators. The steam from the boiler
rives the turbine which is connected to the
enerator. The generator provides the
lectricity by rotating a sophisticated version
f a magnet in coils of wire. Each one of the
oiler/generator units, which can provide
ufficient electricity for a city the size of
Liverpool, is controlled remotely from the
ontrol tower room.

Having expended all its energy in the turbine
he steam must then be converted back into
vater. This is done by passing the steam over
housands of brass tubes cooled by a separate
ircuit of cooling water. The temperature of

Massive cooling towers at Fiddler's Ferry

the warm cooling water leaving the condenser
is reduced in the cooling towers so that it can
be reused again, with only topping up
supplies needed from the nearby river.

The cooling towers create a draught which
passes through the warm cooling water as it
sprinkles down a lattice inside the base of the
tower. This produces some water vapour and
it is this (and not smoke) which can be seen
coming from the top of the towers. These
towers are characteristic of inland power
stations. By the coast, sea water can be used for
cooling purposes — this is a much cheaper
system.

Practical details: Contact the station manager
by post or telephone 051-424 2020. Groups of
up to twenty-one are preferred; the maximum
number is twenty-eight. Conducted tours start
at 2 pm and 7 pm by previous arrangement.
No visitors are accepted at weekends or bank
holidays. There is a charge, depending
on the size of the party, which includes tea

and biscuits at the end of the visit. School parties free of charge.

Visitors in the control room, Fiddler's Ferry

4   Commercial Rabbit Farm

Hylyne Rabbits Limited
Woodacre Farm, Statham
Lymm, Cheshire
Tel: Lymm 3005

Woodacre Farm is a commercial rabbit farm where rabbits are bred for their meat and fur. A tour of the farm will show you some of the methods of commercial rabbit breeding.
Practical details: Tours around the farm last an hour and can be arranged on Wednesdays, Thursdays and Fridays. It is necessary to book at least one month in advance. Individuals and parties of up to twenty people are welcome. There is no admission charge. The farm is suitable for the disabled and there are catering facilities nearby.

5   Saddlery

J. W. Wycherley and Son
Church Street, Malpas, Cheshire SY14 8NU
Tel: Malpas 316

J. W. Wycherley and Son make saddles and

harnesses. Visitors may watch the various stages involved in the making of a saddle which begins as a saddle tree made of laminated wood and steel. Jute web is stretched over the tree to form the seat and this in turn is covered with wool and serge. The leather is then cut and designed to fit the saddle.
Practical details: The saddlery is open on weekdays from 8 am to 1 pm and from 2 pm to 6 pm but it is closed on Wednesday afternoon.

6   Candles and Crafts

Cheshire Workshops
Burwardsley, Near Tattenhall
Chester, Cheshire
Tel: Tattenhall 70401

In a converted farm in the hills of Cheshire are the workshops of Bob and Anne Sanderson who make candles in a style used in the seventeenth century. Visitors can watch demonstrations of this craft and they can browse round one of the largest craft centres in the region.
Practical details: The workshops are open seven days a week throughout the year from 1 am to 5 pm for casual visitors but are closed on Christmas Day and Boxing Day. Groups should make prior arrangements for day or evening visits. There is parking for cars and coaches and there is a large restaurant.

7   Block Salt Manufacturer

Lion Salt Works
Marston, Northwich, Cheshire CW9 6ES
Tel: Northwich 2066

Lion Salt Works is the only open pan salt works making natural Cheshire salt. The additive-free salt is made in the form of crystal for salt grinders and as cut lump salt for use by housewives in preserving vegetables. It is sold to the consumer in fine food shops throughout Britain.

isitors can see the pump house with the iginal steam engine which pumps brine om below the works, and they can view a n-working salt pan and stove restored to uthentic turn-of-the-century condition. hey can also see the present-day method of lt production, with its steaming pan and ry hot drying stove.

ractical details: The works is open from May September seven days a week including ank holidays from 2 pm to 5 pm. There is a nall charge. Party visits by appointment lease, and evening visits by arrangement. A a room is open on Sunday afternoons and for arty visits, and there is also a shop.

lock salt being raked from a salt pan

8 Jodrell Bank

Jodrell Bank
Lower Withington
Macclesfield
Cheshire SK11 9DL
Tel: Lower Withington 339

Jodrell Bank's 250 foot radio telescope is still one of the largest of its kind in the world. It is driven by electric motors controlled by a computer.
Photographs and diagrams show the investigations of the astronomers and visitors can steer a smaller 25 foot radio telescope which picks up radio signals from the sun. There are several working models.

The changing night sky is depicted on the undersurface of the planetarium's dome and a recorded commentary explains the movements of the stars and planets.
Practical details: Jodrell Bank is open seven days a week, 2 pm to 6 pm from mid-March to October 31st and from November 1st to Easter at weekends only, 2 pm to 5 pm. It is closed at Christmas and New Year. There is an admission fee.
For further details write or telephone the director, Mr. R. G. Lascelles.

9   Industrial Machinery

Monks Hall Museum
42 Wellington Road
Eccles, Manchester
Tel: 061-789 4372

This is a museum where you can see static industrial machinery. Amongst the items are a steam hammer, a slotting machine and a shaping machine by James Nasmyth. There is also a Gardner gas engine, a Browett and Lindley steam engine and a water pump. Other locally produced artefacts and machine are also on view.
Practical details: The museum is open from 1 am to 6 pm from Monday to Friday and on Saturday from 10 am to 5 pm. School partie and disabled people must book in advance.

10   Victorian Workshops

Salford Museum and Art Gallery
The Crescent, Peel Park, Salford M5 4WU
Tel: 061-736 2649 and 061-737 7692

This is a museum and not strictly a place to se modern Britain at work. But there is a complete reconstruction of a period street wit

orkshops and shops such as those used by lacksmiths, cloggers, printers, chemists and awnbrokers. "Lark Hill Place" contains one f the largest collections of British folklore naterial in the North West. And in the Art allery there is the largest publicly owned ollection of works by L. S. Lowry.

ractical details: Schools and other organised roups should telephone to arrange their isits. The museum is open to the public londay to Friday, 10 am to 5 pm, and Sunday, 2 noon to 5 pm. It is closed on public olidays.

1   Manchester Airport

lanchester International Airport
lanchester M22 5PA
el: 061-437 5233 Ext: 3712

lanchester International Airport is Britain's argest airport outside London, with a apacity of over seven million passengers. The irport opened in 1938 and dealt with 4,500 assengers in its first year. It now handles that ame number in an hour and passenger hroughput in the 1980's is expected to be over our million.

he airport claims that more aircraft are liverted to it than from it on account of bad veather. The runway has been overlaid with a orous friction course which improves its haracteristics in wet weather, and enables ircraft to operate in higher crosswinds.

 new airfield lighting system, possibly the nost technically advanced in the world, has ecently been installed at Manchester nternational. This, together with the nstrument Landing System, gives the airport ategory IIIb status which, in simple terms, neans that aircraft are able to land in virtually he worst possible weather conditions.

n future the number of passengers is expected o rise again, though less aircraft will be in use ecause of the capacity of the latest planes. he smaller planes seat about one hundred assengers, but the new Lockheed 1011 Tristar

takes four hundred and the Boeing 747 'Jumbo Jet' seats nearly five hundred people. You should be able to spot a couple of the new wide-bodied aircraft on your tour of the airport.

Practical details: The airport is open every day of the year and individuals and parties of any size who do not want a guided tour may visit the spectators' terraces. These are open from dawn to dusk and no notice is required. Entry to the terraces is by tokens, which can be

4 typical northern street of 1900

bought for a small fee from the kiosk at the entrance. Groups who advise the airport authority of their proposed visit in advance can get a ten per cent discount, and parties of retired people who are visiting midweek (except on public holidays) can get in free. Conducted tours are free and are booked up well in advance. The airport director needs to know the number of people in your group, dates and times of the proposed visit and alternative dates. There are two tours each day, for up to twenty-five people at a time, starting at 10.30 am, 2.30 pm or 7.30 pm. Tours cover the check-in hall, concourse, flight information control room and domestic lounge. The tours are general, not technical, and are suitable for children aged eight or over. There are no tours from midday Friday to midday Monday, nor on public holidays. Tours take about forty-five minutes, and afterwards you can eat and drink in the airport's restaurants and licensed bars.

12   Manchester Stock Exchange

The Stock Exchange
6 Norfolk Street
Manchester M2 1DS
Tel: 061-833 0931

London has no monopoly on stock exchanges: others are found in Liverpool, Glasgow, Sheffield, Leeds, Newcastle, Birmingham and Manchester.
The only people allowed on the stock exchange floor are the brokers, jobbers and stock exchange staff.
School parties are given a simple explanation of how the stock exchange works, what brokers and jobbers do and how to invest money. If sufficient notice is given, groups such as technical students, chartered accountants and bank employees can be given specialised talks relating to their particular interests.
For the layman it is fascinating enough to hear about 'bulls', 'bears', brokers and jobbers. The 'bull' (think of a bull in a china shop) is the optimist who expects the market to rise. He

buys low before prices rise and sells when prices are high — hopefully just before they fall. The 'bear' (think of him as a grizzly misery of a pessimist) thinks the market will fall. He sells and hopes to buy back stocks and shares later when prices are low.
Practical details: Parties of up to twenty people, who have booked in advance, are shown a film and hear a talk from the guide. All groups, especially school parties, are welcome. Individuals may join pre-arranged groups if they book in advance. Contact the public relations department for a suitable date.

13   Reproduction Coal Mine

The Salford Museum of Mining
Buile Hill Park
Eccles Old Road, Salford M6 8GL
Tel: 061-736 1832

As so many real mines are not open to the public, this museum, which contains a reproduction coal mine, provides an excellent opportunity for people who might not otherwise have the chance to see how a mine works.
Practical details: The museum is open Monday to Friday from 10 am to 12.30 pm and 1.30 pm to 5 pm and on Sunday from noon until 5 pm. It is closed on Good Friday, Christmas Day, Boxing Day and New Year. Members of the public are welcome. There are no tours but advance booking is essential for parties, who may also see a deep mine. Admission is free.

14   Terry Towelling Weavers

W. M. Christy & Sons
Fairfield Mills
Droylsden
Manchester M35 6PD
Tel: 061-370 3403

Fairfield Mills became famous for Terry towel weaving in the early 1850s after this unusual abric was discovered in Turkey. Today the company employs about 400 people and Terry abric is used for baby wear, beach clothes, dressing gowns, curtains, hospital blankets, ea towels and bar mats.

Processes include winding, creeling, sizing he ground warps, weaving on looms — some of which have attachments for Jacquard patterns, inspecting and side sewing, making up — including putting in labels, embroidery, folding, shrink-wrapping, boxing and the final despatch of the completed towel.

Practical details: Christy's tours take place on Wednesday starting at 2 pm and ending at 4 pm. Groups of people up to thirty in number can be accepted, and as tours are usually fully booked several months ahead you should write to the personnel officer well in advance. There are no arrangements for individuals.

Huge weaving looms at Christy's

15   Liverpool Law Courts

St. George's Hall, Liverpool
Tel: 051-709 3752

Members of the public can attend court
sessions and are welcome at the recitals held in
the main hall.
St. George's Hall itself is of great architectural
interest and experts have described it as the
finest example of Greco-Roman building in
Europe. Today it is used primarily as the
City's Law Courts — there are seven courts of
law — and concerts and exhibitions are
occasionally held here.
Practical details: The courts are in session and
open to the public Monday to Friday, 10.30 am
to 1 pm and 2.15 pm to 4.30 pm.
To obtain details of recitals and possible
private visits (outside the hours courts are in
session) and public viewing contact St.
George's Hall direct.

16   Municipal Government

The Town Hall
Liverpool L2 3SW
Tel: 051-236 5181

Public debates take place in the City
Council Chamber and from the public gallery
you will see that the chamber is divided, with
the controlling party on one side of the Lord
Mayor and the opposition on the other. Each
member's seat is equipped with microphone
and speaker, controlled from a panel behin
the dais. The ninety-nine members have ha
many marathon sittings including one in 196
which lasted thirteen hours. The building
itself has a splendid classical facade and th
amazing chandeliers and golden decoration
of the ballrooms are of great interest.
Practical details: Visitors must make prior
arrangements to attend Council Day which i
on a Wednesday. The exact times can be
checked by a telephone enquiry. No notice
need be given to visit during the two week
in August when attendants are on duty and
thirty-minute tour is given.

17   Liverpool Airport

Liverpool Airport
Liverpool L24 8QQ
Tel: 051-427 4101

Liverpool Airport started operations in 193
Scheduled flights operate within the UK an
Ireland, and holiday flights to resorts in
Europe. The main runway is 2286 metres lon
and is highly developed to give 97% usabilit
allowing for a 20 knot crosswind.
Practical details: Guided tours of the airpo
are available for organised parties. A writte
application to the Airport Director is
necessary. The spectators' balcony is open t
all from April to September each year.

18   Motor Car Manufacturers

Ford Motor Company Limited
Halewood, Liverpool L24 9LE
Tel: 051-486 3900

This famous factory produces more than on
thousand cars every day, and is the only ca
factory in the country where complete cars a
produced under one roof. Visitors can watc
the whole process of manufacture, from the
introduction of the sheet steel into the
building, right through to the despatch of
shiny new cars to showrooms all over the
world.

Three of the stages in the manufacturing process of Ford cars

Naturally you will not be able to see the progress of any one particular car as it takes twenty-five hours to build one from start to finish, but you will be able to see each separate process in operation. These include the panels of steel being pressed into shape, the several coats of paint, the engines going into the body shells, the wheels, seats, controls and such like being fitted.

Eventually come the stringent tests that cars undergo before being allowed out of the factory. Ford of Halewood are currently producing Ford Escorts only.

Practical details: Contact Mr. R. Knight on extension 6291 to arrange an appointment. Tours operate Monday to Friday starting at 9.30 am and 1.30 pm, and it is essential to book well in advance, as they are booked up as much as six months ahead. When writing it is advisable to give alternative dates. Individuals and all types of parties are accepted, but there is a lower age limit of twelve years, and a maximum of twenty-five people per party. Light refreshments are served free of charge during the two-hour tour.

Visitors should report to Number One gate. The factory is on the main Liverpool to Widnes road.

Soapmaking plant at Lever Brothers

19   Soap Factory and Employees' Village

Lever Brothers Limited
Port Sunlight, Wirral, Merseyside
Tel: 051-644 9444 Ext: 8040

There is a choice of tours at Lever Brothers. One can firstly see the factory which is the largest of its kind in the world. Here soap and detergents are produced and packed.

The soap factory was founded by the first Lord Leverhulme, who had a vision of creating a village community where 'our workpeople will be able to live and be comfortable. . . .'. It is this award-winning community scheme that one sees on the village tour.

About three thousand employees and older people live in the nine hundred houses, flats or maisonettes.

There is a dell with trees and flower beds, a ballroom, hotel and restaurant, school, library, theatre and training centre.

Practical details: Anyone interested in factor tours should apply to Mr. J. E. Threadgill a the above address. Tours are usually held o Tuesday, Wednesday and Thursday afternoons.

Organised groups of up to twenty people ar accepted. Individuals can arrange to join smaller groups but should apply in advance For *village* tours contact The Manager, Th Bridge Inn, Bolton Road, Port Sunlight, Wirral, Merseyside. Tel: 051-644 8555 Ext: 32

20   Boat Restoration

The Boat Museum
Dock Yard Road, Ellesmere Port
South Wirral, Cheshire L65 4EF
Tel: 051-355 1876

This is the largest collection of floating inlan navigational boats in Europe and has been visited by the Queen. In the dock complex, against a background of modern shipping, visitors can see restoration work on boats buil of wood, iron, steel and even concrete, usin the same tools as 19th century boatbuilders Planks are made pliant in a steambox and damaged timber is still repaired with metal patches sealed with a mixture of horse dun nd tar!

.mong the boats are icebreakers, and a reedcutter, some of them built as recently as 950 and used as recently as 1980. Rubbish oats in Birmingham are still horse-drawn. 'isitors see an exhibition about the life of people who lived on canal boats, climb aboard everal of the craft, and take a trip on a horse-drawn narrow boat.

Practical details: The museum is open daily from Easter until late in October, between 10 m and 5 pm. The admission charge is reduced or booked groups of 20 or more. Guided tours an be arranged, and facilities are provided for he disabled. Parking is free.

1   Glass Museum

The Pilkington Glass Museum
Prescot Road, St. Helen's, Merseyside
Tel: St. Helen's 28882 Ext: 2492

This is an industrial museum which illustrates the evolution of glassmaking and the various applications of glass.

Practical details: The museum is open Monday to Friday from 10 am to 5 pm. On Wednesdays from March to October it is open until 9 pm. At weekends and on bank holidays, excluding Christmas and New Year, it is open from 2 pm to 4.30 pm. Admission is free but groups must book. There is a free coach and car park.

2   Natural Cosmetics Producers

Cottage Cosmetics
Castle Lane, Garstang
Preston, Lancashire
Tel: Garstang 2131 or Blackpool 53915

Cottage Cosmetics is a family firm which makes natural cosmetics by hand. The cosmetics are made in a converted shippon by Bernard Shilco and his family. They extract oils from fruits and plants including limes, oranges, cucumbers, avocados and various

Repairing a 19th century boat in the traditional manner

flowers. These oils are then combined with a base of beeswax to produce cosmetics ranging from carrot oil cream to oil of orchid cream. Visitors can watch the oils being extracted and see how cosmetics are made. There are 40 different products for the visitor to try, and these, as well as a do-it-yourself kit for making your own cosmetics, are on sale in the craft and gift shop.

Practical details: Cottage Cosmetics is open daily from 11 am to 5 pm. It is closed on Friday and Saturday. Evening visits can be arranged by appointment. Allow one and a half hours for a visit. Parties of up to sixty people can be accommodated, but an appointment must be booked in advance. Admission is free. There is a snack bar, a craft and gift shop and a free car park. Cottage Cosmetics is between Preston and Lancaster off the A6 and M6.

23   Premium Bond Office — ERNIE

Department for National Savings
Bonds and Stock Office
Lytham St. Anne's, Lancashire FY0 1YN
Tel: St Anne's 721212

A talk is given and a film about ERNIE is shown, followed by a demonstration of ERNIE in action. ERNIE is probably the best-known piece of electronic equipment in Britain. It is the Premium Bond draw machine at Lytham St. Anne's on the Lancashire coast. Every month ERNIE, whose initials stand for Electronic Random Number Indicator Equipment, pays out millions of pounds in Premium Bond prizes. Constant checks are made to ensure that ERNIE remains strictly impartial and that each eligible bond unit has an equal chance of winning a prize. Since the scheme began in 1956 more than £800 million has been distributed in prizes.
Premium Bonds differ from ordinary investments in that the distribution of prizes takes the place of interest or dividends. In addition, holders can always be sure of getting a pound for pound repayment of the money they have invested.
Practical details: The office is open for visits Monday to Friday except Christmas, New Year, Easter and bank holidays. Visits start at 2 pm and last about two hours.
Parties of up to sixty people can be accepted and the minimum booking is for twenty-five people. Individuals are welcome if they book in advance and are prepared to fit in with a pre-booked group. Educational groups of older children are also accepted.

24   Thornton Pottery

Thornton Pottery
Potters Barn, 2 Fleetwood Road North
(Four Lane Ends), Thornton
Cleveleys, Blackpool
Lancashire
Tel: Cleveleys 855045

Potters Barn is more than 250 years old. The building now has a studio, kiln room, store room and two display galleries.
The pottery is hand-made in porcelain, stoneware and high fired earthenware. There should be something new to see every year because the potters experiment to produce new and original finishes when the pottery is closed to the public during the winter. They believe that experimental work is one of the main functions of the studio potter.
The kilns are fired by electricity to temperatures between 1120°C to 1280°C in an oxidising atmosphere. These temperatures ensure the durability of the pottery. All the goods can be bought on the premises.
The pottery's trade mark is a mill. You might look out for the windmill at Thornton. It is one of the few left in England which is in perfect condition.
Practical details: The pottery is open to individuals and small parties from 2 pm to 5 pm every day from June until the end of October, and closed from Christmas until Whitsun. It opens at other times by appointment. Parties of between twenty and thirty are shown the process of pottery making in the mornings and evenings.
Potters Barn is on the corner of the B5268 to Fleetwood and the B5412 at Cleveleys. It is only five miles from Blackpool.

ERNIE — electronic equipment extraordinary!

25 Nuclear Power Station

Heysham Nuclear Power Station
Heysham, Morecambe, Lancashire
Tel: Heysham 53131

Construction of the first stage of the Heysham
nuclear power complex began in 1970. When
it is brought into full use towards the end of
1981 it will be able to provide enough
electricity to meet the peak power demands of
four cities the size of Manchester. Stage two,
begun in 1979, will be of a similar design and
the same output. Construction of both power
stations can be viewed from a hill top
observation tower containing an exhibition
on nuclear power.
Practical details: The observation tower is
open daily from 10 am to dusk from 1 April to
30 September. Admission is free. Parties of
between ten and thirty people can visit the
stage one power station, by prior arrangement
in writing with the station manager. Smaller
numbers can write in to ask if they can join a
group which has already booked. Children
under fourteen years cannot be taken on tours.

26 Railway Centre

Steamtown Railway and Museum
Warton Road, Carnforth
Lancashire
Tel: Carnforth 4220

The largest railway centre in the north-west,
Steamtown has a collection of preserved steam
locomotives including the Flying Scotsman,
plus engines from Britain, France and
Germany. Also on view are restored vintage
coaches, a Midland Railway signal box, an 00
gauge model railway and a working coaling
plant.
Practical details: The museum is open daily
from 9 am to 6 pm in summer and until 4.30
pm in winter. Railway passenger rides operate
daily in July and August, on Sundays between
Easter and October and on bank holiday
weekends.

Construction at Heysham Power Station

27 Large Popular Pottery

Hornsea Pottery (Lancaster)
Wyresdale Road
Lancaster LA1 3LA
Tel: Lancaster 68444

This spotless new pottery, with its 42-acre
leisure park, is a branch of the famous
Hornsea Pottery at Hornsea in Yorkshire, and
offers similar varied entertainment for all
the family.
The original Hornsea Pottery was started by
two hard-working brothers with a second-hand
kiln. They decided that their huge Hornsea
site had been developed to capacity. So
they looked for a second site. Lancaster was
chosen because of the encouragement they
received from the City Council, and this
enabled the brothers to 'link the white rose
and the red'. (In the 15th century Wars of
the Roses the Lancastrian emblem was the red
rose.)
Production started at the pottery in 1974 and

'Contrast' emerging from the kiln at Lancaster

it was opened to the public in 1976. In 1979 the pottery received an estimated 82,000 visitors.

The Lancaster products are manufactured by an entirely new ceramic process, with kilns operating at infinitely higher temperatures. The end product is a range of tableware which is fully vitrified, rock hard, chip resistant, oven, dishwasher and freezer safe. Production at Lancaster began with 'Contrast' oven-to-tableware which won the 1975 Design Council Award and gained a place for posterity in the Victoria and Albert Museum. The name is apt because the white glazed surfaces

contrast with the rich, brown, pebble-smooth finish of the remainder.

The pottery also makes a wide variety of mugs including special commemorative mug 'Young Lovers' mugs are a striking range made in the vitrimic body. A set of twelve designs depicts young lovers pursuing their courtship in a whimsical yet romantic manner.

The absorbing factory tour shows the whole production process from claymaking to firing.

Practical details: Everything in the factory and immediately around it is on one level, so the outing is very suitable for the elderly. The landscaped parkland has a picnic area, cafe, tea garden and children's

playground.
Miniature golf and a small children's farmyard have been added to entertain the children,
and in 1979 a Rare Breeds Survival Farm
which preserves a collection of domestic farm
animals, some of which were in danger of
extinction, was established on the hillside
above the factory.
The pottery is open all day every day from 10
am except for one week at Christmas.
For party bookings write to: The Visits
Organiser, Hornsea Pottery Company Limited
(Lancaster), Wyresdale Road, Lancaster
LA1 3LA. There is ample free parking for
cars and coaches. The factory is just off
the M6 motorway, exit 33 or 34.

28   Green Slate Workshop

Lake District Green Slate Co. Limited
Fence Gate, Fence, Near Burnley, Lancs.
Tel: Nelson 66952

Slate comes in various colours — blue, black,
purple and brown, but here in the Lake
District it has a greenish tinge. The local slate,
excavated from Coniston and Elterwater,
about eighty miles away, is brought to the
slate workshop in ten ton loads.
Six or seven of the workforce of ten can be seen
at any one time making the slate into fancy
goods and gifts. You will see slate being cut
with diamond saws and made up. If slate is
used as a mount for a clock or thermometer the
object being mounted is glued on. The slate is
finished with a sealant which stops it getting
dirty and gives it a slight eggshell glaze. Some
of the slate is made into house signs — names
and numbers are engraved with a hammer and
chisel. Holidaymakers can order house signs
and have them sent on by post a week later.
Other pieces of slate are made into parts for
DIY fireplaces.
Products are sold in the shop by the entrance.
Practical details: The workshop can be visited
at any time of year except Christmas week by
individuals and groups of up to ten people.
Workshop and shop are open Monday to
Friday from 8 am to 5 pm and on Saturday

until 4 pm. Visitors are welcome to walk in
and look around without prior notice. There
is no charge.
The workshop is on the A6068 Padiham-
Nelson by-pass.

29   Forge

Trapp Forge
Simonstone, Near Burnley, Lancashire
Tel: Padiham 71025

There are usually three forges going in this
family business and hand methods persist
beside the most modern machinery. They
produce ironwork gates and staircases, fire-

Working with iron at Trapp Forge

Kathy Cartledge decorates a jug

grates, lights, fire-irons and paper-knives.
Practical details: Pre-arranged groups can
watch the forging of iron, hear something of
the history and legends of blacksmithing and
browse in the showroom where ironwork,
brass and copperwork — antique and modern
— are for sale.

30   Weaving Museum

Tonge Moor Textile Museum
Tonge Moor Library, Tonge Moor Road
Bolton, Lancashire
Tel: Bolton 21394

Tonge Moor Textile Museum houses a
collection of important early textile machines
including Crompton's Spinning Mule,
Hargreave's Spinning Jenny and Arkwright's
water frame. It illustrates the history of the
development of the fine cotton spinning
industry.
The museum leaflet covers early spinning and
weaving, the revolutionary eighteenth century
inventions and twentieth century inventions,
including man-made fibres.
Practical details: The museum is open to the
public on Monday and Tuesday from 9.30 am
to 7.30 pm; on Friday from 9.30 am to 5 pm

and on Saturday from 9.30 am to 12.30 pm. It is
closed on bank holidays. Groups should
telephone in advance. There is no guided tour
but the museum's leaflet is given to school
parties.

31   Small Pottery

Kathy Cartledge
Bentham Pottery, Oysterber Farm
Low Bentham, Lancaster
Tel: Bentham 61567

This is a pottery where visitors are welcome to
watch pottery being made and decorated.
There is a large showroom with a good range
of pottery on view. Clay and raw materials are
sold to schools, other potters and hobbyists.
Practical details: The workshop is open from 9
am to 5 pm, Monday to Friday. Groups need to
book in advance. The shop is open at
weekends in the summer.

32   Stoneware Sculpture

Shelf Pottery Limited
Spout House Lane, Hove Edge
Brighouse, West Yorkshire
Tel: Brighouse 710618

Shelf Pottery produces an extensive range of
exclusive sculptured stoneware including
lamp bases, table lights, decorative flower
vases, planters and hanging bowls. The whole
range is produced in natural brown and beige
stoneware glaze. The lamp bases and vases
have been designed to match one another and
are made in many shapes and sizes. The
pottery has between twenty and thirty
employees. Shelf Pottery have recently opened
their own retail shop, "Hipperpottery" in
Halifax. This stocks a complete range of Shelf
Pottery as well as a wide choice of
international craftware.
Practical details: The pottery is open Monday
to Friday 10 am to 4 pm. (Closed Christmas
and bank holidays.) Individual visitors are

welcome to look around during these times and see "Shelf" ware being made. Children under sixteen should be accompanied by an adult. Group visits are also welcome during the above times and in the evenings, but by appointment only; please write or telephone.

33 Pot Luck Pottery

Pot Luck
The Old Fire Station', Cragg Road
Mytholmroyd, Hebden Bridge
West Yorkshire HX1 5EG
Tel: Halifax 3651

Pot Luck Pottery is owned by Mr Edward Underhill, a friendly, talkative man, who worked in silk-screen printing for six years before taking a degree in ceramics as a mature student. You will see him and his four or five part-time staff at work.
Mr. Underhill shows visitors all the processes, including high-speed industrial methods, how to use plaster moulds, slip casting and so on, plus printing on tiles.
The pottery made here ranges from domestic and kitchenware to ornamental and decorative pieces. Most of it has on-glaze decoration. Mr Underhill designs and hand-prints tiles, which can be used for bathrooms, kitchens or coffee tables. These are sold in the shop. He also welcomes commissions, making limited editions of commemorative pieces and presents.
The pottery produces both earthenware and stoneware. For their commemorative pieces they buy china produced in Stoke-on-Trent which they then decorate. For example, in 1976 they depicted the Piece Hall (cloth and wool exchange) in Halifax, 6 miles away. In 1977 they decorated a Jubilee plate with the places in Yorkshire visited by the Queen during her reign, and in 1979 they will probably decorate another plate to show the Piece Hall for its bicentenary.
Other goods are displayed in the shop.
Practical details: The shop is open daily and visitors can view work in progress through a glass partition. Groups of up to twelve people

can arrange to have a two hour demonstration and for this there is a fixed charge. Mytholmroyd is on the A646 and the pottery is on the B6138.

34 Industrial Museum

Bradford Industrial Museum
Moorside Mills, Moorside Road
Bradford BD2 3HP
Tel: Bradford 631756

Bradford Industrial Museum is housed in a typical worsted spinning mill. You can see working machines used to convert raw wool into lengths of worsted material. It shows development from prehistoric times to the days of the huge mills. There is a stationary steam engine, a working waterwheel, the last surviving Bradford tram and a trolley bus. In the grounds is the home of the mill owner which is furnished to show the life of a middle-class family in late Victorian times.
Practical details: The museum is open from 10 am to 5 pm, six days a week. It is closed on Christmas Day, Boxing Day, Good Friday and all Mondays except bank holidays. There are extensive educational facilities; information is available from the Keeper of Education. There is no admission charge and all visitors are welcome. A car park is available and there are refreshment facilities. The recommended maximum size of groups is forty-five people but larger numbers may be taken by special arrangement.

Exhibits at Bradford Industrial Museum

35   Hand Loom Weaving

Bronte Tapestries
Ponden Hall, Stanbury, Near Haworth
West Yorkshire BD22 0HR
Tel: Haworth 44154

Bronte Tapestries is a partnership of three
people. It was started in 1962 by Roderick
Taylor and moved to Ponden Hall in 1975.
Ponden Hall was built in 1560 and was made
famous as "Thrushcross Grange" in
Wuthering Heights. Demonstrations of
weaving are given. The products of the studio
are displayed in the Ponden Hall entrance hall
and tearoom.
Practical details: The studio at Ponden Hall is
open to visitors at any time but it is
inaccessible to coaches. It is advisable to
telephone first. There is a small admission fee.

36   Hand Tool Manufacturers

Record Ridgway Limited
Parkway Works, Sheffield S9 3BL
Tel: Sheffield 449066

Hand tools are manufactured here under the

brand names of Record, Ridgway, Marples
and Gilbow. The group is a large public
company employing about 1,200 workers in
four factories.
Practical details: Organised trade groups
are accepted, but arrangements must be made
in advance.

37   Tape Measures and Rules

Rabone Chesterman Limited
Pomona Street, Sheffield
South Yorkshire S11 8JP
Tel: Sheffield 660044

Rabone Chesterman Limited manufactures
various tape measures and rules. Printing and
engraving of long steel tape measures, steel
rule engraving and the making of measuring
instruments are among the processes to be
seen.
Practical details: Educational groups,
consumer associations and other interested
groups can tour the works on weekdays
between 9 am and 4 pm. In the evening a few
processes can also be seen. Visits must be
arranged by appointment.

38   Scythe and Steelworks

Abbeydale Industrial Hamlet
Abbeydale Road South, Sheffield
South Yorkshire S7 2QW
Tel: Sheffield 367731

Here on the River Sheaf you will see a restored
waterpowered scythe and steelworks dating
from the late eighteenth and early nineteenth
century with associated domestic housing.
Souvenirs are available from the museum
shop.
There are special working days held in March,
October and November and an annual
Craftsman's Fair held in June.
Practical details: Abbeydale Industrial
Hamlet is open Monday to Saturday from 10

Record Ridgway—vices near completion

m to 5 pm and on Sunday from 11 am to 5 pm.
t is closed on Christmas Eve, Christmas Day
nd Boxing Day. There is a small charge and
arking is available. A cafe is open during
ummer. Guides are available if booked in
dvance and teachers are advised to read the
uidebook as a pre-visit teaching aid.
Also enquire about Shepherd Wheel,
Vhiteley Wood, Sheffield. A waterwheel drives
wo cutlery grinding systems. It is open from
0 am to 12.30 pm and 1.30 pm to 5 pm
Vednesday to Sunday and on bank holiday
Mondays. It is closed on Christmas Eve,
Christmas and Boxing Day. Individuals are
velcome and groups must contact Abbeydale
ndustrial Hamlet first.)

9 Unusual Jigsaws

Puzzleplex
tubbs Walden, Doncaster
outh Yorkshire DN6 9BY
Tel: Doncaster 700997

Puzzleplex is run by Peter and Dinah Stocken
vho specialise in three–dimensional jigsaws,
devised by Peter. The puzzles are very difficult
o put together as the average number of pieces
s about thirty and each piece interlocks in
very direction!
Most people take more than two hours over the
puzzles, though the occasional puzzle
genius has been known to assemble a puzzle in
wenty minutes.
The usual size of the jigsaws is three and a
half inches across, and one and a half inches
deep. Simple shapes include a heart, a
diamond and a circle.
There are also complex shapes such as a four-
leaf clover, a whale, a cello or a dragon.
Care is taken to select woods with an attractive
grain and in the case of home grown woods the
Stockens even choose a tree which is still
standing. The woods which they use include
English beech, red Paduak, yew, walnut
and holly.
Precious woods include Indian rosewood,
ulipwood and ebony.
Jigsaws are popular with people of all ages

and here at Puzzleplex they make jigsaws to
fascinate even those who are not jigsaw fans,
and jigsaw enthusiasts will be amazed and
delighted.
Practical details: Peter and Dinah Stocken
welcome individuals and small parties by
appointment only. Visitors will see the
making of handmade puzzles. Goods can be
ordered, or purchased when in stock.
Puzzleplex is 'impossible' to find, they say,
so get directions from them before you set
off.

40 One-man Pottery

Pear Tree Potteries, Firbeck Lane
Laughton, near Sheffield
Tel: Dinnington 4788

Mr. Newman makes pots in the traditional
manner — he decorates, glazes and does
everything himself — even sweeping up! He
gets a large number of overseas visitors in
summer.
The pottery is in a 180-year-old chapel — a
lovely old building.
Practical details: The pottery is open seven
days a week from 10 am to 5 pm, including
bank holidays. At weekends visitors can see
pottery being made all day at the wheel. Mr
Newman has now increased his work force by
a hundred per cent — he now employs his
young son.
School children are accepted by prior
arrangement. Evening visits for groups can be
arranged by appointment and include a talk
on pottery, a demonstration on the wheel and
a chance for one or two people to have a go
themselves.

41 Edwardian Street and Craft Workshops

Castle Museum
York YO1 2RY
Tel: York 53611

The most famous part of the Castle Museum is

a Victorian cobbled street of tiny shops, their windows and shelves crammed with old-fashioned goodies. The museum sets out to show how people have lived and worked in Yorkshire during the last four hundred years. Parents enjoy this nostalgic scene even more than the children.

The museum has period rooms, a tithe barn interior, an Edwardian street. The debtors' prison to the right of the entrance hall has a military collection, costumes and toys, the Edwardian street and craft workshops. Outside the museum is the working water-driven cornmill.

Practical details: The museum is open to everyone all year on Monday to Saturday, from 9.30 am to 6.30 pm (closing at 5 pm from October to March); and on Sunday from 10 am to 6 pm (closing at 5 pm in winter). The turnstiles shut half an hour before closing time. The museum is closed on Christmas Day, Boxing Day and New Year's Day but open on other bank holidays from 9.30 am to 6.30 pm. Prior booking is required for school parties in May, June and July — ring York 33932 to book. Evening visits can be arranged. As well as extensive teaching materials, the museum sells a variety of books, guides, transparencies and postcards.

Working an 18th century printing press

42   RNLI Life-boats

Royal National Life-boat Institution
Life-boat Museum, Pier Road, Whitby
Tel: Whitby 2001

At Whitby you can see the old and the new — perhaps the best RNLI Museum in the country and a modern life-boat station. The main feature of the Whitby Life-boat Museum is the last life-boat to be pulled by oars in this country — used as recently as 1957. The old life-boat house was turned into a museum in 1955 by Mr. Eric Thomson and displays hundreds of photographs, line-throwing guns, anchors and all sorts of paraphernalia connected with life-boats. Mr. Thomson, who is now retired, repairs and renovates the museum models in his workshop and his son Peter, coxswain mechanic of one of the Whitby life-boats, has painted a scene showing how in 1881 the Whitby life-boat was hauled overland through deep snow to Robin Hood's Bay. There is a full page account from the Whitby Gazette of February 1861: 'Loss of the crew of the Whitby life-boat'.

The oldest life-boat still in existence in the world, the Zetland, can be seen at Redcar (approximately twenty miles north of Whitby). By way of contrast there is also a modern life-boat at Redcar

On the opposite bank of the river to the Whitby Museum, about two hundred yards away, you can see an example of one of today's RNLI sea-going boats. (You might also see the inshore life-boat, if it is called out or goes on an exercise.)

The Whitby lifeboat is typical of one of the boats based on latest American designs. These are built of steel, not wood. They have seats fitted with car-type seat belts to keep you anchored in rough weather. Their technical equipment includes radar, VHF/UHF radio and an intercom between the after cabin and the wheelhouse, so that the helmsman and radio operator can communicate. Another of these modern boats can be seen at Hartlepool.

The RNLI—launching for a practice run

Practical details: Whitby Life-boat Museum is open at weekends from Easter to Whitsun, and daily from Whitsun to the end of September. There are no set times but opening hours are roughly 10 am to 4 pm. The museum can be opened specially out of season for school parties and even individuals. There is no charge. Parties can write to Mr. Eric Thomson, 4 Wentworth Crescent, Whitby. Tel: Whitby 2001.

If you are interested in visiting another life-boat station, send a stamped addressed envelope to RNLI, West Quay Road, Poole, Dorset (Tel: Poole 71133) and they will send you the address of the secretary of your nearest life-boat station.

43   Country Furniture Workshop

Treske Ltd
Station Works, Thirsk
North Yorkshire YO7 4NY
Tel: Thirsk 22770

This furniture workshop uses one wood — Yorkshire grown ash, and is probably the only workshop in the country specialising in English ash. The modern workshops are in an imaginatively converted 150-year-old maltings. Machine work is done on the ground level, where the old quarry-tiled floor has been preserved. Pillars support an upper floor in the centre of the building, where hand craft work is carried out. Around the upper floor a 300-foot gangway has been built specifically to enable visitors to walk around watching work at both levels.

When the timber has been sawn at local mills it is stored on the premises to dry out. If wood is not thoroughly dried it shrinks and warps later, particularly in centrally-heated homes. Ash has one great advantage. It takes only six months to a year to be dried out. At Treske's they make a wide range of tables, chairs, dressers, sideboards and chests; also smaller items such as bread and pastry boards, napkin rings, children's building blocks and book ends. The two showrooms and the illustrated walkway enable you to see every aspect of the processes — wood being sawn and planed, mortice and tenon joints being made, high speed router work (cutting at 24,000 revolutions per minute) — right through to the final polishing.

Ash is a porous wood, and to get a smooth finish they have perfected a method of sealing it with cellulose and coating the surface with clear melamine. This is more expensive than using polyurethane, but produces a softer feel and a more durable finish. Tables treated this way are heat-resistant and do not need table mats.

Ash is a hard wood, and their standard range is all solid wood — no veneer. Dining tables include round, rectangular or refectory styles and there are chunky solid-looking rockers as well as upholstered dining chairs. The light-coloured ash, which looks not unlike stripped pine, suits modern homes. Ash comes in a variety of colourings — white, brown, tan and olive. It can also be stained. Some stained black ash furniture is sold in a major department store under the house brand name but most of Treske's products are sold here, direct to the public. The majority of their sales are to farmers and others living in the area. The firm also make up furniture to individual requirements. They aim to appeal to English taste though they use intenationally known designers for the main lines, and have exported to an Arabian palace or two. Traditionally, oak is used in churches, but Treske's are trying to get ash accepted in modern churches. Photographs in their display show where ash has been used. About ten people work here full-time and an unusual feature of the place is that it is residential. The manager and his wife, and the apprentices live at the old kiln end of the factory, so it is open to visitors at all times.

Practical details: Treske Ltd is a mile from Thirsk and buses and trains stop beside the workshops. Groups should give a few days' notice. Tea can be provided by arrangement. There is no charge. Individuals can walk in unannounced. The name Treske is from the Anglo-Saxon spelling of Thirsk.

Carving the famous mouse at Thompson's

4   Oak Carvings and Furniture

Robert Thompson's Craftsmen Limited
Kilburn, York YO6 4AH
Tel: Coxwold 218

The trademark of Robert Thompson's is the mouse. Robert Thompson, who died in 1955, never intended to advertise, but it has become a very successful advertising symbol. Thompson used to describe how he thought of the idea. 'I was carving a beam on a church roof when another carver, Charlie Barker, murmured something about us being as poor as church mice, and on the spur of the moment carved one. Afterwards I decided to adopt the mouse as a trademark, because I thought how a mouse manages to scrape and chew away the hardest wood with its chisel-like teeth, working quietly with nobody taking much notice. I thought that was maybe like this workshop hidden away in the Hambleton Hills. It is what you might call industry in quiet places — so I put the mouse on all my work.'

Robert Thompson loved English oak and succeeded in reviving the craft of oak carving. His work is to be seen in seven hundred churches, including Westminster Abbey and York Minster, as well as in numerous schools, colleges, official buildings and in homes throughout the country.

His work is now continued under the direction of his two grandsons and his timber frame cottage has been converted into a showroom. The workshop itself is relatively modern.

Every year hundreds of visitors go to Kilburn hoping to buy something with a mouse carved on it. In addition to domestic furniture, ranging from grandfather clocks to rocking chairs and carvings, small articles can be ordered or bought from stock. These include book-ends, bowls and cheeseboards — all adorned with the mouse.

Practical details: The workshop and showroom are open Monday to Friday from 8 am to 12 noon and 12.45 pm to 5 pm, and on Saturday from 10.30 am to 12 noon. Individuals are welcome to arrive without prior notice and walk around the workshop and showroom. No coach parties or school parties are allowed. Conducted tours are not arranged.

45   English Oak Furniture Maker

Albert Jeffray
Sessay
Thirsk YO7 3BE
Tel: Hutton Sessay 323

There is usually a small amount of finished work in the showroom and visitors are welcome to look round the workshop. Ninety per cent of the work is furniture made of English oak but other woods are used when specified by customers.

Carvings and furniture are produced to customers' requirements. Items include dining, occasional and church furniture. Small items, such as fruit bowls, ash trays, bread and cheese boards, trinket boxes, table lamps, book racks and leaf dishes are also made here.

Practical details: The workshop and showroom are open to visitors in all daylight hours. It is advisable to make an appointment for visits at weekends and on bank holidays.

Sessay is two miles off the A19 between Thirsk and Easingwold and seven miles from the A1.

46   Herbal Products

The Herb Centre
Middleton Tyas, Richmond, North Yorkshire
Tel: Barton 686

Heather Bates grows herbs. She sells plants, fresh and dried herbs and manufactures craft goods containing herbs grown on her herb farm. She also sells herb doll kits and pot pourri for filling pot-pourri holders. The herbs used are lemon balm, eau de Cologne, mint, hyssop, rosemary and applemint. The herbs are processed from July to October. Visitors will see Heather Bates and her assistants working when they visit the herb centre. There is less to see in winter but herb products can always be purchased.
Practical details: The centre is open from 2 pm to 5 pm every day except Friday. It is open at weekends and bank holidays. Conducted tours for groups of twenty or more can be arranged. The herb centre is situated two miles from Scotch Corner on the road between Scotch Corner and Middleton Tyas.

47   Stoneware Clay Figures

Manor Farm Studio
Stokesley, Middlesbrough
Cleveland TS9 5AG
Tel: Stokesley 710267

Mrs. Sheila Kirk specialises in hand-carved stoneware clay figures of old country folk and craftsmen. She has studied the methods, tools and clothes of these folk and each figure is made individually, without using a mould, for fine and accurate reproduction. They are finished with a simple oatmeal glaze.
Sheila Kirk also makes the usual variety of pots, bowls, dishes, vases and lamps, as well as flower-arrangers' pots, wall reliefs and ceramic sculpture, but concentrates on one-off pots rather than repetitive design. Pots can be made to customer's requirements and, indeed, are often made to the customer's own design. Inspiration for decoration and form often comes from natural objects and the cultures of past civilisations. Another interesting idea which you will see formulated here is the creation of composite pots combining different methods of construction.
The wide variety of wares together with a range of glazes ensures changing displays in the tiny showroom.
Practical details: This is Sheila Kirk's home so please telephone first to check that she will be in. The workshop is small so large parties cannot be accommodated.

48   Large Popular Pottery

Hornsea Pottery
Hornsea, Yorkshire HU18 1UD
Tel: Hornsea 2161

The Rawson brothers started the pottery in their home with a tiny second-hand kiln. They had no experience but their success has been phenomenal. Hornsea Pottery now employs about three hundred people and produces four million pots a year.
Hornsea is noted for its modern designs and for its special decorative effects. All Hornsea tableware is Design Council accepted and safe for use in freezers, ovens and dish-washers.
The absorbing factory tour (30 minutes) shows the production process right through from clay making to glazing and firing. Hornsea Pottery has broken away from traditional methods of decorating tableware by perfecting its own method of screen-printing on to pots, with a specially formulated (and patented) ink. The results are unique after firing — a contrast between the colour of the glaze and the pattern, and between the texture of the smooth and glass-hard glaze and the matt decoration.
The pottery is popular, and provides plenty of entertainment for a family day out. It is set in a twenty-eight acre landscaped leisure park featuring a lake, playground, picnic areas, pony rides, aviary and mini-zoo for

Clay figures, hand-modelled by Sheila Kirk

the children, and a tea garden.
An added attraction and providing a new
dimension is Minidale, a charming model
village reflecting life in miniature (open
Easter to September).

The magnet for most visitors, however, is the
famous pottery shop stocked with Hornsea's
selected seconds where you can browse at
leisure and pick up a basketful of bargains.

Practical details: The pottery is open all day,
every day from 10 am except for one week at
Christmas. For party bookings write to the
Visits Organiser. There is ample free parking
for coaches and cars.

49   Oak Furniture and Workshops

Oak Rabbit Crafts
Wetwang, Driffield
North Humberside YO25 9XJ
Tel: Driffield 86257

Oak Rabbit Crafts was established in 1970 and
all the articles are made in English oak and
bear the registered trademark of a carved
rabbit. There are no specific talks or
demonstrations but visitors can look around

Packing kiln trucks at Hornsea Pottery

e showroom and the workshop.
the showroom visitors can see small articles
nging from ashtrays to nests of tables and
ining furniture, all with an adzed finish.
the workshops craftsmen can be seen
rving the rabbit which is on each piece of
rniture, or carving lattices for dining-chair
acks, or perhaps turning fruit bowls, and
aking up furniture.
he locally produced oak can be seen stacked
n the premises where it is seasoned for years
efore it is ready for use.
ractical details: The workshop and
howroom are open Monday to Friday from 8
m to 5 pm, and most weekends from 11 am
 5 pm. Individuals and groups are welcome
ut parties should book well in advance to
rrange a suitable time. If they wish to see
ork being done, visits must be arranged
uring the week before 5 pm, although
vening visits can be made by prior
rrangement.
isitors may purchase goods.

0   Ropemaking

. R. Outhwaite & Son, Ropemakers
own Foot, Hawes, North Yorkshire
el: Hawes 487

his is a rural workshop where visitors can
atch rope being made by traditional
ethods. Apart from agricultural products
ke halters, lead ropes and haynets, a number
f specialist ropes are made such as church bell
pes, bannister ropes, skipping ropes and
oat fenders. Ropes, twines and cords and an
mazing number of rope and twine related
raft items are on sale. These include dog
ads, rope dolls, hammocks, lanyards,
opping bags, quoits, key rings and rope
dders.
ractical details: Entry is free. Open in
orking hours for individuals and families.
roup visits by arrangement only; please send
n sae. Closed on Sundays. Situated at the
ntrance to the old station car park and Dales
useum, opposite a children's playground.

Ropes made by traditional methods

51   Mining, Farming and Railway Museum

Beamish Museum
Beamish Hall, Near Stanley, Co. Durham
Tel: Stanley 31811

Beamish is an open-air museum showing the
way of life in the north-east at the turn of the
century. It includes a rebuilt colliery with a
winding engine house and furnished pit
cottages. Visitors can go down a real drift mine
(a drift mine is one you can walk into, without
taking a lift) to see how coal was worked. The

Baking bread at the coal-fired range

visitors on a tour of the brewery. Visitors are also taken to the stables to see the shire horses which are used for local deliveries.
Practical details: Visits must be arranged in advance. Groups of up to thirty people can be accommodated and are welcome to go on conducted tours during the day or evening from Monday to Friday.

53   Decorative Stoneware

Washington Studio Pottery
Old Hall Smithy, The Green
Washington Village, District 4
Tyne and Wear

The stoneware made here is influenced by pottery produced during the Middle Ages. Tiles, murals and sculptural items are manufactured and commissions are undertaken for interior designers.
Practical details: The pottery is open from 9.30 am to 5 pm Monday to Saturday and from pm to 5.30 pm on Sundays. Groups of up to ten people can be accommodated.

54   Ale Brewing and Bottling

Scottish and Newcastle Breweries Ltd.
Tyne Brewery, Gallowgate
Newcastle-upon-Tyne NE99 1RA
Tel: Newcastle 25091

Visitors are given a conducted tour of the Tyne brewery, where the famous Newcastle Brown Ale and other 'Blue Star' ales are brewed. You will see the step-by-step process of making beer, from the hop store where the hops are kept ready for selection and blending before being added to the coppers, right up to the bottling and despatching of the beer in delivery tankers. At the end of the tour you are given an opportunity to sample the ales.
Practical details: The brewery is open to visitors Monday to Friday at 2.30 pm. Up to

farm area has animals and exhibitions of farm tools and machinery. There is also a railway area with a station, signal box, goods shed and a transport collection and visitors may take tram and loco rides. Craft workers demonstrate how to throw pots, make proggy mats (rag rugs) and bake bread in a coal-fired oven.
Practical details: Beamish is open every day from 10 am to 6 pm April to September and from October to March it is open every day except Monday from 10 am to 5 pm. The last admission is one hour before closing time. There are reduced rates for groups and worksheets for schoolchildren are available.

52   Brewery

Vaux Breweries Limited
Castle Street, Sunderland SR1 3AN
Tel: Sunderland 76277

The brewing and bottling of ale are shown to

enty people can be accepted in a group, but
u must book well in advance with the
ewery guide, in the public relations
partment. Individuals can often join groups
 arrangement.

5   Lindisfarne Liqueurs

he Lindisfarne Liqueur Company
t. Aidan's Winery
he Holy Island of Lindisfarne
Jorthumberland
el: Holy Island 230

he managing director of this most unusual
ompany tells us that due to Customs & Excise
estrictions visitors are not actually allowed
nto the working area of the winery. However,
hey are welcomed into the winery showroom,
vhere groups can have the processes
xplained. Every visitor over the age of
ighteen is allowed to sample the famous
Lindisfarne Mead.
Lindisfarne Liqueur Marmalade, Strawberry
reserve with Lindisfarne Liqueur and their
amous lemon curd with Lindisfarne
Advocaat are also offered for sale.
The recipe for the mead is still a closely
guarded secret, but it is safe to say that
ermented grape juice, water from an artesian
vell on the island, honey and locally gathered
herbs are used.

Practical details: The Lindisfarne Liqueur
Company is open from Easter 10 am to 5 pm,
seven days a week, including all bank
holidays.
All visitors are accepted into the showroom.
However, it will be appreciated that if school
parties are brought into the showroom, ten
people at a time will be the maximum, and
they should be under strict supervision.

56   Kipper Curers

L. Robson & Sons Limited
Haven Hill, Craster
Alnwick NE3 66K
Tel: Embleton 223

The process of curing kippers will be
explained to visitors and it is interesting to
note that this has not been changed for more
than a hundred years. The original smoking-
houses which were built in 1856 are still being
used. Kippers are available in the factory shop,
but this depends on herring catches, so

The traditional method of kipper curing

there is no guarantee that you will be able to buy them every day.

Practical details: The factory is open from June to mid-September, excluding bank holidays. Working hours are Monday to Friday from 9.30 am to 5 pm (closed for lunch from 12 noon to 1 pm), and open Saturday from 9.30 am to 12 noon. The factory is not always working in the opening times stated above, as this depends on the herring catches. However, someone is always available to explain the processes which take place there. Individuals are welcome to arrive without prior notice and walk around the works. Large parties and schools must give notice.

57   Engraved Glassware

Dent Glass
Crossfield Mill, Kirkby Stephen, Cumbria
Tel: Kirkby Stephen 71543

Visitors can watch all stages of prepared sandblast engraving on tableware, decanters and window panes. Commissions are undertaken and, for example, visitors can choose to order glasses with their own choice of delicately decorated initials engraved. Other engraved items are also on sale.

Practical details: Dent Glass is open all year from 9 am to 4 pm Monday to Friday, but it is closed on public holidays.

58   Craftsman-built Furniture

Peter Hall Woodcraft
Danes Road, Staveley
Kendal, Cumbria LA8 9PL
Tel: Staveley 821633

Peter Hall makes solid oak and mahogany furniture, dining-tables and chairs, joint stools, sideboards and Welsh dressers, coffee tables and bookcases. Visitors can watch the work in progress at the time of their visit: much of the time is spent making items to order, but some time is also spent restoring antiques.

Peter Hall—polishing an oak stool

Practical details: The workshop is open to individuals and small groups from 9 am to pm, Monday to Saturday. It is situated on th A591 on the Windermere side of Staveley.

59   Industrial Museum

Museum of Lakeland Life and Industry
Abbot Hall, Kendal
Cumbria LA9 5AL
Tel: Kendal 22464

The museum was the first winner of the Museum of the Year Award in 1973 and is wel worth seeing. Farming is illustrated by a display of equipment and photographs shov the implements in use. A farm-house parlou is furnished as it would have been in the last century. Other sections show printing and weaving.

Upstairs there is a fascinating display of blacksmiths', wheelwrights', mechanics', painters', brewers', miners' and bobbin-makers' equipment. Children will be particularly interested in a classroom from Kendal's Old Grammar School, displaying early toys and games.

Changing exhibitions show the activities of present-day local industries such as K Shoes and the Abbey Horn Works. There is a craft shop.

Practical details: Open 10.30 am to 5 pm on weekdays and 2 pm to 5 pm on Saturdays and Sundays. Closed on Good Friday and over Christmas and the New Year.

60   Snuff Makers

Illingworth's Tobaccos Limited
Aynam Mills, Kendal, Cumbria
Tel: Kendal 21898

Visitors are usually given a sample of snuff and are told about the history of snuff-taking in general and about this particular firm. Snuff-taking had its heyday during the Regency times in the reign of George IV, when the tobacco came into the ports on the west coast of Britain from the West Indies.

At one time there were snuff factories all over Kendal; now there are very few left. This particular factory was founded in 1867, and the original grinding and mixing machinery is still used every day. Mr. Edmondson, the director of Illingworth's, tells us that there are now only three firms left here in Kendal and two in Sheffield which still grind their own snuff. These five factories supply blenders, who add their own perfumes to previously ground tobacco. He estimates that there are about half a million snuff takers in Britain, of whom thirty per cent are women. Snuff can be bought by visitors in sets of a dozen tins at reduced prices. There is a choice of a dozen perfumed snuffs, including wallflower, rose, jasmine and patchouli.

There are also six medicated snuffs, including menthol, menthol and eucalyptus, and camphor. The snuffs are made from tobacco, ground into perfumed and medicated brown powders, some in dainty pill-box size tins.

Practical details: The factory is open Monday to Friday, but closed on bank holidays. Telephone or write to Mr. K. Edmondson, the director, a fortnight in advance. Individuals and groups of up to about ten people are welcome, and children aged twelve years and over. The free tour takes about an hour.

61   Hand Screen Printing

Wendy Todd Textiles
Corn Mill Galleries, The Old Town Mill
Ulverston, Cumbria
Tel: Ulverston 55456

This workshop, in a 17th century corn mill, is arranged to enable visitors to watch the

process of hand screen-printing. All the textiles are designed by Wendy Todd and they are made into a variety of fashion and furnishing items.
Practical details: Corn mill galleries, workshop and museum are open 9.30 am to 5.30 pm, Tuesday to Saturday. Special demonstrations of screen-printing for parties of up to 50 people can be arranged by appointment. There is a small admission fee.

62   Reproduction Antique Glassware

Cumbria Crystal Limited
Lightburn Road
Ulverston LA12 0DA
Tel: Ulverston 54400

Cumbria Crystal came into being because five collectors of antique glass decided that the beautiful old English designs should be preserved. The company started in 1975 and it makes reproduction glass based on seventeenth and eighteenth century designs. About fifty people work here including eleven glassmakers. You will see men blowing glass and making wineglasses and decanters.
Practical details: The glassworks' hours are 9 am to 4 pm Monday to Friday. All visitors including children are welcome. Notice would be preferred for parties of more than thirty people. There is a small admission charge. The *shop* is open 9 am to 5.30 pm Monday to Friday, 9 am to 5 pm on Saturday

and 9 am to 12 pm on Sunday. Prices in the shop are often 50 per cent below normal.

63   Nuclear Power Station and Re-processing Plant

Calder Hall Nuclear Power Station
Windscale and Calder Works
British Nuclear Fuels Limited
Sellafield, Seascale, Cumbria CA20 1PG
Tel: Seascale 333 Ext: 220

Calder Hall was the first nuclear power station large enough to produce electricity on a commercial scale and it was opened by the Queen in 1956. A visit consists of an illustrated talk followed by a tour of the reactors and turbine hall. Windscale re-processes nuclear fuel and any electricity generated which is surplus to the plant's own requirements is passed on to the national grid.
Practical details: Visits are arranged by appointment at 10 am and 1.30 pm Monday to Friday, excluding bank holidays. Parties of up to forty people are accepted for the two-hour tour and the minimum age limit is twelve years. Write to the visits liaison officer two months in advance.

64   Handloom Mill

St. George's Woollen Mills Limited
Laxey, Isle of Man
Tel: Laxey 781395

Holiday-makers are invited to see the handlooms being operated and turning out pure wool Manx tweeds and travel rugs.
Practical details: The handloom unit and showrooms are open Monday to Friday from 10 am to 5.30 pm. On Saturday the showroom only is open from 10 am to 5 pm. The mills are open on bank holidays. Individuals and groups are welcome but school parties must telephone or write in advance for confirmation.

Work with molten glass at Cumbria Crystal

SCOTLAND

Dumfries and Galloway, Borders, Lothian, Strathclyde, Central Fife, Tayside, Grampian, Highlands, Orkney, Western Isles

▌ Weaving Mills

Glen Cree Limited
Cree Mills, Newton Stewart
Wigtownshire, Scotland DG8 6DH
Tel: Newton Stewart 2990

Glen Cree brushed 100% Mohair products are made at Cree Mills on the banks of the River Cree. They are made by craftsmen from the finest Mohair yarns which are woven and gently brushed using natural teazles. The unique properties of Mohair (the fleece of the Angora goat), are its softness, lightness, and warmth, combined with clarity and brilliance of colour.
Practical details: Visitors are welcome Monday to Friday at 10 am, 10.30 am, 11 am, 11.30 am, 2.30 pm and 3 pm, when they will be guided round the mill and have the weaving, brushing, and finishing processes described by a guide.

2   Gem Rock Workshop

Creetown Gem Rock Museum
Chain Road, Creetown by Newton Stewart
Wigtownshire DG8 7HJ
Tel: Creetown 357

Creetown's local beaches, especially those facing west, provide a rich hunting ground for the gem-stone collector. You can pick up agate and jasper, and a map in this museum shows you where to look. In the museum's open view workshop lapidary work is carried out.
You can see one of the largest collections of walking sticks in the world. There are also displays of wood and stone, North Sea oil wells and a picture gallery.
Practical details: The museum and workshop are open seven days a week from 9.30 am to 5.30 pm. Parties should make arrangements in advance. A small fee is charged for admission. At the museum there is a shop selling gemstones, jewellery fittings and equipment and jewellery made on the premises. Refreshments are available.

3   Hydro-electric Power Station

Tongland Hydro-Electric Power Station
Near Kirkcudbright
Kirkcudbrightshire
Tel: Kirkcudbright 30114

Parts of the Tongland reservoir and gorge can be seen from the road but visitors on the Tongland tour can take a closer look, not only at the interesting engineering of the power station and dam, but also at the impressive scenery.
Tongland Dam is sharply curved against the pressure of the water and measures nearly three hundred metres along the top. It rises

more than twenty metres above the river bed and creates a reservoir of twenty hectares in area. Below the dam the spectacular gorge is accessible because some of the water is diverted. Visitors will also see one of Scotland's famous fish ladders, which curves round the eastern side of the gorge in a series of stepped pools.

Each summer the salmon return from their Atlantic feeding grounds to mate and spawn in the fresh water: they can be seen leaping up the ladder or resting in the top pool before entering the reservoir. The salmon are counted electronically and in a good year about four thousand pass through the system of ladders.

The power of the water turbine depends upon the volume of water which flows through it and the height or 'head' from which it is piped. The engineers manage the dam and reservoir so that there is enough water at a sufficient height to produce electricity. Hydro-electric power stations have the great advantage that they can start up quickly to meet an unexpected demand. In summer, when the water supply may be limited, they are used mainly at times of peak load to supplement the output of other power stations. In winter, when the demand for electricity is high, the heavier rainfall enables the hydro-electric power stations to work longer hours.

Practical details: The Tongland tour is run from the end of June to late September. Visitors should telephone the tour centre to reserve a place. Parties of up to sixteen people are met at the Information Kiosk in Kirkcudbright, and are driven in a minibus to the power station. At the tour centre next to the power station buildings visitors are given a short talk.

They are then taken by bus to the dam, where there is an observation area with seats, tables and information panels. From here the guide leads the party across the dam and down the side of the fish ladder. An audio-visual presentation is laid on when the weather is bad. Visitors who do not wish to view the ladder and prefer to enjoy the scenery from the dam can do so.

4 Glass Craftsman

North Glen Gallery
Palnackie, Castle Douglas
Kirkcudbrightshire
Tel: Palnackie 200

Half-a-mile up a narrow farm lane from the small port of Palnackie, stone buildings, sheep, free-range hens and coastal scenery provide a retreat for a former research scientist, Edward Iglehart. He has developed his own methods of glass working, including making his own colours and decorative materials. Molten glass is rolled in a combination of oxides and colourants, mixed in the fire, and drawn into rods, which are used to shape and form hollow pieces. No fixed range is produced, because all Mr Iglehart's work is original — but bottles, vases and drinking vessels are usually well represented.

His eventual aim is to produce glassware made entirely of local materials, fired using methane from an organic composter, which also provides the fertilizer for the vegetable garden. This, by the way, is where you should search if there is no-one in the workshop.

Edward Iglehart—individual glassware

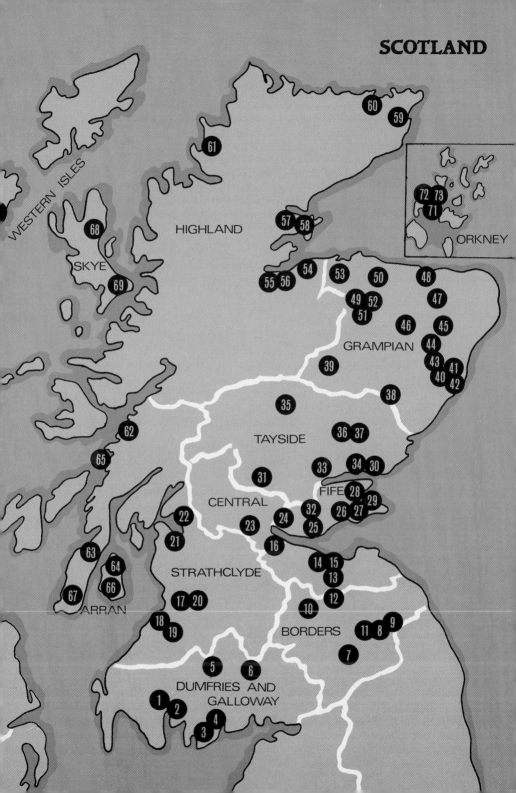

SCOTLAND

WESTERN ISLES

HIGHLAND

SKYE

ORKNEY

GRAMPIAN

TAYSIDE

CENTRAL

FIFE

STRATHCLYDE

ARRAN

BORDERS

DUMFRIES AND
GALLOWAY

Practical details: The pottery is open from 10 am to 6 pm Monday to Saturday and at other times by arrangement. Individuals or groups should telephone in advance, when arrangements can be made for them to watch steel being cut and welded into sculpture, or glassblowing.

Practical details: The workshop is open Monday to Saturday, from 9 am to 5 pm and limited numbers of visitors are welcome, although not in parties. Please write or telephone in advance.
Craigdarroch is two miles west of Moniaive or the B729.

5   Spinning Wheel Maker

H. Pouncey
The Stables, Craigdarroch
Moniaive, Thornhill, Dumfriesshire
Tel: Moniaive 230

The stable workshop is a one-man craft shop situated in the grounds of Craigdarroch House, former home of Annie Laurie, immortalised in the Scottish song.
Mr. Pouncey produces a range of spinning wheels to meet the needs of all kinds of spinners. They are all made to traditional designs used in Scotland, Scandinavia, Saxony, Holland, Finland and Austria.

6   Wrought Ironwork

E. Martin and Son
Closeburn, Thornhill, Dumfriesshire
Tel: Closeburn 267

The Martins do all kinds of general blacksmithing in these premises and the wrought-iron work is only one aspect of their business. They also do horse-shoeing and other related iron-forging assignments.
Practical details: Contact Mr. E. Martin before paying them a visit as the wrought-iron forging is done only on specific orders and is not, therefore, a continuous process.

Industrial Weaving

Crow Mill Weavers
Trow Mill, Hawick
Roxburghshire TD9 8SU
Tel: Hawick 2555

This most picturesque of mills produces Hawick Honeycomb Gold Medal cellular blankets, tweeds and travel rugs, which are all available direct to the public at mill prices. The technically minded can visit the mill itself with a guide, going through the various stages of tweed and blanket manufacture.
Practical details: The mill and showroom are open Monday to Friday from 8 am to 5 pm. The showroom alone is open on Saturdays 9 am to 5pm and in winter from 2 pm to 5 pm; other times by arrangement.

Weaving a decorative wall hanging

The mill receives a large number of visitors so coach parties must book at an early date. The tour of the mill lasts about forty-five minutes and they are well prepared for groups. There is a snack bar where light refreshments may be purchased and, in addition, they have arranged with hotels in Hawick to provide lunch or high tea. The mill is 2½ miles from Hawick on the A698.

8   Woven Wall Hangings

Mr. Macdonald Scott
Walton Hall, Kelso, Roxburghshire
Tel: Kelso 3863

Mr. Macdonald Scott makes decorative wall-hangings for churches and homes. The tapestry is handwoven in wool on cotton

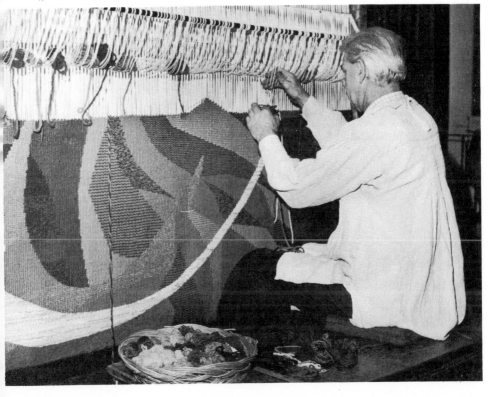

warp. The subjects of the wall-hangings are abstract, symbolic or as commissioned. There is an art gallery with work for sale.
Practical details: A phone call is necessary to arrange a visit.

9 Borders Pottery

The Kelso Pottery
The Knowes, Kelso, Roxburghshire
Tel: Kelso 2027

Piggy banks, hens and plates are specialities at this pottery where you can watch as pots are thrown and glazed. The richly coloured slip decoration is influenced by the landscape of the Borders Region and Scots pines sometimes feature in the design. In addition to domestic pottery a small amount of Raku ware, fired in straw, hay or sawdust, is produced. Another speciality is the making of portrait models of buildings.
Practical details: The studio shop is open from 10 am to 1 pm and from 2 pm to 5 pm Monday to Saturday. Up to ten people can be accommodated at the pottery, which is situated behind Kelso Abbey in the large car park.

10 Tweed Manufacturers

D. Ballantyne Brothers & Co. Limited
March Street Mills
Peebles EH45 8ER
Tel: Peebles 20146

The mill employs three hundred people, and visitors may observe all the manufacturing processes involved, from preparation of the yarn to weaving and finishing. Around 300 pieces of tweed are produced here every week.
Practical details: The mill is open Monday to Thursday 9 am to 4.30 pm. Contact Mr. Roland Brett by phone or letter. Groups of twenty to forty-five people should give at least a week's notice. Individuals are welcome with children aged thirteen or older. Tours last an hour.

11 Costume Doll Maker

Anne Carrick
Walton Hall, Kelso, Roxburghshire
Tel: Kelso 3863

Anne Carrick makes costume figures with wire and fabric. Each one is individually made, sometimes based on a portrait of an historical character, sometimes drawn from imagination. Most work is commissioned but a few items are on sale in the gallery.
Practical details: The house-cum-studio is open every day. A telephone call is advisable

12 Loom-making and Weaving

Whim Looms
Whim Square, Lamancha
Peeblesshire EH46 7BD
Tel: Penicuik 77474

Visitors can see the processes of sawing

ardwoods from the trunk, seasoning,
vorking and finishing wood for the final
oom. About fourteen kinds of tapestry and
veaving looms plus accessories are made,
nostly on commission. Some looms are also
n sale in the showroom. In the weaving
vorkshop, the looms can be seen in use and
here are articles for sale. The workshops and
howroom are set in an A-listed Georgian
table square, currently under restoration.
Practical details: Individuals and small
roups are welcome, but it is best to phone
rst.

3   Cut Crystal Glassware

dinburgh Crystal Glass Company
astfield, Penicuik
Midlothian EH26 8HB
Tel: Penicuik 72244

isitors see all the processes of making
dinburgh Crystal in this ultra-modern and
fficient factory. Particularly fascinating are
he glass-blowing and cutting which turn the
nolten glass into the beautiful crystal articles.
Practical details: Parties of up to twelve people
re conducted round the factory at regular
ntervals starting from 9.15 am to 11 am and
rom 1.15 pm to 3 pm daily, Monday to Friday
xcluding holidays. Special arrangements can
e made for large parties and for disabled
ersons by telephoning in advance. You
vill find the factory about ten miles south of
dinburgh.

4   Whisky Blending and Bottling

Wm. Sanderson and Son Limited
7 The Loan, South Queensferry
Vest Lothian
el: 031-331 1500

isitors may watch the blending and bottling
f Vat 69 and The Antiquary de luxe whiskies

Loom-making at Whim Looms

for the United Kingdom and all export
markets. The Company's bond is operated
under surveillance of HM Customs and Excise
and no shop is allowed to sell the products on
the premises.
Practical details: The plant is open Monday to
Friday from 7.30 am to 5 pm, except on Friday
afternoons. Visiting parties are normally
received at 10 am and 2 pm. The Visits Officer
can be contacted between 9 am and 5 pm.
Bookings should be made by telephone or
letter — large parties two to three weeks in
advance — and individuals three to four days.
Thirty-five to forty people can be accepted at
one time. They do not usually take parties of
school children. However, they do not object
to children accompanied by parents. There is a
car and coach park on the premises and
admission is free.
The plant is situated on the Firth of Forth
between the Forth road and rail bridges.

15   Modern Brewery

Scottish & Newcastle Breweries Ltd.
Abbey Brewery
Holyrood Road
Edinburgh EH8 8YS
Tel: 031-556 2591

Scottish and Newcastle Breweries' Fountain
Brewery is one of the largest and most
automated complexes in the world. On the
tour you see the complete brewing process,
including a look at the high-speed canning
lines. You may try a sample of the end product
in the visitors' room at the end of the
tour.
Practical details: Tours are held on Monday to
Thursday at 10.30 am and 2.30 pm and on
Friday at 10.30 am, and the brewery is closed
on all bank holidays. Individuals and groups
of up to twenty people are accepted, also
children and school parties. Visitors should
write or telephone in advance as visits depend
on time available.
The ninety-minute tour is physically
demanding, which is something club leaders
should bear in mind.

16   Rocking Horses

Peter Walmsley
18 Main Street, Larbert
Stirlingshire
Tel: Larbert 4030

When visiting Peter Walmsley at his
workshop you will have to take a chance as to
what you will see. Sometimes he will be
merely cutting up pieces of wood, but at other
times he may be working on an intricate and
detailed carving. A rocking horse may be 'on
the blocks', or finished and waiting delivery,
or not even started. However, he likes a chat
and may offer you a cup of tea.
Practical details: Usually open Tuesday to
Saturday 10 am to 5 pm, but phone first to
make sure he is there.
Individuals and small groups up to five
please.

17   Whisky Blending and Bottling

John Walker & Sons Limited
Kilmarnock, Ayrshire KA3 14D
Tel: Kilmarnock 23401

'Johnnie Walker' is the brand name of the
world's largest selling Scotch whisky — se
the Guinness Book of Records. Whisky fron
all over Scotland is brought here for
blending and bottling.
The tour starts with a visit to Barleith to s
whiskies being blended. Coopers can be see
at work, repairing the oak casks which sto
the whisky, by hand. Back at Kilmarnock,
visitors tour the bottling halls and taste a we
'dram'.
Practical details: Visiting parties must mal
prior bookings. The tour, which lasts abou
two hours, is not suitable for children under
years or the elderly as there is a fair amount

alking and a number of steps to climb.
elephone or write to the above address.
ndividuals and small groups may come along
nd join larger groups on tours at 10 am or 2
m. Again, prior booking is needed.

8   Aircraft Manufacture

ritish Aerospace Aircraft Group
cottish Division
restwick International Airport
trathclyde, Ayrshire KA9 2RW
el: Prestwick 79888

ritish Aerospace Aircraft Group is
cated on an eighty-six acre site
. Prestwick Airport. Over one thousand
mployees produce light transport and
aining aircraft, major airframe assemblies,
recision machining of engine components
nd overhauling complete engines.
ractical details: Visitors are accepted
nfrequently because of security and other
asons, therefore requests for visits must be
ade well in advance and are accepted only
om recognised organisations.

9   Horncraft

harles Fairns Horncraft
yr Road, Dalmellington, Ayrshire
el: Dalmellington 265

n this workshop visitors can see the
roduction of horn tableware and fancy
oods. The horn is selected and cut according
o its natural shape to make items such as
hips, fish and hunting horns. In the case of
hoehorns and spoons, where the natural
hape cannot be preserved, the horn is heated
nd manipulated into the required shape.
inally, there are several stages of grinding
nd polishing which bring out the wide
ariety of colours and natural beauty of the
orn.
ractical details: The workshop, situated on
he main Ayr to Castle Douglas road in the

Doon valley, is open all year, Monday to
Friday from 8.30 am to 4.30 pm. Individuals
and groups are welcome.

20   Carpet Manufacture

Blackwood Morton and Sons Limited, BMK
Burnside Works, Kilmarnock, Strathclyde

Blackwood Morton and Sons provide tours
round their carpet factory. Visitors can watch
the weaving and finishing of Axminster,
Wilton and tufted carpets. A film about
carpets is shown and a question and answer
session follows.
Practical details: Tours take place on weekday
afternoons at 2 pm and should be booked one
month in advance.

21   Vacuum Cleaner Manufacturers

Hoover Limited
Somervell Street, Cambuslang
Glasgow G72 7TZ
Tel: 041-641 5111

Lady guides dressed in tartan uniforms take
visitors round the factory and answer
questions. The factory produces all models
from the Hoover range, including the vacuum
cleaners, and the small products like kettles,
toasters and irons.
Practical details: Schools, colleges, women's
organisations and other specialist groups may
visit the Hoover factory. Requests should be
made in writing to J. Valentine at least three
weeks in advance of the proposed visit. Hoover
do not cater for individual visitors.

22   Knitwear Factory

Lomondside Knitwear
Lomond Industrial Estate
Alexandria, Dunbartonshire
Tel: Alexandria 52517

At this small modern factory visitors can see

the manufacture of fully-fashioned knitwear through all its processes from the yarn to the finished article. A large mill shop sells goods at factory prices and also Scottish-made crafts and tartans.
Practical details: The factory is open Monday to Friday from 9 am to 5 pm, and opens at 9.30 am on Saturday and 11.30 am on Sunday, closing at 5 pm. Visitors, including coach parties, are welcome during these times without prior notice.

23   Hand-thrown Stoneware

Barbara Davidson Pottery
Muirhall Farm, Muirhall Road
Larbert, Stirlingshire FK5 4EW
Tel: Larbert 4430

The pottery is usually visited by people who are interested in seeing the manufacture of hand-thrown stoneware .
There are two potters and one apprentice at work making coffee sets, mugs and bowls, etc. The showroom is situated in the farm's byre (cowshed) and there is always an interesting selection of pottery for sale.
Practical details: Pottery-making can be seen in progress Monday to Friday.
The showroom is open Monday to Saturday from 9 am to 5.30 pm, and also on Sundays from 2 pm to 5.30 pm. All members of the public are welcome to watch the potters at work through large studio windows and browse in the showroom.
There is no entrance fee and ample car parking space is provided.
Muirhall Farm is on the A88 twenty-six miles from Glasgow.

24   Scottish Crafts

Tron Shop
Culross, Fife
Tel: Newmills 880271

The Tron shop sells Scottish handcrafts and woollen goods. The family specialises in patchwork, hooked rugs and screen printing Other articles made to order are dulcimers and bodhrans. It is always possible to see patchwork being made on the premises.
Practical details: The shop is open from Monday to Saturday from 10 am to 1 pm and from 2 pm to 6 pm. On Sunday it is open from 2 pm to 6 pm.

25   Small Pottery

Anne Lightwood
68 Main Street
Lower Largo, Fife KY8 6BN
Tel: Lundin Links 320686

Anne Lightwood makes pottery for domestic use — such as mugs, soup bowls and casseroles — and decorative stoneware pieces. She makes a narrow stemmed vase, not unlike a flower with holes in the flared top to help you arrange dried grasses. This is a studio pottery with only two people working in a row of converted cottages so there is not always a great deal to see. But all the processes are carried out here, from preparing the clay to throwing, turning, bisque firing, glazing and glost firing in a gas kiln.
Practical details: Individuals and small groups (not more than twenty people) may visit in the afternoons during summer, and at other times by appointment. Normally demonstrations can be arranged. All finished work is transferred to the shop which is open daily, from 2 pm to 5 pm, from April to December.

26   Mixed Craft Centre

Balbirnie Craft Centre
Balbirnie, Near Markinch
Fife KY7 6MR

Balbirnie Craft Centre, which is part of the Balbirnie Park, is open to visitors daily and you may wander round on an informal basis. In order to pay a special visit to any of the workshops it is advisable to make prior rrangement by contacting the craftsmen ndividually. The workshops are housed in he eighteenth-century stable buildings of the state.

here are no catering facilities and large arties cannot be accommodated, but pecialist groups may write to the secretary for n appointment. There is no charge for dmission to the park and centre.

Contact each workshop separately as follows:
tained glass artist—John Blyth
el: Glenrothes 756839

ractical details: Saturday 2 pm to 4 pm when onvenient. Work is on a commission basis.
Knitwear — Susan Emmerson.

ractical details: Tuesday to Saturday, from 10 m to 6 pm and Sunday from 2 pm to 6 pm.
Reproduction furniture—Joe Chartris
el: Glenrothes 758273

ractical details: Saturday only. Commission asis only.
ottery and ceramics—David Heminsley
Tel: Glenrothes 755975

ractical details: Monday to Saturday from am to 6 pm, and Sunday from 2 pm to 6 pm.
Articles are for sale.

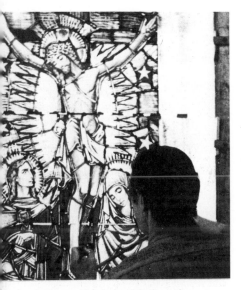

Stained glass artist John Blyth at the Balbirnie Craft Centre

Fashion designer—Marjorie Heminsley
Tel: Glenrothes 755975

Practical details: Monday to Saturday from 9 am to 6 pm, and Sunday from 2 pm to 6 pm. Garments for sale, and to order.

Furniture & woodwork — Donald McGarva
Tel: Glenrothes 758759

Practical details: Monday to Friday from 9 am to 6 pm, and Saturday and Sunday from 2 pm to 6 pm. Wooden objects are on sale but the furniture is made on a commissioned basis, with a standard range available.

Jewellery—Alison and Roy Murray
Tel: Glenrothes 753743

Practical details: Monday to Saturday from 10 am to 6 pm. Articles may be purchased.

Leatherwork—Ron and Susan Muir
Tel: Glenrothes 758753

Practical details: Monday to Sunday from 10 am to 6 pm. Articles may be purchased.

27   Calligraphy and Letter Carving

George L. Thomson
The White Cottage
Balgrie Bank
Leven, Fife

Mr. Thomson's work includes writing manuscript books and panels, and carving inscriptions on wood and stone. He works on burgess tickets, the illuminated addresses which are presented to outstanding citizens with the Freedom of the Burgh. He also makes personal seals which he cuts by hand and which may take the form of a sign of the zodiac or a logo using initials.

Practical details: A limited amount of Mr. Thomson's work can be seen at his home where visitors may watch him carrying out the work on which he is currently engaged. Parties cannot be accommodated and visitors are advised to make an appointment in writing. Access to the farm is difficult and neither refreshments nor toilet facilities are available. Larger displays of Mr. Thomson's work may be seen at the Scottish Craft Centre in Edinburgh.

28 Deer Farming

Reedie Hill Farm
Auchtermuchty, Fife KY14 7HS
Tel: Auchtermuchty 369

This is the first commercial red deer farm i
Britain in which the deer are fully
domesticated and approachable. On an
informal tour of the farm visitors will find ou
some interesting facts about red deer.
Practical details: Visitors, including the
disabled, are welcome Monday to Friday bι
must telephone at least twenty-four hours i
advance. There is an admission charge. Dog
should not be brought to the farm.

29 Tapestry, Macramé and Embroidery

Loudens Close Workshop and Gallery
1–2 Loudens Close
St. Andrews, Fife

The workshop and gallery are located in a
restored eighteenth century close in central Sι
Andrews. In the workshop spinning, tapestry
loom weaving and macramé can be seen. Th
main products are wallhangings in tapestry
with handspun wool and in macramé with
tapestry embroidery. Exhibitions featuring
work from the workshop and other craftsmeι
are held four times each year.
Practical details: The workshop is open to
visitors in the morning from 9 am to 1 pm anι
on some afternoons, during the week. The
exhibitions are open from 10 am to 5 pm.

30 Computers and Terminals

NCR (Manufacturing) Limited
Engineering & Manufacturing
Kingsway West, Dundee DD2 3XX
Tel: Dundee 60151

Visitors see all the latest in electronic

technology. 'To those who know little of electronics it will be like opening a magic box,' they promise. There are electronic modules and machines being assembled, self-service terminals, document handling equipment, system peripherals using the latest in micro-computer technology and computers.

Practical details: The factory is open Monday to Friday from 8.45 am to 4.15 pm. Groups of up to ten people, aged over fourteen years, can be taken round the factory. Contact the information liaison co-ordinator at least two weeks in advance to arrange a visit.

The guided tour, lasting over an hour, is free of charge.

31   Mouthblown Hand-made Glass

Stuart Strathearn Limited
Muthill Road, Crieff, Perthshire
Tel: Crieff 2942

The glassware made is for the international prestige market and consists of ranges of modern and more traditional clear and coloured vases, bowls, table-lamp bases, ashtrays and candleholders. High quality paperweights, both modern and traditional millefiori, are a speciality, and doorknobs, too, are made in millefiori designs. Millefiori, Italian for thousands of flowers, looks like clusters of tiny pieces of edible rock.

The engraving department accepts special commissions for goblets, decanters and vases in full lead crystal and crystalline.

The glassworks is one of the most modern and beautifully sited in the country.

Practical details: The factory is open Monday to Friday from 9.30 am to 11.30 am and 1.30 pm to 4.30 pm. On Saturday the showroom alone is open from 9.30 am to 5 pm.

Individuals and groups are welcome. Parties of ten or more should make an appointment one week in advance. There is no admission charge.

The showroom shop sells 'seconds' at reduced

Engraved glass from Strathearn Ltd.

prices and takes orders for 'firsts'. The modern building is set in landscaped grounds between the A822 and the River Earn.

32   Leather Craftsman

Eddergoll Studios
Eddergoll House, 29 Bonnygate
Cupar, Fife KY15 4BU
Tel: Cupar 54757

Raymond Morris of Eddergoll and his wife Margaret have restored an early 18th century

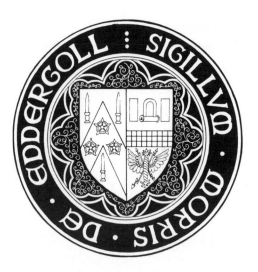

most impressive and he makes them to order in
any size.
He describes himself as 'a dedicated craftsman
striving to keep alive traditional Scottish
crafts to a high standard in the face of inflation
and imported "Scottish souvenirs".'
Margaret Morris teaches tapestry weaving and
metal thread embroidery on the premises.
The Morrises have a shop which supplies a
wide range of craft materials.
Practical details: As they live on the premise
the workshop is open every day from about 1(
am. Individuals can call without giving
notice. Groups should telephone prior to a
visit. Cupar is 12 miles inland from St
Andrews and is on the Edinburgh-Dundee
railway line.

33   Whisky Blending and Bottling

John Dewar & Sons Limited
Inveralmond, Perth PH1 3EG
Tel: Perth 21231

Six guides are in charge of taking visitors
round to see blending and bottling of Scotch
whisky. All the processes are on view, from the
receipt of casks from the distilleries to the
despatch of cases of whisky to the markets of
the world. The plant, which cost two million
pounds to build, occupies twenty-four acres
and about seven hundred people are
employed. More than forty whiskies are used
to produce Dewar's blend. They are blended in
a huge vat, then transferred to oak casks, where
they mature. From there the whisky is pumped
to the automatic bottling plant which handles
more than a quarter of a million bottles a day.
Practical details: The warehouses are open
Monday to Friday throughout the year except
for the annual holiday fortnight during July,
plus the local and factory holidays — not
necessarily the same as bank holidays. Visitors
are received by prior arrangement only.
Individuals or small parties should write or
telephone at least twenty-four hours before
their intended visit. Groups of up to forty
people can be accepted but large parties are

Georgian house and 17th century
workshop, in the centre of the Royal
Burgh of Cupar. Cupar is the county
town of Fife (once known as the Kingdom of
Fife). Raymond Morris is one of the few master
leather carvers left in Britain and produces a
wide range of items. One of his specialities is
reproduction targes, the circular shield of the
Scottish clans used during the 17th and 18th
centuries until the Battle of Culloden in 1746,
after which the English government banned
the use of all weapons in Scotland. The targe
could be an offensive weapon when a spike
was fixed to the centre. The targes you can see
and buy here have been meticulously copied
from historic originals. They are made of
wood covered with leather and decorated with
hundreds of brass studs. Some have intricate
patterns tooled into the leather.
Chevalier Raymond Morris of Eddergoll (he is
a Knight of the Military and Hospitaller Order
of St Lazarus of Jerusalem, which dates back
to the crusades) also specialises in heraldic art.
This can range from hand-carved or tooled
wall panels of heavy leather showing coats of
arms, either painted or left natural, to
medieval style jewel boxes, coffee tables,
table mats or coasters.
His three dimensional leather wall panels of
historical figures, heraldry or Celtic art look

Targemaking at Eddergoll Studios

advised to write months ahead as the diary soon becomes booked. Children under eighteen are not admitted. Parties should arrive at 10.15 am or 2.15 pm. The warehouses close at 4.15 pm. Contact the Visits Organiser. A sample of the product is usually provided before visitors leave.

The Dewar warehouses are at Inveralmond, one mile north of Perth on the A9.

34 Basket, Bedding and Brush Making

The Royal Dundee Institution for the Blin
59 Magdalen Yard Road, Dundee DD1 4LJ
Tel: Dundee 644433

About one hundred blind, partially sighted and severely disabled sighted people work this factory using a blend of craftwork and machine operations. They make baskets an baby basinettes in cane and willow, as well a mattresses, divans, continental quilts, pillows, brushes, canetex furniture and novelty pouffes. These products can be boug on the spot and, if necessary, delivered or sen to your home.

Practical details: The showroom can be visite without an appointment from 9 am to 12 noon and 1.30 pm to 4.30 pm, Monday t Friday, except during annual and public holidays. Individuals who wish to visit the factory should give one day's notice. Parties o up to ten people are accepted and they shoul give two days' notice. The factory is in the we end of Dundee.

Top: Whisky bottling at Dewar's

Left: Basket-making at Dundee Institution

Whisky casks at John Dewars

35   Power Station and Fish Ladder

North of Scotland Hydro-Electric Board
Pitlochry Power Station
Pitlochry, Perthshire
Tel: Pitlochry 2271

Pitlochry Dam fish ladder is a great tourist attraction, visited by 500,000 people every year. Through windows in a specially built viewing chamber visitors can see salmon passing upstream to spawn. Fish go upstream throughout the year. An electric recorder counts the salmon distinguishing between fish passing up and those returning after spawning, also between the smaller grilse and the heavier mature fish. Inside the Pitlochry Dam a hatchery has accommodation for a million salmon eggs.

Practical details: There is a Hydro-Electric Board Exhibition, including an audio-visual display. It is open to the public daily from Easter to October. There are working models, a fish ladder, pump storage schemes and hydro-electric generators.

days.
Practical details: Piob Mhor is open Monda to Friday from 9 am to 5.30 pm. As space facilities are limited only parties of up to a dozen people can be accommodated on a tou of the premises, which takes half an hour.

37   Farming and Fruit Picking

Rosemount Farms
Rosemount, Blairgowrie, Perthshire
Tel: Blairgowrie 3578

Rosemount Farms is a mixed arable-dairy-fruit enterprise consisting of four farms. The main attraction to visitors would be during the fruit-picking season which start early in June with strawberries, then raspberries and finally blackcurrants. Visitor are welcome to participate by picking fruit fo themselves, or merely to watch.
Practical details: To fix an appointment for a visit contact the farm manager, Mr. W. S. Courts.
You will find Rosemount Farms on the roa to Balmoral Castle.

38   Lavender Farm and Factory

Dee Lavender
Ingasetter Limited
North Deeside Road
Banchory, Near Aberdeen, Grampian
Tel: Banchory 2600

The smell of lavender hits you the minute you open the door of this small factory. The lavender grows in neat rows in a field at th back. Picking of lavender only takes place ir July, so visitors are shown a short film covering all the processes, including distilling the lavender and making cosmetics.
A guide, often the chemist himself, in his white coat, takes you through the laborator where the mixing takes place and the rows o test tubes are sniffed and watched for changes in colour. Distilling is done in a large vat. Containers are filled and packages are

36   Kilt and Bagpipe Makers

Piob Mhor
39 High Street, Blairgowrie
Perth PH10 6DA
Tel: Blairgowrie 2131

Piob Mhor is a small firm of six people that specialises in making kilts, bagpipes, sporrans and feather bonnets. The products are made for individuals and for pipe bands, and the kilts and skirts are hand-made to measure. Visitors may watch various stages of work in progress although it is rarely possible to see any of the work from start to finish as a kilt takes approximately fourteen hours to complete and bagpipes take two and a half

rapped and despatched by women in an
adjoining room. Products for sale include
vender water, lily of the valley hand-cream,
cansing cream, vitamin cream, aftershave,
rfume and an insect repellent stick.
ractical details: Between March and October
dividuals and groups of up to forty-five
ople are welcomed. Tours are given
onday to Friday between 9 am and 5 pm
arting every half hour, so there is no need to
ok. The tour itself lasts about half an hour.
he shop remains open throughout the year.

9 Woodcarving

. &. I. Crichton, Woodcarvers
raemar, Aberdeenshire
el: Braemar 657

hese woodcarvers make wooden moulds for
rinting patterns on shortbread and butter.
ne traditional design is the thistle. You can
so watch them making tea-caddy spoons,
irtles (wooden sticks for stirring porridge),
ead-boards and cheese-boards.
ractical details: The workshop is open from 9
m to 12 noon and from 1 pm to 5 pm Monday
Friday. Individuals and groups of up to ten
ople can be accommodated.

0 Papermaking

'iggins Teape Limited
toneywood Mill, Bucksburn
berdeen AB2 9AB
el: Aberdeen 712841

toneywood Mill, one of ten papermaking
nits of the Wiggins Teape Group, has a
istory of making fine papers going back to
770. Four production lines, with their
ecialised machinery and processes, make
aper for a worldwide market. The range
cludes fine writing papers, cheques, filing
nd coated papers. The mill has an annual
apacity of over 40,000 tonnes.
ractical details: Tours and visits can be

arranged Monday to Friday, with the
exception of July, and the Christmas and New
Year holidays. Two weeks' advance
notification is required. The mill is sited on
the River Don approximately 6 miles from the
centre of Aberdeen.

41 Village Crafts

The Camphill Village Trust
Newton Dee Village
Bieldside, Aberdeen, Grampian AB1 9DX
Tel: Aberdeen 868701

Camphill communities, based on the work of

One of the many crafts at Camphill

Rudolf Steiner, help mentally handicapped adults to work within a sheltered and secure community, developing their skills and independence. The Newton Dee village has 14 houses where 165 people live. They work in the houses, in the workshops or on the land. The farm of more than a hundred acres is a mixed one, producing crops such as oats, hay and potatoes. There are also pigs and cattle. Workshops include the bakery, dollmaking, joinery and weaving. There are tie-and-dye, metal and rug-weaving shops. Goods which you buy, and perhaps watch being made, include pure silk squares in batik and tie-and-dye patterns. There are pull-along wooden toys made from hardwood, and African, Asian and European rag dolls.

Early morning at Aberdeen's fish market

Practical details: The workshops are open from 9 am to 12 noon and from 2 pm to 5 pm Monday to Friday, and from 9 am to 12 noon on Saturdays. There is a coffee bar and a shop which are open from 10 am to 12 noon and from 3 pm to 5 pm Monday to Saturday. Free guided tours lasting about two hours are provided without notice for small groups. For larger groups of up to 70 people a week's notice should be given to the secretary.

42   Fish Market

The Fish Market
Aberdeen, Grampian
Tel: Aberdeen 52932

Although looking at dead fish is not

erybody's idea of fun, there is an air of
citement in the market-place which is very
fectious, and it is fascinating to find out how
e fish you eat get from net to table.
ne fish start arriving at Aberdeen market as
rly as 4 am. They are brought overland from
naller ports, as well as being unloaded
rectly from ships at Aberdeen. Aberdeen is
otland's largest processing port and it
ndles more than twenty million pounds
orth of fish every year. The local fish
eciality is haddock — you've probably heard
 Finnan haddock. You will see all kinds of
h arriving packed in ice, having been boxed
at way at sea.
ne catch is winched ashore in baskets,
eighed, and laid out in lines of boxes for the
uyers to inspect. Everything happens very
st. Competition is keen, with two to three
undred firms out to buy fish, and many of the
uyers radio news about prices back to their
fices.
he auctions start at 7.30 am and, on days
hen there is a good supply of fish, they carry
n until midday. After the fish have been sold
ey are whisked off in lorries to processing
ants in Aberdeen and elsewhere.
ractical details: The market is open Monday
 Friday from 7.30 am to 11 am.
fter you have finished seeing the market the
eal lunch or breakfast is, of course, fish! You
n eat a Scottish breakfast in the New Market
f Union Street. Or, take a tip from somebody
ho has lived in Aberdeen and buy a whole
noked salmon before leaving. It costs less
ere and it ought to be the best you have ever
sted.

3   Creamery and Dairy Products

berdeen & District Milk Marketing Board
win Spires, Bucksburn, Aberdeen
el: Aberdeen 696371

he creamery is highly automated and
roduces milk, milk powder, cream and butter
il and a wide range of dairy products. It is
quipped with highly sophisticated
achinery and is one of the leaders in spray-

Milk Marketing Board—quality control

drying technology.
Practical details: Visitors are welcome by
appointment on two afternoons each week, in
groups of ten to twenty-five people. Mrs. A.
Hay requires three weeks' notice. Individuals
and small parties can join groups, by
appointment, provided they are willing to fit
in with times arranged for a group visit. The
tour takes two hours.

44   Gemstone Cutting and Polishing

Lapidary Workshops Company
Garlogie School, Skene
Aberdeenshire AB3 6RX
Tel: Skene 381

This is the home of Scotland's national
gemstone, 'The Cairngorm'. Interesting local
minerals and specimens from all over the
world are on display. You can watch
gemstones being cut, polished and drilled.
Glass engraving also takes place. Most of the

company's business is with manufacturing jewellers and goods are on sale to the public at the same price. Commissions are undertaken.
Practical details: The workshop is open to individuals and small groups during normal working hours.

45   Highland Whisky Distillery

Glengarioch Distillery
Oldmeldrum, Aberdeenshire
Tel: Oldmeldrum 235

Glen Garioch highland whisky is made from barley which is malted (meaning soaked) in local soft water, with nothing but the water and peat smoke to give it colour and flavouring. The result is a 'light, fragrant, flowery whisky, not very smoky, and surprisingly mild on the palate'. This distillery is one of the few which still produces its own malted barley.
One large building has a number of floors where the malt is laid to germinate. If you burrow into it with your hand you can feel the heat that it generates. In another building the malt is 'peated' for twelve hours with peat smoke to give it flavour. After it has been dried, the barley is sent through the malt mill. The first mill removes the dust and the second removes the roots and developing stems. Next the malt is ground.
Then comes the mashing which dissolves the sugar and takes seven hours. Several waters are used and conditions have to be kept the same every week, so that there is no variation in the characteristic taste of the whisky.
The liquid is cooled, the yeast is added, and during the fermentation a head comes up in the huge vats — it looks rather like boiling milk.
After fermentation the malt is distilled. It is boiled to evaporate some of the alcohol, and after maturing, water is added to dilute the whisky to the British standard for whisky. The whisky is matured in oak casks which have previously been used for storing sherry. The casks are sixty or seventy years old and the whisky is matured in them for eight years.

Practical details: Individuals can phone in advance. Parties should give two to three weeks' notice.
Oldmeldrum is fifteen miles from Aberdeen on the rural bus route, and the tour lasts 1½ 2 hours. There is no age limit for visitors. The distillery is open all year except for one week New Year and three weeks in the July and August period. Visitors can taste a tiny tot in the newly-built visitors' centre. The bus back to Aberdeen takes half an hour, just right for sobering up, and the scenery looks even nicer than on the ride out.

46   Malt Whisky Distillery

William Teacher & Son Limited
The Glendronach Distillery
Forgue, By Huntly, Aberdeenshire
Tel: Forgue 202

This distillery is set in rolling farmland in the Forgue Valley ('Glen' is Gaelic for valley). By the Dronac burn are the ancient buildings of the distillery where you can see the process of distilling malt whisky and learn about the delicate single malt, Glendronach, which is bottled at eight and twelve years old and which is used as an ingredient of blended whisky.
Practical details: The distillery is open Monday to Friday by appointment and tours lasting 1½ hours are held at 10 am and 2 pm. Members of the public are accepted singly or in groups of up to 50 people. One day's notice is required.

47   Hand Weavers

Russell Gurney Weavers
Brae Croft, Muiresk, Turriff
Aberdeenshire AB5 7HE
Tel: Turriff 3544

Russell Gurney Weavers are a cottage based industry on a ten-acre croft and specialise in the production of handwoven ladies' and gentlemen's suitings, ties, evening-skirt

ngths, and overshot shawls. Visitors are
elcome to come and see them at work and
ill have the weaving process explained to
em. Cloths are all woven in short lengths
nd patterns are never repeated.
or those interested in actually learning the
aft a limited number of weaving and
inning courses are offered each year.
ractical details: The weavers are open
onday to Saturday from 9 am to 5.30 pm.
hey are seldom away, but a telephone call to
. R. Gurney will ensure their availability.
arties of up to twenty people are accepted,
ut these should make prior arrangement.
here is no charge for the handweaving
emonstration, which lasts about half-an-
our. Goods may be purchased.
rae Croft is 600 yards off the B9024 Turriff to
untly road, 2½ miles from Turriff.

8 Marble Cutting and Polishing

ortsoy Marble Company
he Marble Workshop
horehead, Portsoy, Banffshire
el: Portsoy 2404

he local serpentine stone, popularly called
Portsoy marble', which has lovely subtle
reen and red colouring was ordered by the
ings of France, who always had the best of
verything. You will see it if ever you go to the
alace of Versailles.
he marble workshop, which is by the
icturesque 18th century harbour, makes and
lls paperweights, penknives, pen-holders,
esk thermometers, table lighters, brooches,
endants and other jewellery. You can watch
e marble being polished and made up into
seful articles. If the work interests you, you
n buy lapidary equipment designed for the
mateur lapidary enthusiast — tumblers,
ws, grinders, instruction books and, of
urse, rough or polished stones and jewellery
ttings.
ext door is Portsoy Pottery where you can see
e potter at work making stoneware.
ractical details: The marble workshop is
pen every day except Sunday, from 8 am to

5.30 pm. Parties are not shown around but
individuals are welcome to watch the work in
progress.

49 Whisky Distillery

The Glenlivet Distillery
Glenlivet, Banffshire
Tel: Glenlivet 202 Ext: 10

The Glenlivet Distillery, established over one
hundred and fifty years ago, provides guided
tours which show visitors the process of
whisky making. Visitors can view a collection
of artefacts connected with the distilling
industry and of special interest is the three-D
recreation of Landseer's, 'The Illicit Still'. An
opportunity to sample twelve-year-old single
malt awaits the visitor.
Practical details: The reception centre is open
from mid-April to mid-October, Monday to
Friday between 10 am and 4 pm. Groups of
approximately eight people are taken on
guided tours which last 25 to 35 minutes.
Stairs make the tour unsuitable for disabled
people and small children. Coach parties are
welcome but groups of over twenty should
give notice. No charge is made. Whisky and
souvenirs are on sale in the shop. The
distillery is ten miles north of Tomintoul on
the B9008.

50 Whisky Distillery

Chivas Brothers Limited
Strathisla Distillery, Seafield Avenue
Keith, Banffshire AB5 3BS
Tel: Keith 7471

At the Strathisla Distillery you can see all the
processes involved in distilling whisky.
Visitors are shown a short film of the entire
process and then taken round the mashing,
fermentation and distillation sections when
the distillery is in operation. Two famous
whiskies produced by this firm are twelve-
year-old Chivas Regal and twenty-one-year-

old Royal Salute.

Practical details: Tours round the distillery
take place Monday to Friday from mid-June to
August at 10 am, 11 am, 2 pm, 3 pm and 4 pm.
Coaches cannot be accommodated.

51 Popular Whisky Distillery

J. & G. Grant
Glenfarclas Distillery
Marypark, Ballindalloch
Banffshire AB3 9BD
Tel: Ballindalloch 245

The Glenlivet area has no fewer than thirty
distilleries bearing the name Glenlivet in their
title and we have chosen to feature Glenfarclas
distillery because it has such excellent
facilities for visitors. They are all cheerful,
friendly people here. 'See round the old
distillery' they say, 'We'll make you really
welcome'.

The Glenfarclas distillery has a reception
centre with an exhibition hall and a craft
shop. They stock booklets such as 'Hamish's
Guide to Glenfarclas Distillery' which
explains the processes with the help of a
cartoon character. Hamish also appears on
one of their tea-towels called DO-IT-
YOURSELF MALT WHISKY. The captions
to Hamish's antics read: '1. Take one sack of
good malt. 2. Grind into a flour. 3. Mix
thoroughly with boiling water. 4. Drain the
liquid and add a wee bit of yeast to it. 5. Stand
and allow to ferment. 6. Drain and distil. 7.
Leave to mature for fifteen years.
'NOTE: DON'T GET CAUGHT! You'll be
quicker and safer buying a bottle of
Glenfarclas Highland Malt Whisky.'

The distillery is on a hillside by the Spey River
and the combination of clear water, peat cut
from the hillside moorland, and locally grown
barley gives the distinctive flavour to whisky
made here. As in France, where wines from
neighbouring vineyards have different
characteristics, so it is with Scottish whiskies.
Glenfarclas Distillery was established in 1836
and the Grant family has owned and
supervised it since 1865. In the 1830s the

development of the patent still led to the
production of grain whisky (what the
Americans call Bourbon). For thirty years
malt and grain whiskies were distilled and
drunk as single whiskies. Then in the early
1860s the practice began of blending malt and
grain whiskies. 'Scotch' is made by blending
several malt whiskies from different
distilleries with grain whisky.

Since 1972 Glenfarclas has bought in malted
barley from outside. You will see mashing,
mixing the crushed malted barley with hot
water to extract the sugar in a mash tun,
fermenting the liquid (called worts) with the
help of yeast, distilling twice in pot stills, and
leaving whisky to mature in casks.

Practical details: The distillery is open

Monday to Friday from 9 am to 5 pm.
Individuals and groups of up to one hundred
people are welcome and should give one day's
notice to Mr. R. MacDonald.

52   Whisky Distilling and Bottling

William Grant and Sons Limited
The Glenfiddich Distillery
Dufftown, Banffshire AB5 4DH
Tel: Dufftown 375

The distillery, which was built nearly one
hundred years ago by William Grant, has
changed little over the years. Here you can see
all aspects of malt distilling including

warehousing and bottling. You can visit the
cooperage, noisy with the hammering of iron
hoops on to oak casks, the washback with its
giant wooden vats, the stillhouse where the
whisky is kept in gleaming copper stills and
the warehouse where for eight years or more
the whisky matures. At the end of your visit
you can look forward to sampling a dram or
two of the matured product. A collection of
items connected with malt distilling and a
number of personal articles belonging to
William Grant are housed in the Glenfiddich
Museum.
Practical details: The distillery is open from 10
am to 12.30 pm and from 2 pm to 4 pm

Copper Pot Stills at William Grants

throughout the year except for Christmas and New Year. Up to twelve persons can be shown around without prior arrangement but coaches should give 24 hours' notice (48 hours in winter). Children must be accompanied by adults. Admission is free and there is a gift shop which is open from April to October. The distillery is situated on the A941 about half a mile north of Dufftown.

53   Glass Engraving

Harold Gordon
Greywalls Studio
Forres, Morayshire IV36 0ES
Tel: Forres 72395

Harold Gordon works at Greywalls, a stone-built stable, which he bought and converted to provide studio and storage rooms after the last war. He now has a flourishing business engraving glass with copper wheels, which he makes himself. He has a stock of more than two hundred, ranging in size from pinhead to four inches. As you watch him at work, he moves the glass across the revolving wheel. Most of his work is done for people wanting designs for special occasions and anniversaries. He prefers not to clutter the glass with dates and inscriptions, but to use pictures and patterns which are meaningful to the people who will own them.

Practical details: Harold Gordon tells us that his studio is open to anyone from Monday morning till 12 noon Saturday, unless he happens to be on holiday which is usually July or early August. He cannot cope with large parties but can manage four to six people. He prefers visitors with a special interest. As he works alone it would be better to ring the studio beforehand.

A lovely glass engraved by Harold Gordon

54   Culloden Pottery

Culloden Pottery
Gollanfield, Near Inverness
Tel: Ardersier 2340

You can see a variety of pottery and pottery making processes here — hand-thrown individual pieces and tableware, earthenware

nd stoneware.
ractical details: The pottery, shop and
estaurant are open every day from 9.30 am
ɔ 6 pm from April to December. They are
losed in January and February.
ndividuals and groups of up to ten people
ʋishing to see the pottery should telephone or
ʋrite to Mr. Park at least seven days in
dvance.

5   Woollen Manufacturers

ames Pringle Limìted
Iolm Woollen Mills, Inverness
'el: Inverness 223311

'he Holm Mill started in 1780 as a small
ɔuntry mill driven by water power, preparing
ιe farmer's wool for home spinning and
eaving. Nowadays modern machinery is at
ork in the old buildings and small farmers

from the Shetlands, Orkneys and the
Highlands, still send wool here to be spun into
knitting wools and turned into goods.
On a tour you see raw wool being dyed,
colours being blended, and carding — which
is the combing of wools ready for spinning
into thread. The single threads are used to
make tartans, tweeds and travel rugs on high-
speed automatic weaving machines.
In the warehouse you will see the wools,
tweeds and tartans which are sold by the yard,
as well as lambswool and knitwear, dresses,
jackets, coats, cashmere knitwear, skirts, kilts,
sports jackets, scarves, stoles and travel rugs.
Practical details: The woollen mills are open
all the year Monday to Friday from 8 am to
5.30 pm, except during the first fortnight in
July, the Christmas and New Year period. The
warehouse, where visitors can buy factory
goods, is open all the year except for
Christmas and New Year's Day, on Monday to

J. & G. Grant's popular distillery

Friday from 9 am to 5 pm and on Saturday
from 9 am to 12.30 pm. From May to October it
is also open from 9 am to 5 pm on Saturday
and Sunday.
Visitors are welcome to arrive without notice
and walk around individually or in groups.
Children and school parties are welcome.

56   Reproduction Weapons

Ancient Scottish Weapons
5 Friars Street, Inverness IV1 1RJ
Tel: Inverness 222465

James McConnell makes reproductions of
ancient Scottish weapons. These include the
Scottish battleshield known as the targe which
Mr. McConnell makes in suede, cowhide or
stagskin. The skin is stretched over a wooden
base which is then studded in traditional
designs. In the centre of the circular targes a
spike or a cast Royal Scottish lion's head is
often featured. Mr. McConnell also makes
thirty-four inch steel swords which have a hilt
made of hand-wrought iron and a leather
hand grip. Other items are Scottish lion belts
and Sgian dubhs.
Practical details: Individuals are welcome
during normal working hours but the
workshop is small so groups are limited to
twenty people and group organisers should
give one week's notice.

57   Cheese Making

Highland Fine Cheeses Limited
Blarliath, Tain, Ross and Cromarty
Tel: Tain 2034

The story of 'Highland Fine' began in 1962
when Reggie and Susannah Stone were
milking cows on the spot where their
colourful creamery now stands. He remarked
that he remembered delicious home-made
'Crowdie', the fresh Highland cheese that he
had eaten on oatcakes long ago. Susannah
made some and, having too much for their

own family, she took the rest to the grocer in
Tain. He came back for more, and more, and
they were in business.
One delicious cheese is 'Caboc', made from
thick cream then rolled in toasted pin-head
oatmeal. Its texture is like butter, its taste very
delicate, and it's curiously addictive. You
might also try Crowdie and Wild Garlic,
Hramsa, and Galic, all made with the
chopped fresh leaves of the local wild garlic
herb. Galic is rolled in nuts.
Practical details: Anybody and everybody is
welcome to visit this pleasant open-plan
building with its background of piped music.
In the summer the 'cheesery' has well over one
hundred visitors each week and the staff are
actively encouraged to talk to people in order
to create a happy atmosphere, so you will find
any one of them eager to answer any
questions. There are also many opportunities
to sample the various cheeses. The factory is
open Monday to Friday from 10 am to 1 pm
and 2 pm to 5 pm.

58   Earthenware Pottery

Cromarty Design Workshop
Fishertown, Cromarty, Ross-shire
Tel: Cromarty 254

Old fishing cottages have been converted into
pottery workshops and a shop. The pottery
made here is hand-thrown or slab-built in
terracotta clay, and often decorated with
coloured slips which are either brushed or
sprayed onto the pot. Sgraffito work is also
done, which involves scratching a design
through a layer of slip to reveal the clay
underneath. Natural forms such as leaves and
flowers are used for the design.
White slip-cast ware is made and hand-
painted in various colours.
Practical details: The workshop and shop are
open from 10 am to 5 pm, May to September.
As the potters live on the premises they
sometimes open at other times. Individuals
and small groups are welcome to watch
whatever work is in progress. Large groups
should book.

59   Modern Glass Factory

Caithness Glass Limited
Inveralmond Industrial Estate, Perth
Tel: Perth 37373

The visitor centre and factory were opened in
July 1979 by HRH The Prince of Wales and
since then many thousands of visitors have
passed through this modern plant. The art of
glass-blowing can be seen from the raw
material stage through to the finished article.
Notice boards are posted throughout the
viewing gallery explaining the different
processes taking place. The gallery leads into
the factory seconds shop where second quality
items may be purchased at reduced prices.
Practical details: No advance notice is
required as there are no guided tours and
visitors may look round at their leisure. No
charge is made for the visit. Glass-blowing can
be seen all year, Monday to Friday, from 9 am
to 4.30 pm. The seconds shop is open in the
summer from 9 am to 6 pm, Monday to
Saturday, and it is open Sunday throughout
the year from 1 pm to 5 pm. The cafeteria is
open in the summer from 9 am to 5 pm,
Monday to Saturday, and Sunday from 1 pm to
5 pm. The factory is situated on the north side
of Perth, about ten minutes from the city
centre and visitors should follow signs for the
A9 to Inverness.

60   Atomic Energy Reactor

UK Atomic Energy Authority
Dounreay, Thurso, Caithness
Tel: Thurso 2121 Ext: 656

Here you can see an exhibition on nuclear
power. There are also tours of the prototype
fast reactor.
Practical details: The exhibition is open every
day from May to September from 9 am to 4 pm.
The tours of the reactor are on weekdays only
and should be booked in advance either at the
Tourist Information Centre, Riverside,
Thurso or at the exhibition.

61   Art and Stone-Craft

Sutherland Gemcutters
Mr. Ian Yates
114 Achmelvich, Lochinver
Sutherland
Tel: Lochinver 312

The workshop is in a beautiful setting about
one hundred feet above an inlet of the sea,
Loch Roe, where terns nest on the small
islands below. Local rock material is used by
the workshop in jewellery, lamps, pen stands
and so on. The tiny workshop also cuts
precious and semi-precious gem materials
from all over the world.
Visitors can have a polished face put on their
own specimens while they wait: information
is given on local collecting areas and rock
types and a booklet is available detailing local
walks for collecting polishable material.
Practical details: The workshop is open
Monday to Saturday from 9.30 am to 5.30 pm.
It is closed for lunch from 1 pm to 2 pm. Only
small groups can be accommodated, but there
is a large viewing window between the
showroom and workshop. Children are not
allowed into the workshop when machinery is

Prototype fast reactor at Dounreay

running. The Yates undertake special commissions and repair work during the winter months.

62   Glass Paperweights

Oban Glass
Lochavullin Estate, Oban, Argyll
Tel: Oban 3386

Opened in 1970, this small, modern glassworks specialises in the production of hand-made paperweights. The skilled crafts of glassmaking geared to paperweight-making techniques can be seen at first hand right from the first gather of hot glass to the beautifully shaped and hand-finished article.
Practical details: No advance notice is required as there are no guided tours and visitors may look round at their leisure. The *factory* is open the whole year, Monday to Friday, from 9 am to 5.30 pm. From May to September the *shop* is open from 9 am to 5.30 pm on Monday to Friday and from 9 am to 12.30 pm on Saturday. From October to April the *shop* is open on Monday to Friday from 9 am to 5 pm. Access to the glassworks is from the main Lochgilphead Road via Market Street in Oban.

63   Hand-wrought Stag Horn

Fiadh Mor Antlercraft
A. and E. Dale, Battery Point
Clachan, By Tarbert, Argyll
Tel: Clachan 226

This business, which began as a hobby, specialises in the fashioning of a variety of articles which use antlers as the basic material. The stag's horn is combined with metal parts to produce a range of cutlery and traditional brass fire irons, shoe horns and toast forks. In the workshop visitors can watch as antlers are cut, shaped and polished and they can view the completed goods which are on display.
Practical details: Visitors are welcome in the afternoons, but are advised to make an appointment in winter. Owing to limited space only small parties can be accommodated.

64   Sculpture and Pottery

Alasdair Dunn
Tigh-an-Droma
King's Cross, Brodick, Isle of Arran
Tel: Whiting Bay 323

The main output of the pottery is Alasdair Dunn's small 'wheel sculptures' which are thown on the wheel. The most popular are the bird shapes and the 'Arran Chuckie-Stanes'. The latter are inspired by local pebbles, and local clay and sand are used to give them an interesting surface texture. Each piece is different. After throwing each one is sculpted on the bench and fired to high stoneware temperature.
Practical details: Alasdair Dunn can be seen at work during the holiday season. Please arrange by telephone.
The workshop is at Tigh-an-Droma, which means house on the ridge, and is best reached on foot.

5 Graphic Design

Old Rectory Design
Longhouse Buttery, Gallery and Workshop
Cullipool, Isle of Luing
By Oban, Argyll PA34 4TX
Tel: Luing 209

Cards, notelets, gift tags, bookmarks and
melamine tablemats are designed and
packaged here. Murals are also produced by
mounting prints and then using heat to seal
them. Visitors can watch as the design work
and packaging of these items takes place.
Practical details: The workshop is open daily
to individuals from 10.30 am to 5 pm from
Easter to mid-October. There is also a gallery,
where Edna Whyte's graphic material is on
display, and a BTA commended restaurant.
The Cuan car ferry, sixteen miles south of
Oban, operates from Monday to Saturday.

66 Cheese Making

The Scottish Milk Marketing Board
Torrylinn Creamery
Kilmory, Isle of Arran
Tel: Sliddery 240

At the Torrylinn Creamery it is possible to
watch the various processes involved in
making the small Arran Dunlop cheese.
Practical details: The creamery is open from
Monday to Friday from 11 am to 3 pm.
Individuals and small parties are welcome but
they should give three days' notice. The visit
lasts forty minutes.

67 Animal Skin Rugs and Grogbottles

Grogport Rugs
Grogport Old Manse
Carradale, Campbeltown, Argyll
Tel: Carradale 255

The business specialises in skins of different
colourings, but all are the natural colours of
the animals, for nothing is dyed or tinted.
Sheepskins are brown, black, grey, white, or
brown and white spotted. Deerskin rugs are
also made here from Red deer, Sika, Roe and
the spotted Fallow deer.
At the other end of this same work-room is the
squashed bottle business. Squashed bottles
(Grogbottles) are wine bottles processed by
heat into dishes and ashtrays. Each one is
unique .
Practical details: Mrs. M. F. Arthur tells us
that visitors are welcome, though it is wise to
phone first, as they also breed ponies and may
not be visible if you call unexpectedly. They
will accept all ages, but not in great numbers
at one time. No charge is made and you can
buy goods at reduced prices.

68 Traditional Weaving

Skye Wool Mill Limited
Portree, Isle of Skye
Tel: Portree 2889

Since the days of Bonnie Prince Charlie, there
has been a small woollen mill at Portree on the
Isle of Skye. Visitors to Portree can still see the
mills where weaving in the traditional
manner is carried on.
Practical details: The warehouse, where
visitors can buy goods, is open all the year
round, except for Christmas and New Year's
Day, Monday to Friday from 9 am to 5 pm and
on Saturday from 9 am to 5 pm, during the
summer season.

69 Knitting Workshop

Muileann Beag a' Chrotail
Sgoil Dhuisdeil
Camus Croise (Camascross)
Isle of Skye, Scotland IV43 8QR
Tel: Isle Ornsay 271

The name of the company is Gaelic and means
'The little Crotal Mill'. You can usually see
ten to fifteen people knitting jerseys, scarves

and hats on hand machines.
The main product is traditional jerseys in colours which were originally derived from vegetable dyes.
Practical details: The factory is open from 9 am to 5.30 pm and usually on Saturday mornings in summer.

70   Hand-woven Harris Tweed

Lachlan MacDonald
'Cnoc-Ard'
Grimsay, North Uist, Western Isles
Tel: Benbecula 2418

Harris tweed has been known for decades as one of the warmest and most durable tweeds and it is still a cottage industry in the Hebrides, where it is woven on hand-looms by individual weavers.
Island and Shetland knitwear is available and he has an expanding mail-order trade for both tweeds and knitwear.
Practical details: Lachlan MacDonald sends this poetic invitation, 'Hiking over the moorland, listening to the song of the birds, the whisper of the breeze, you could also hear the familiar click-clack, click-clack of the loom and, of course, you are very welcome to stop for a chat and see how it is all done.' You may also drive up to the gate (though public transport is very limited).

71   Silver and Gold Jewellery

Ortak Jewellery
Hatston Industrial Estate
Kirkwall, Orkney KW15 1RH
Tel: Kirkwall 2224

Silver and gold jewellery is manufactured here by Scotland's leading jewellery manufacturers. Ortak produce a full range of jewellery in sterling silver and 9 carat gold with agates, diamonds, emeralds, rubies and sapphires as well as many other precious and semi-precious stones. Designs are traditional, Nordic, Celtic, Scottish and modern.

Practical details: The *workshop* is open Monday to Friday from 9.30 am to 12.30 pr and 2 pm to 4.30 pm. The *showroom and salesroom* are open Monday to Friday from am to 1 pm and 2 pm to 5 pm and on Saturday from 10 am to 1 pm and 2 pm to 5 pm. Th workshop and showroom are closed on loca holidays and during Christmas the New Yea Visitors are allowed to walk around the workshop and the processes are demonstrate on request.

72   Orkney Creamery

Swannay Farms Limited
Birsay, Orkney KW17 2NP
Tel: Birsay 365

Visitors see the making of various British cheeses including Orkney Farmhouse chees The visit lasts about twenty minutes.
Practical details: The creamery is open Monday to Friday from 10 am to 12 noon. Individuals can visit the creamery by giving one day's notice to the office. Groups of up to fifteen people can be accepted at one week's notice.

73   Orkney Sheepskins

Lindor Sheepskins
Braevilla, Rendall
Orkney Islands
Tel: Finstown 356

This is a husband and wife business. Mr. and Mrs. Plant use only Orkney sheepskins. Eac skin is chrome tanned, shaped and finished and is in its natural colours. The skins can be hand washed or dry cleaned.
Practical details: The workshop is open all year Monday to Saturday from 11 am to 4 pm Visitors are shown around in groups of abou six and advance booking is necessary.

Agricultural museum
Lackham Agricultural Museum 41

Aircraft
British Aerospace Aircraft Group......................195
Cardiff–Wales Airport 126
East Midlands Airport 100
Fleet Air Arm Museum...33
Gatwick Airport...61
Liverpool Airport 162
Luton International Airport...............................76
Manchester International Airport 159
Royal Air Force St. Athan 126

Animal hospital
Little Creech Animal Centre 33

Antique restoration
Czajkowski, Edmund, & Son.............................96
Hamlyn Lodge Cottage Industry 98

Artists' supplies factory
Winsor & Newton Ltd...72

Bagpipe maker
Piob Mhor...204

Bakery
Moores, S...34

Basketry
Cirencester Workshops 114
Royal Dundee Institution for the Blind..........202
Smith, Thomas, (Herstmonceux) Ltd.................54

Batik
Camphill Village Trust.....................................206
Mary Potter Studio 56

Bee-keeping
Bickleigh Mill...26
Cornwall Education Committee Demonstration
  Garden...12
Quince Honey Farm 21

Blacksmiths
Hyders Ltd..50
Martin, E., & Son...190
Penpompren Smithy...135
Price, John M., & Son 135
Trapp Forge...169

Wing & Staples 40

Boat building
Denis Ferranti Laminations Ltd......................146

Boat restoration
Boat Museum..164
SS Great Britain..43
Waterways Museum 95

Bookbinding
Powell, Roger 81

Breweries
Ansells Ltd...108
Bird Paradise...9
Carlsberg Brewery Ltd...93
Eldridge Pope & Co Ltd.......................................37
Fuller, Smith & Turner Ltd 66
Scottish & Newcastle Breweries Ltd
  (Edinburgh)..193
Scottish & Newcastle Breweries Ltd
  (Newcastle)..182
Shepherd Neame..50
Vaux Breweries Ltd 182

Butterfly breeding
Worldwide Butterflies Ltd 35

Calligraphy
Guild of St Dunstan 58
Thomson, George L. 197

Candle-making
Cheshire Workshops...156

Car Manufacturers
Ford Motor Co Ltd, Dagenham 47
Ford Motor Co Ltd, Halewood 162

Carpet manufacturers
Axminster Carpets Ltd 24
Blackwood Morton & Sons Ltd.........................195
Wilton Royal Carpet Factory Ltd 41

Cheese-making
Highland Fine Cheeses Ltd...............................214
Nuttall, J. M. & Co...100
Swannay Farms Ltd...218
Torrylinn Creamery..217

China clay mining
English China Clays Ltd......................................15

Cider-making
Bulmer, H. P., Ltd...119
Drusillas...55
Merrydown Wine Co Ltd 60
Sheppy, R. J., & Son..29

Coal-mining
National Coal Board..6

Cosmetic production
Cottage Cosmetics..165

Council meetings
Greater London Council 66

Guildhall, London 68
Liverpool Town Hall...................................162
Country life museums
Acton Scott Working Farm Museum 121
Ashley Countryside Collection..........................27
Dairyland 13
Craft centres
Abbey Green Studios 153
Balbirnie Craft Centre 196
Bickleigh Mill..26
Camphill Village Trust...................................205
Cheshire Workshops.......................................156
Cirencester Workshops 114
Clevedon Craft Centre 42
Craftsman Gallery..53
Guild of St Dunstan 58
Old Granary...80
Tron Shop..196
Viables Activities Trust Ltd 83
Wellow Crafts 41
Wimborne Pottery..40
Worcestershire Guild of Artist-Craftsmen........117
Workshop Wales...134
Creameries
Aberdeen & District Milk Marketing Board......207
Milk Marketing Board H.Q............................. 6

Deer farm
Reedie Hill Farm...198
Design
Design Centre..64
Diamond production
London Diamond Centre 65
Doll houses
Young, Den...93
Doll-making
Carrick, Anne...192
House of Nisbet Ltd 42
Dye-crafts
Dylon International Ltd....................................66
Electrical goods factory
Hoover Ltd..195
Electronic equipment
NCR (Manufacturing) Ltd...............................198
Embroidery
Abbey Green Studios 153
Loudens Close Workshop................................198
Engines
Bressingham Live Steam Museum 90
Dogdyke Pumping Station Preservation Trust...96
Kew Bridge Engine Trust..................................74
Middleton Top Engine House 101
Silk Mill...98

Ernie
Department for National Savings ....1(
Fabric printing
Sanderson Fabrics......................................
Falconry
Falconry Centre....................................1
Farms
Acton Scott Working Farm Museum 1
Ashley Countryside Collection....................
Bibury Trout Farm.................................1
Bickleigh Mill.....................................
Dairyland ....
Farmyard at Chatsworth..........................
Hobbs Cross Farm 4
Hylyne Rabbits Ltd 15
Kentish Town City Farm 7
Lullingstone Silk Farm.........................5
National Association of City Farms.............
Oakridge Farms Ltd 7
Park Lodge Farm Centre.........................7
Reedie Hill Farm 19
Rosemount Farms..................................20
Fashion Design
Balbirnie Craft Centre 19
Feathercraft
Pettitts Rural Industries Ltd 9
Fish breeding
Bibury Trout Farm................................11
Cynrig Salmon Hatchery..........................13
Fish curing
Robson, L., & Sons Ltd..........................18
Fish ladder
Pitlochry Power Station 20
Folk museums
Beamish Museum...................................18
Castle Museum....................................17
Old House Museum.................................9
Food manufacture
Colman Foods....................................8
Lion Salt Works.................................15
Fur fabric manufacturer
Richesse Furs....................................6
Furniture-making
See **Woodworking**
Garden
Cornwall Education Committee Demonstration
  Garden..12
Gemstone workshops
Creetown Gem Rock Museum 187
Lapidary Workshops Co..........................207
Sutherland Gemcutters..........................215

lass factories
aithness Glass Ltd 215
umbria Crystal 186
artington Glass Ltd 19
dinburgh Crystal Glass Co 193
ban Glass 216
oyal Brierley Crystal 112
uart & Sons Ltd 110
uart Strathearn Ltd 199
ebb Corbett Ltd 108
ebb, Thomas, & Sons 107
edgwood Glass 91

lass workshops
eckhurst Glass Studio 53
owdy Glass Workshops Ltd 116
ent Glass 184
lasshouse 71
lass Workshop 95
ordon, Harold 212
le of Wight Studio Glass Ltd 84
ichael Rainer Island Glass 83
orth Glen Gallery 188

raphic design
ld Rectory Design 217

erbs
ee Lavender 204
erb Centre 178
orfolk Lavender Ltd 91

oney farm
uince Honey Farm 21

orncraft
harles Fairns Horncraft 195
iadh Mor Antlercraft 216

orse-drawn waggons
ngram, Peter 80

orses
ourage Shire Horse Centre 78

ndustrial museums
bbeydale Industrial Hamlet 172
voncroft Museum of Buildings 119
ass Museum 106
eamish Museum 181
oat Museum 164
radford Industrial Museum 171
ladstone Pottery Museum 104
orsham Museum 60
ronbridge Gorge Museum 120
onks Hall Museum 158
orwellham Quay Centre 18
useum of Lakeland Life & Industry 184
ilkington Glass Museum 165
alford Museum 158
ilk Mill 98
onge Moor Textile Museum 170

Waterways Museum 95

Jewellery-making
Balbirnie Craft Centre 196
Michael Rainer Jewellery 149
Old School 78
Ortak Jewellery 218

Jigsaw-making
Puzzleplex 173

Knitwear manufacturer
Lomondside Knitwear 195
Muileann Beag a' Chrotail 217

Lace-making
Kennet, Isobel 52

Law courts
Central Criminal Court 71
Liverpool Law Courts 162

Leatherwork
Balbirnie Craft Centre 196
Candles in the Rain 142
Devon Leathercrafts Ltd 23
Eddergoll Studios 199
Grogport Rugs 217
Halford, S. W., & Son 97
Inskin Leather 133
Lindor Sheepskins 218
Wood, John, & Son (Exmoor) Ltd 29
Wycherley, J. W., & Son 156

Life-boats
Life-Boat Station, Rhyl 143
Royal National Life-Boat Institution 174

Lighthouses
Press Officer, Lighthouses 5

Liqueur production
Lindisfarne Liqueur Co 183

Loom-making
Whim Looms 192

Macrame
Loudens Close Workshop 198

Maritime museum
National Maritime Museum 67

Markets
Aberdeen Fish Market 206
Spitalfields Market 69

Mining museum
Chatterley Whitfield Mining Museum 102
Llywernog Silver-Lead Mine Museum 137
Salford Museum of Mining 160
Wheal Martyn 12

Musical instrument makers
Arnold Dolmetsch Ltd 60
Boosey & Hawkes 72
Piob Mhor 204

Rose, Malcolm ... 58

Musical museum
National Musical Museum ... 72

Naval air station
Fleet Air Arm Museum ... 33

Newspaper production
Berrow's Newspapers Ltd ... 118
Birmingham Post & Mail Ltd ... 110
Cambridge Evening News ... 93
Coventry Newspapers Ltd ... 113
Daily Mail ... 71
Express Newspapers Ltd ... 67
Western Mail and Echo Ltd ... 123

Painters
Anahid ... 82
Southwell, Sheila ... 56

Paint manufacturer
Winsor & Newton Ltd ... 72

Paper-making
Wiggins Teape Ltd ... 205
Wookey Hole ... 31

Patchwork
Stables Studio ... 76
Tron Shop ... 196

Photography
Gnome Photographic Products Ltd ... 124

Pokerwork
Studio Craft-Workshop ... 135

Poppy-making
Royal British Legion Poppy Factory ... 62

Post office
Reading Head Post Office ... 78

Pottery factories
Denmead Pottery Ltd ... 81
Foster's Pottery Co ... 12
Henry Watson's Potteries Ltd ... 87
Hornsea Pottery ... 178
Hornsea Pottery (Lancaster) ... 167
Jersey Pottery Ltd ... 85
Minton Factory ... 102
New Devon Pottery Ltd ... 23
Poole Pottery Ltd ... 38
Royal Crown Derby Porcelain Co Ltd ... 100
Royal Doulton Tableware Ltd ... 104
Spode Ltd ... 103
Wedgwood, Josiah, & Sons Ltd ... 105
Worcester Royal Porcelain Co Ltd ... 117

Pottery workshops
Abaty Pottery ... 137
Ark Pottery ... 96
Babbacombe Pottery ... 24
Balbirnie Craft Centre ... 196

Beddgelert Pottery ... 15
Brannam, C. H., Ltd ... 2
Brixham Pottery Ltd ... 2
Bryn Coch Pottery ... 14
Carmelite Friary ... 4
Cartledge, Kathy ... 17
Cooper, Waistel and Joan ... 2
Craftsman Gallery ... 5
Cromarty Design Workshop ... 21
Culloden Pottery ... 21
Davidson, Barbara ... 19
Derbyshire Craft Centre ... 9
Dunn, Alistair ... 21
Ewenny Pottery ... 12
Harlech Pottery ... 15
Hastings Pottery ... 5
Island Pottery ... 8
John Hughes Gallery ... 12
Kelso Pottery ... 19
Lake, W. H., & Son Ltd ... 1
Leach Pottery ... 9
Lightwood, Anne ... 19
Manor Farm Studio ... 17
Old Forge Pottery ... 8
Owen, Trefor and Gillian ... 14
Owl Pottery ... 8
Pear Tree Potteries ... 17
Pennant Crafts ... 14
Porthmadog Pottery ... 148
Pot Luck ... 17
Rumney Pottery ... 12
Rye Pottery ... 55
Saundersfoot Pottery ... 131
Seckington Pottery ... 19
Shelf Pottery ... 170
Surrey Ceramic Co Ltd ... 61
Tenby Pottery ... 130
Thornton Pottery ... 166
Three Kings Studios ... 153
Tremaen Pottery Ltd ... 8
Ventnor Pottery Studio ... 83
Washington Studio Pottery ... 182
Wharf Pottery ... 63
Wimborne Pottery ... 40
Wood End Pottery ... 97
Wye Pottery ... 142

Power stations (coal-fired)
Aberthaw 'A' & 'B' Power Stations ... 126
Brighton Power Station ... 52
Carmarthen Bay Power Station ... 128
Didcot Power Station ... 77
Drakelow 'A', 'B' and 'C' Power Stations ... 107
Fiddler's Ferry Power Station ... 153
Staythorpe 'A' and 'B' Power Stations ... 97

ower stations (hydro-electric)
ary Tavy Power Station ...19
itlochry Power Station ...203
heidol Power Station ...138
ongland Hydro-Electric Power Station ...187
ower stations (nuclear)
erkeley Nuclear Power Station ...117
alder Hall Nuclear Power Station ...186
ungeness Power Station ...50
eysham Nuclear Power Station ...167
inckley Point 'A' & 'B' Power Stations ...31
ldbury-on-Severn Power Stations ...44
rawsfynydd Power Station ...152
.K. Atomic Energy Authority ...215
'ylfa Power Station ...145
ower stations (oil-fired)
awley Power Station ...79
embroke Power Station ...131

ublishing
bson Press & Abson Books ...43

uilting
tables Studio ...76

abbit breeding
Iylyne Rabbits Ltd ...156

ailway centres
ast Somerset Railway ...31
teamtown Railway ...167

ocking-horse maker
Valmsley, Peter ...194

opemaking
)uthwaite, W. R., & Son ...181

ug-making
ormer's Farmhouse ...55
rogport Rugs ...217
indor Sheepskins ...218
ron Shop ...196

addlers
Ialford, S. W., & Son ...97
Vycherley, J. W., & Son ...156

alt manufacturer
ion Salt Works ...156

cience museums
ost Office Telecommunications Museum ...30
cience Museum ...64

creen printing
eckford Silk ...114
ron Shop ...196
Vendy Todd Textiles ...185
Vorkshop Wales ...134

culpture
ailey, Keith ...93
)unn, Alistair ...216

Guild of St Dunstan ...58
Hastings Pottery ...54
Jarrett, Audrey ...56
John Hughes Gallery ...128
Manor Farm Studio ...178
Self-sufficiency
National Centre for Alternative Technology 142
Shellcraft
Tropical Shells Co Ltd ...51
Shoe manufacture
Clark, C. & J., Ltd ...32
Silk production
Lullingstone Silk Farm ...36
Silversmithing
Abbey Green Studios ...153
Slate working
Dinorwic Quarry Museum ...147
Gloddfa Ganol Slate Mine ...151
Lake District Green Slate Co Ltd ...169
Old Delabole Quarry ...14
Quarry Tours Ltd ...149
Snuff maker
Illingworth's Tobaccos Ltd ...185
Soap factory
Lever Bros Ltd ...164
Spinning
Speen Weavers and Spinners ...76
Spinning-wheel maker
Pouncey, H. ...190
Stained glass
Balbirnie Craft Centre ...196
Stock Exchanges
London Stock Exchange ...68
Manchester Stock Exchange ...160
Stone carvers
Bailey, Keith ...93
Bedwyn Stone Museum ...40
Portsoy Marble Co ...209
Tapestry-making
Hecquet, Patricia ...55
Loudens Close Workshop ...198
Taxidermy
Pettitts Rural Industries Ltd ...90
Snowdonia Taxidermy Studios ...146
Telecommunications
Jodrell Bank ...157
Post Office Telecommunications Museum ...30
Television studios
Associated Television ...5
BBC ...6
HTV Cymru/Wales ...123
IBA ...5

Theatres
Congress Theatre 53
Redgrave Theatre 62

Tin Mill
Tolgus Tin Co. 9

Tin Mine
Geevor Tin Mines Ltd 8

Tool manufacturers
Rabone Chesterman Ltd 172
Record Ridgway Ltd 172

Town planning
Barbican, London 69
Lever Bros Ltd 164
Thamesmead Information Centre 66

Vehicle manufacturers
Coventry Climax Ltd 112
Ford Motor Co Ltd, Dagenham 47
Ford Motor Co Ltd, Halewood 162

Vineyards
Cavendish Manor Wines 87
Cranmore Vineyard 84
Drusillas 55
Hambledon Vineyards Ltd 78
Pilton Manor Vineyard 30

Water mills
Alvingham Water Corn Mill 96
Yafford Mill 84

Waterwheels
Morwellham Quay Centre 18

Weaponry
Ancient Scottish Weapons 214
Calcraft Products 18

Weaving factories
Cash, J. & J., Ltd 114
Christy, W. M., & Sons 160

Weaving workshops
Bronte Tapestries 172
Dyserth Hand Weavers 145
Fenweave 92
MacDonald, Lachlan 218
Macdonald Scott 191
Malvern Weavers Ltd 119
Old Weavers House Ltd 48
Pennant Crafts 147
Royal British Legion 140
Russell Gurney Weavers 208
Speen Weavers and Spinners 76
Stoney Park Weavers 130
Whim Looms 192

Whisky distilleries
Brecon Brewery Ltd 140
Chivas Bros Ltd 209

Dewar, John, & Sons Ltd 2
Glengarioch Distillery 2
Glenlivet Distillery 2
Grant, J. & G. 2
Grant, William, & Sons Ltd 2
Sanderson, Wm., & Son Ltd 1
Teacher, William, & Son Ltd 2
Walker, John, & Sons Ltd 1

Wine-making
Hambledon Vineyards Ltd ....
Harveys (of Bristol) Wine Museum ....
Merrydown Wine Co Ltd ....
Pilton Manor Vineyard ....
Southern Vineyards Ltd ....

Woodworking
Balbirnie Craft Centre 19
Charles Jones Woodcarving Workshop ... 14
Crichton, J. & I. 20
Cwmduad Mill 13
Czajkowski, Edmund, & Son 9
Grahame Amey Ltd 14
Hamlyn Lodge Cottage Industry 9
Ingram, Peter 8
Jeffray, Albert 17
John Makepeace Furniture Workshops 3
Kings Somborne Craft Centre 8
Loughborough, Hugh 13
Maltings ....
Oak Rabbit Crafts 18
Owen Hughes, J., Workshop 13
Peter Hall Woodcraft 18
Rake Factory 8
Ridgewell Crafts 4
Robert Thomson's Craftsmen Ltd 17
Treske Ltd 17
Walmsley, Peter 19

Woollen mills
Afonwen Woollen Co 14
Dartington Hall Tweeds Ltd 2
Glen Cree Ltd 18
Holywell Textile Mills Ltd 14
James Pringle Ltd 21
Penmachno Woollen Mill 14
Skye Wool Mill Ltd 21
St George's Woollen Mills Ltd 18
Trefriw Woollen Mills 14
Tregwynt Woollen Mill 13
Trow Mill Weavers 19
Wallis Woollen Mill 13